Lecture Notes in Artificial

Subseries of Lecture Notes in Compt

Edited by J. G. Carbonell and J. Siekmann

Lecture Notes in Computer Science

Edited by G. Goos, J. Hartmanis and J. van Leeuwen

Springer

*Berlin
Heidelberg
New York
Barcelona
Budapest
Hong Kong
London
Milan
Paris
Santa Clara
Singapore
Tokyo*

Hyacinth S. Nwana   Nader Azarmi (Eds.)

Software Agents and Soft Computing

Towards Enhancing Machine Intelligence

Concepts and Applications

Springer

Series Editors
Jaime G. Carbonell, Carnegie Mellon University, Pittsburgh, PA, USA
Jörg Siekmann, University of Saarland, Saarbrücken, Germany

Volume Editors

Hyacinth S. Nwana
Nader Azarmi
BT Laboratories, Intelligent Systems Research
Martlesham Heath, Ipswich, IP5 7RE, United Kingdom
E-mail: azarmin@info.bt.co.uk

Cataloging-in-Publication Data applied for

Die Deutsche Bibliothek - CIP-Einheitsaufnahme

Software agents and soft computing : towards enhancing machine intelligence ;
concepts and applications / Hyacinth S. Nwana ; Nader Azarmi (ed.). - Berlin ;
Heidelberg ; New York ; Barcelona ; Budapest ; Hong Kong ; London ; Milan ;
Paris ; Santa Clara ; Singapore ; Tokyo : Springer, 1997
  (Lecture notes in computer science ; 1198 : Lecture notes in artificial intelligence)
  ISBN 3-540-62560-7

NE: Nwana, Hyacinth S. [Hrsg.]; GT

CR Subject Classification (1991): I.2, D.2, C.2.4, D.1.3, H.5.1, H.3.4, J.1

ISBN 3-540-62560-7 Springer-Verlag Berlin Heidelberg New York

© Springer-Verlag Berlin Heidelberg 1997
Printed in Germany

Typesetting: Camera ready by author
SPIN 10548961   06/3142 – 5 4 3 2 1 0   Printed on acid-free paper

Preface

Over the last several years, there has been a distinct flurry of research and development activity under the '*agents*' banner in universities and research laboratories world-wide. It is worrying that agent technology is being promulgated by some as a panacea to a whole host of problems. Rampant use and misuse of the word 'agent', exaggerated claims and overselling of this nascent technology are giving currency to many sceptical detractors to claim that this technology is just the current passing AI fad and craze, as were expert systems in the 1980s. At BT Laboratories, we believe such detractors are wrong: expert systems are now established in permanent and secure roles in industry, and so will agent technology be in a decade. By early in the next millenium, we expect software agents to play numerous roles, including managing and controlling networks, enabling customers to buy and sell miscellaneous services on vast wide-area networks such as the WWW, managing the information explosion problem, mining vast databases, assisting in the control of air traffic, facilitating command and control in military systems, and providing many other 'value-added' services.

This book largely presents some of the work of the Intelligent Systems Research group at BT Laboratories, and some of the work of its collaborators. Much of our work is related to agents, as is this book. However, we are also carrying out work in the emerging area of *soft computing*, and this volume contains several defining papers on this new area, including one which exemplifies this new paradigm.

Naturally, as members of a group with the name 'Intelligent Systems Research', we are all engaged in the broader endeavour of enhancing the 'intelligibility' of machines, with all its attendant benefits to a company like BT. In this vein, this volume also includes some papers propounding valuable views on the past, present, and future of the *machine intelligence* endeavour.

In short, this book contains seventeen papers which cover the concepts and applications of agent technology, the concepts of soft computing, and some viewpoints on current work towards improved machine intelligence. It is our hope and expectation that this book will provide an informative guide to the promises of these still nascent AI research areas.

December 1996   Hyacinth S. Nwana
BT Laboratories   Nader Azarmi

Acknowledgements

The authors of the papers are the *sine qua non* of the endeavour of creating an edited volume. We are deeply grateful to them and we do apologise if they found us demanding; hopefully it has enhanced the quality of the volume. We would like to thank Robin Smith and Divine T. Ndumu who reviewed many of the papers.

Contents

Introduction

This book emanates from a special issue of the BT Technology Journal, Volume 14, Number 4, October 1996 which we edited in collaboration with Professor Robin Smith. We believe it is a valuable resource for many more beyond the usual readership of this journal, hence we have 'converted' it into this volume.

This book consists of four sections. The first section, *Software Agents — Concepts,* contains four papers which introduce agents, psychological agents, co-ordination in multi-agent systems, and software agent technologies respectively.

The second section, *Software Agents — Applications,* contains six papers on agent-based demonstrators, most of them developed at BT Laboratories or with its support. These systems demonstrate the practical and industrial applicability of agent technology.

The third section, *Soft Computing — Concepts and Applications,* contains three defining papers which cover the rationale, philosophy, and techniques of the emerging area of soft computing, which thrives on dealing with imprecise, uncertain, or vague information. Indeed, the founder of soft computing, Professor Lofti Zadeh, has argued cogently that high Machine Intelligence Quotient (MIQ) systems will have to be hybrid systems, and the soft computing paradigm celebrates hybridism. The third paper in this section exemplifies such hybridism. The fourth paper is a philosophical critique of soft computing — indeed it is a critique of AI as a science. Soft computing, however, is bound, sooner or later, to have an impact upon agent technology in many ways.

Section 4, the last of the book, is on *Machine Intelligence.* This is the broader context of all the work reported in the preceding three sections. This section contains three papers which look at the past, present, and future of the machine intelligence endeavour in general, and intelligent software systems in particular.

Section 1: Software Agents — Concepts

H. S. Nwana and D. T. Ndumu — An Introduction to Agent Technology — Intelligent agent technology is a rapidly developing area of research. However, in reality, there is a truly heterogeneous body of work being carried out under the 'agent' banner. In this paper, software agent technology is introduced by briefly overviewing the various agent types currently under investigation by researchers.

S. N. K. Watt — Artificial Societies and Psychological Agents — Agents have for a while been a key concept in artificial intelligence, but often all that the word refers to is a computational process or task with a capability for autonomous action, either alone or in an artificial society of similar agents. However, the artificial nature of these societies restricts the flexibility of agents to a point where social interaction between people and agents is blocked by significant social and psychological factors not usually considered in artificial intelligence research. This paper argues that to overcome these problems it will be necessary to return to the study of human psychology and interaction, and to introduce the concept of 'psychological agents.'

H. S. Nwana, L. Lee and N. R. Jennings — Co-ordination in Multi-Agent Systems — The objective of this paper is to examine the crucial area of co-ordination in multi-agent systems. It does not attempt to provide a comprehensive overview of the co-ordination literature; rather, it highlights the necessity for co-ordination in agent systems and overviews briefly various co-ordination techniques. It critiques these techniques and presents some conclusions and challenges drawn from this literature.

H. S. Nwana and M. Wooldridge — Software Agent Technologies — It is by now a cliché that there is no one, universally accepted, definition of intelligent agent technology, but a number of loosely related techniques. Yet there are certain themes that appear common to agent-based systems, and, correspondingly, certain problems that must be addressed and overcome by all agent system builders. The aim of this paper is to briefly survey the tools and techniques that can be used to address these common issues, and that hence form a substrate for software agent systems. This paper begins with a review of agent communication languages, focusing particularly on the emerging standard known as KQML. Then a thumbnail sketch of various programming languages for building agent-based systems is presented, and there follows a discussion on support for ontologies, which allow agents to communicate using commonly defined terms and concepts. Then other computing infrastructure support for agent-based systems is considered, in particular, the use of client/server architectures and distributed object frameworks. Finally, some general comments and conclusions are presented.

Section 2: Software Agents — Applications

N. J. Davies, R. Weeks and M. C. Revett — Information Agents for the World Wide Web — This paper describes a distributed system of intelligent agents, Jasper, for performing information tasks over the Internet World Wide Web (WWW) on behalf of a community of users. Jasper can summarise and extract keywords from WWW pages and can share information among users with similar interests automatically. Jasper provides agents which can retrieve relevant WWW pages quickly and easily. A Jasper agent holds a profile of its user, based on observing their behaviour and learning more about their interests as the system is used. A novel three-dimensional front end on to the Jasper system has been created using VRML (virtual reality modelling language), a language for 3-D graphical spaces or virtual worlds networked via the global Internet and hyperlinked within WWW. This and other ongoing research using keyword and document clustering techniques are described.

L. Foner and I. B. Crabtree — Multi-Agent Matchmaking — Many important and useful applications for software agents require multiple agents on a network that communicate with each other. Such agents must find each other and perform a useful joint computation without having to know about every other such agent on the network. This paper describes Yenta, a matchmaker system designed to find people with similar interests and introduce them to each other. It describes how the agents that make up the matchmaking system can function in a decentralised fashion, yet can group themselves into clusters which reflect their users' interests. These clusters are then used to make introductions or allow users to send messages to others who share their interests. The algorithm uses referrals from one agent to another in the same fashion that word-of-mouth is used when people are looking for an expert. A prototype of the system has been implemented, and the results of its use are presented.

D. Fisk — An Application of Social Filtering to Movie Recommendation — The system described in this paper (MORSE — movie recommendation system) makes personalised film recommendations based on what is known about users' film preferences. These are provided to the system by users rating the films they have seen on a numeric scale. MORSE is based on the principle of social filtering. The accuracy of its recommendations improves as more people use the system and as more films are rated by individual users. MORSE is currently running on BT Laboratories' World Wide Web (WWW) server. A full evaluation, described in this paper, was carried out after over 500 users had rated on average 70 films each. Also described are the motivation behind the development of MORSE, its algorithm, and how it compares and contrasts with related systems.

P. D. O'Brien and M. E. Wiegand — Agents of Change in Business Process Management — Successful enterprises are built on change. Increasingly, businesses operate in a rapidly evolving environment where the response to changing markets may of necessity be measured in hours and days instead of months and years. Responsiveness and adaptability will be the hallmarks of business success. BT is strategically placed as a major potential facilitator of this change, as well as benefiting from its technology. This paper describes how agent-based process management systems can provide powerful tools for managing the enterprise of the future. It explores recent work combining distributed computing technology with autonomous software agent techniques for business process management, and argues that these represent a viable supplement and even an alternative to existing workflow management systems. This is supported by the results of a number of projects, including ADEPT, BeaT and a number of other related schemes, which are exploring how leading edge technology can improve the way business processes are managed. This paper provides a vision of how agent-based process management systems can support the needs of the 'virtual' enterprise of the future and the integration of the information systems of small to medium-sized enterprises (SME).

R. Titmuss, I. B. Crabtree and C. S. Winter — Agents, Mobility and Multimedia Information — This paper describes the design philosophy and implementation of a system which manages the location, retrieval and processing of multimedia information for mobile customers. The system uses intelligent agents in all aspects of management and allocation of service components to perform the most appropriate translation and movement of information through the network. The agents use an open market model to provide the services. The strategy of the management agents is to stimulate demand to use their services, which is offset by quality-of-service factors, leading to balanced utilisation of the network. Agents also act as proxies for the user to take into account personal preferences.

A. Chavez, D. Dreilinger, R. Guttman and P. Maes — A Real-Life Experiment in Creating an Agent Marketplace — Software agents help people with time-consuming activities. One relatively unexplored area of application is that of agents that buy and sell on behalf of users. The authors recently conducted a real-life experiment in creating an agent marketplace, using a slighly modified version of the Kasbah system. Approximately 200 participants intensively interacted with the system over a one-day (six-hour) period. This paper describes the set-up of the experiment, the architecture of the electronic market, and the behaviours of the agents. It discusses the rationale behind the design decisions and analyzes the results obtained. It concludes with a discussion of current experiments involving thousands of users interacting with the agent marketplace over a long period of time, and speculates on the long-range impact of this technology upon society and the economy.

Section 3: Soft Computing — Concepts and Applications

L. A. Zadeh — The Roles of Fuzzy Logic and Soft Computing in the Conception, Design and Deployment of Intelligent Systems — The essence of soft computing is that, unlike the traditional, hard computing, it is aimed at an accommodation with the pervasive imprecision of the real world. Thus, the guiding principle of soft computing is: '...exploit the tolerance for imprecision, uncertainty and partial truth to achieve tractability, robustness, low solution cost and better rapport with reality'. In the final analysis, the role model for soft computing is the human mind. Soft computing is not a single methodology. Rather, it is a partnership. The principal partners at this juncture are fuzzy logic, neuro-computing and probabilistic reasoning, with the latter subsuming genetic algorithms, chaotic systems, belief networks and parts of learning theory. In coming years, the ubiquity of intelligent systems is certain to have a profound impact on the ways in which man-made intelligent systems are conceived, designed, manufactured, employed and interacted with. It is within this perspective that the basic issues relating to soft computing and intelligent systems are addressed in this paper.

B. Azvine, N. Azarmi and K. C. Tsui — An Introduction to Soft Computing — A Tool for Building Intelligent Systems — "The essence of soft computing is that unlike the traditional, hard computing, soft computing is aimed at an accommodation with the pervasive imprecision of the real world. Thus, the guiding principle of soft computing is: '...exploit the tolerance for imprecision, uncertainty and partial truth to achieve tractability, robustness, low solution cost and better rapport with reality'. In the final analysis, the role model for soft computing is the human mind." [Zadeh]. In this paper terms associated with soft computing are defined and its main components are introduced. It is argued, using a number of practical applications, that the hybrid approach of soft computing can provide a methodology for increasing machine intelligence.

J. F. Baldwin and T. P. Martin — Basic Concepts of a Fuzzy Logic Data Browser with Applications — A fuzzy data browser for classification and prediction is described and its use demonstrated with several examples. The browser is written in the AI language Fril and provides a friendly user interface for the user to test performance, see the effect of changes in the rules, visualise performance and try various different forms of modelling. The rules with their associated fuzzy sets are automatically determined from a learning set of examples given in the form of a database. The fundamental theory of this approach to the automatic extraction of rules from data and the method of inference using these rules to generalise is described in simple terms. The method has wide application to data mining, fuzzy AI modelling, pattern recognition, and computing with words.

E. H. Mamdani — Towards Soft Computing — It is not clear who coined the term soft computing but one of its greatest promoters has been none other than Lotfi Zadeh, the inventor of fuzzy set theory. He sees soft computing as an extension of fuzzy logic by merging it with neural networks (or neurocomputing — NC as he puts it) and evolutionary computing. He should certainly be acknowledged as one of the earliest founders of soft computing which he promoted as head of the Berkeley Initiative in Soft Computing (the BISC group). Zadeh advocates soft computing as the means by which we may go beyond what AI has been able to achieve during its 40 years' existence. In this paper we try and look more deeply into what Zadeh has to say about both the motivation for and the methodology of soft computing.

Section 4: Machine Intelligence

H. S. Nwana, N. Azarmi and R. Smith — The Rise of Machine Intelligence — This paper provides a brief historical introduction to the machine intelligence endeavour, and to the discipline of artificial intelligence (AI) whose techniques are employed in building intelligent software systems. It also presents some AI success stories both outside and within BT.

R. Smith and E. H. Mamdani — *Intelligent Software Systems* — During the last four decades the field of artificial intelligence has made impressive progress. It is true that not all the promises generated during the enthusiasm of the early years have yet been delivered. But the fact remains that today's systems do provide impressive levels of machine intelligence. There are many examples of intelligent software systems which can match human capabilities. However, we must not fall into the trap of wanting computer systems to emulate fully human performance, for therein lie many subtle philosophical, scientific, and engineering pitfalls. This paper provides a personal account of the progress of AI and offers an optimistic viewpoint.

S. Muggleton and D. Michie — *Machine Intelligibility and the Duality Principle* — The scale and diversity of networked sources of data and computer programs is rapidly swamping human abilities to digest and even locate relevant information. The high speed of computing has compounded this problem by the generation of even larger amounts of data, derived in ways that are generally opaque to human users. The result is an increasing gulf between human and computer abilities. Society's ever more wide-scale dependence on rapidly growing networked sources of software threatens severe breakdowns if machine intelligibility issues are not given high priority. We argue that lack of machine intelligibility in human/computer interactions can be traced directly to present approaches to software design. According to the duality principle in this paper, software involved in human/computer interaction should contain two distinct layers — a declarative knowledge-level layer and a lower-level functional or procedural-knowledge layer. This extends the formal methods separation of specification and implementation by requiring that the declarative layer be capable of extensive human interrogation at run time. The declarative layer should support simple deductive and inductive inference. The ease with which declarative knowledge can be translated to natural language could be used to provide a human-comprehensible 'window' into the properties of the underlying functional layer. Adaptation of the declarative knowledge in response to human interaction could be supported by modern machine-learning mechanisms. In addition, declarative knowledge could be used to facilitate human-comprehensible communication between programs. Existing well-developed technologies can be commandeered to implement the declarative layer. The obvious language of choice is pure Prolog, augmented with machine-learning mechanisms based on inductive logic programming. The underlying functional layer would be composed of normal procedurally encoded computer programs. It is argued that the duality principle in software design is a necessity for dealing with the demands of wide-scale computer usage in the information age and should be an urgent goal for computer science research at the start of the 21st century.

December 1996
BT Laboratories

Hyacinth S. Nwana
Nader Azarmi

Section 1

Software Agents — Concepts

An Introduction to Agent Technology

H S Nwana and D T Ndumu

Intelligent Systems Research, Advanced Applications & Technology Department,
BT Laboratories, Martlesham Heath, Ipswich, Suffolk, IP5 7RE, UK.
E-mail: hyacinth/ndumudt@info.bt.co.uk

Intelligent agent technology is a rapidly developing area of research. However, in reality, there is a truly heterogeneous body of work being carried out under the 'agent' banner. In this paper, software agent technology is introduced by briefly overviewing the various agent types currently under investigation by researchers.

1. Introduction

The word 'agent' is currently in vogue in the popular computing press and within the artificial intelligence (AI) and computer science communities. It has become a buzzword because it is both a technical concept and a metaphor. However, its rampant use could conjure up the problems faced with other flamboyant titles including 'artificial intelligence' itself; far too ambitious claims precede the real technical work that follows.

This paper presents the real challenges and potential benefits of agent research. The main goal is to overview the rapidly evolving area of software agents; the overuse of the word 'agent' has tended to mask the fact that, in reality, there is a truly heterogeneous body of research being carried out under this banner. This paper places agents in context, defines them and then goes on to overview critically the rationales, hypotheses, goals, challenges and state-of-the-art demonstrators of the various agent types currently under investigation. It also proceeds to overview some other general issues which pertain to all the classes of agents identified.

2. Software Agents — History and the Context of this Paper

Arguably, software agents date back to the early days of AI work, indeed, to Carl Hewitt's concurrent actor model [1]. In this model, Hewitt proposed the concept of a self-contained, interactive and concurrently-executing object which he termed an 'actor'. This object had some encapsulated internal state and could respond to messages from other similar objects.

Along with distributed problem solving and parallel AI, software agents and multiagent systems (MAS) form collectively one of the three broad areas which fall under distributed AI (DAI). Hence, they inherit many of DAI's motivations, goals and potential benefits, for example, modularity (which reduces complexity), speed (due to parallelism), reliability (due to redundancy) and flexibility (i.e. new tasks are composed more easily from the more modular organisation). They also inherit benefits from AI such as operation at the knowledge level, easier maintenance, reusability and platform independence [2].

Broadly, for the purposes of this paper, the research on agents is split into two generations — the first spanning the period 1977—1990, and the second from 1990 to the current day. First generation work on agents concentrated mainly on deliberative-type agents with symbolic internal models[1]. Particularly, they concentrated on macro issues such as the interaction and communication between agents, the decomposition and distribution of tasks, co-ordination and co-operation, and conflict resolution via negotiation. These 'macro' aspects of agents emphasise the society of agents over individual agents. The goal was to specify, analyse, design and integrate systems consisting of multiple collaborating agents. Chaib-draa et al [3], Bond and Gasser [4] and Gasser and Huhns [5] present excellent reviews of work on the first generation of agents. It is important to note that this work still progresses.

Second generation work on agents is viewed as being characterised by two major and distinct strands — research and development of agent theories, architectures and languages, and a significant broadening of the typology of agents being investigated. The former research is well summarised in Wooldridge and Jennings [6, 7] and Wooldridge et al [8]. This paper complements them by concentrating on overviewing the broadening typology of agents being investigated by agent researchers.

3. Agent Applications

The range of firms and universities actively pursuing agent technology is quite broad and the list is ever growing. It includes small non-household names, medium-size organisations and the large multinationals. The scope of the applications being developed is arguably more impress-ive — it really does range from the mundane to the moderately 'smart'. Towards the smart end of the spectrum are the likes of Sycara's visitor hosting system [10] at Carnegie Mellon University (CMU). In this system, agents co-operate in order to create and manage a visitor's schedule to CMU.

To achieve this, the agents firstly access on-line information resources in order to determine the visitor's name, organisation, status in their organisation, areas of interest and projects being worked on. Secondly, using the information gathered about the visitor, they retrieve information (e.g. rank, telephone number and e-mail address) from personnel databases in order to determine appropriate faculty members to meet the visitor. Thirdly, the visitor hosting agent composes messages which it despatches to the

---

[1]A deliberative agent is "one that possesses an explicitly represented, symbolic model of the world, and in which decisions (for example about what actions to perform) are made via symbolic reasoning" [9].

calendar agents of these faculty members, asking whether they are willing to meet this visitor and at what time. Next, the responses are collated and the visitor hosting agent creates the schedule for the visitor which involves booking rooms for the various appointments with faculty members. Naturally, the system interacts with the human organiser, seeking confirmation, refutations, suggestions and advice.

Application domains where agent solutions are being applied or researched include work-flow management, network management, air-traffic control, business process re-engineering, data mining, information retrieval/management, electronic commerce, education, personal digital assistants (PDAs), e-mail filtering, digital libraries, command and control, smart databases, scheduling/diary management. Indeed, as Guilfoyle notes:

> "...in 10 years' time most new IT development will be affected, and many consumer products will contain embedded agent-based systems." [11]

4. What is an Agent?

There is as much chance of agreeing on a consensus definition for the word 'agent' as there is of AI researchers arriving at one for 'artificial intelligence'! When necessary an agent is defined as referring to a component of software and/or hardware which is capable of acting exactingly in order to accomplish tasks on behalf of its user. However, it would be preferable to say it is an umbrella term which covers a range of other more specific agent types, and then go on to list and define what these other agent types are.

4.1 A Typology of Agents

There are several dimensions to classifying existing software agents. Firstly, agents may be classified by their mobility, i.e. by their ability to move around some network — this yields the classes of static or mobile agents. Secondly, they may be classed as either deliberative or reactive. Deliberative agents derive from the deliberative thinking paradigm which holds that agents possess an internal symbolic reasoning model, and they engage in planning and negotiation with other agents in order to achieve their goals. Work on reactive agents originates from research carried out by Brooks [12] and Agre and Chapman [13]. These agents do not have any internal symbolic models of their environment, and they act using a stimulus/response type of behaviour by responding to the present state of the environment in which they are embedded [14].

Thirdly, agents may be classified along several attributes which ideally they should exhibit. At BT Laboratories, a minimal list of three has been identified — autonomy, learning and co-operation. Autonomy refers to the principle that agents can operate on their own without the need for human guidance, even though this would sometimes be invaluable. A key element of autonomy is proactiveness, i.e. the ability to 'take the initiative' [6]. Co-operation with other agents is paramount — it is the *raison d'être* for having multiple agents. Further, the communication required to ensure co-operation generally involves high-level messages. The use of high-level messaging leads to lower communications costs, easy re-implementability, and concurrency. Lastly, for agents to be truly 'smart', they would have to learn as they react and/or interact with their external environment, so that, with time, their performance increases. These three characteristics are used in Fig 1 to derive three types of agent to include in this typology — collaborative agents, interface agents and truly smart agents.

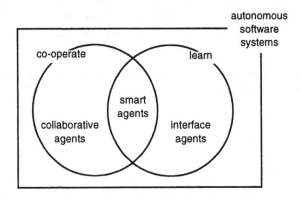

Fig. 1.   A part view of an agent typology.

It is emphasised that these distinctions are not definitive. For example, with collaborative agents, there is more emphasis on co-operation and autonomy than on learning; but it is not implied that collaborative agents never learn. Anything else which lies outside the 'circles' is not considered to be an agent. For example, most expert systems are largely autonomous; but, typically, they do not co-operate or learn. Ideally, agents should do all three equally well, but this is the aspiration rather than the reality. Truly smart agents do not yet exist.

Fourthly, agents may sometimes be classified by their roles (particularly, if the roles are major ones), e.g. World Wide Web (WWW) information-gathering agents. Es- sentially, such agents help manage the vast amount of information in wide area networks like the Internet. This class of agent is referred to as an information or Internet agent. Again, information agents may be static or mobile and deliberative or reactive.

Fifthly, also included is the category of hybrid agents which combine two or more agent philosophies in a single agent.

There are other attributes of agents which are considered secondary to those already mentioned. For example, is an agent versatile (i.e. does it have many goals or does it engage in a variety of tasks)? Is an agent benevolent or non-helpful, antagonistic or altruistic? Does an agent lie knowingly or is it always truthful? Is it temporally continuous? Perhaps unbelievably, some researchers are also attributing emotional attitudes to agents — do they get 'fed up' being asked to do the same thing time and time again [15]? Some agents are also imbued with mentalistic attitudes such as beliefs, desires and intentions [16, 17]. Such attributes as these provide for a stronger definition of agenthood.

In essence, agents exist in a truly multi-dimensional space. However, for the sake of clarity of understanding, this space has been 'collapsed' into a single list of six types of agent:

- collaborative;

- interface;

- mobile;

- information/Internet;

- reactive;

- hybrid.

There are some applications which combine agents from two or more of these categories, and these are referred to as heterogeneous agent systems.

5.   A Panoramic Overview of the Different Agent Types

This section contains an overview of all the types of agents identified in the typology of the previous section in terms of some or all of the following — their essential metaphors, hypotheses/goals, motivations, roles, prototypical examples, potential benefits, and key challenges. This overview does not include smart agents on the grounds that this is the aspiration of agent researchers rather than the reality.

5.1   Collaborative Agents — An Overview

As shown in Fig 1, collaborative agents emphasise autonomy and co-operation with other agents in order to perform tasks for their owners in open and time-constrained multi-agent environments. They may learn, but this aspect is not typically a major emphasis of their operation, though some perform limited parametric or learning by rote. To co-ordinate their activities, they may have to negotiate in order to reach mutually acceptable agreements. Collaborative agents tend to be static, large, coarse-grained agents. They may be benevolent, rational, truthful, some combination of these or neither. Most of the work classified in this paper as first generation investigated this class of agent. As noted earlier, some researchers are providing stronger definitions to such agents, and, as a result, the class of collaborative agents may itself be perceived as a broad grouping.

5.1.1 Hypothesis, Motivation and Benefits

The rationale for having collaborative agent systems is a specification of the goal of DAI. It may be stated as: "...creating a system that interconnects separately developed collaborative agents, thus enabling the ensemble to function beyond the capabilities of any of its members" [2]. Some other motivations for DAI research, and hence collaborative agent research, not already mentioned, include:

- solving problems that are too large for a centralised single agent to do due to resource limitations or the sheer risk of having one centralised system;

- allowing for the interconnecting and interoperation of existing legacy systems, e.g. expert systems, decision support systems, conventional programs, etc;

- providing solutions to inherently distributed problems, such as solutions which draw from distributed information sources such as distributed on-line information sources or distributed sensor networks (e.g. DVMT [18]), and solutions where the expertise is distributed, such as in health-care provisioning or air-traffic control (e.g. OASIS [17]).

5.1.2 A Prototypical Example — The Pleiades System

The Pleiades project [19] applies collaborative agents in the domain of organisational decision making over the 'infosphere' (which refers essentially to a collection of Internet-based heterogeneous resources).

Pleiades is a distributed collaborative agent-based architecture which has two layers of abstraction — the first layer contains task-specific collaborative agents and the second information-specific collaborative agents (see Fig 2). This architecture was used to develop the visitor hosting system which was described earlier. Task-specific agents (TA) perform a particular task for their users, e.g. arranging appointments and meetings with other task agents. These agents co-ordinate and schedule plans based on the context. They collaborate with one another (within layer 1) in order to resolve conflicts or integrate information. In order to garner the information required at this level, they request information from information-specific agents (IA). Information agents, in turn, may collaborate with one another (i.e. within layer 2) in order to provide the information requested back to the layer 1 requesting agent. The sources of the information are the many databases (DB) in the infosphere. Ultimately, the task agents propose a solution to their users.

Task agents encode a model of the task domain and knowledge of how to perform tasks, as well as an acquaintance model detailing the capabilities of other task or information agents. They also possess some learning mechanisms. Information agents possess knowledge of the various information sources and how to access them, and an acquaintance model specifying the abilities of other information agents [10]. Individually, an agent consists of a planning module linked to its local beliefs and facts database. It also has a local scheduler, a co-ordination module and an execution monitor. Thus, agents can instantiate task plans, co-ordinate these plans with other agents and schedule/monitor the execution of their local actions. Interestingly, the architecture has no central planner and hence agents must all engage in co-ordination by communicating to others their constraints, expectations and other relevant information.

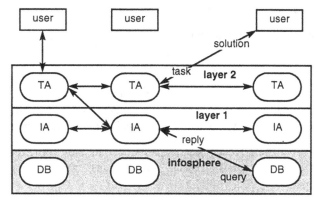

Fig. 2.   The Pleiades distributed system architecture (adapted from Sycara [10]).

5.1.3   A Brief Critical Review of Collaborative Agent Systems Work

There are many other useful pieces of work on collaborative agents. At BT Laboratories, two prototype collaborative agent-based systems, ADEPT and MII, have been developed recently. ADEPT [20] employs collaborative agents in the application area of business process re-engineering while MII [21] uses collaborative agents to perform decentralised management and control of consumer electronics, typically PDAs or PCs integrated with services provided by the network operator.

The key criticism of collaborative agents levelled by some researchers stems from their grounding in the deliberative thinking paradigm. Researchers in the reactive agents camp argue that this results in brittle and inflexible demonstrators with slow response times. In section 5.5 the deliberative versus reactive agents debate is briefly discussed.

5.1.4   Collaborative Agents — Some Key Challenges

Despite successful demonstrators like the Pleiades system and ADEPT, collaborative agents have been deployed in few real industrial settings, e.g. the ARCHON project [22]. There are still many teething problems.

• Engineering the construction of collaborative agent systems — to paraphrase BT's Professor Robin Smith: 'We must move away from point solutions to point problems, and design methodologies which allow for quicker, more structured implementation of collaborative agent-based systems'.

- Inter-agent co-ordination — co-ordination is essential to enable groups of agents to solve problems effectively because of the constraints of resource boundedness and time. Without a clear theory of co-ordination, anarchy or deadlock can set in easily in collaborative agent systems. Much work is required to address the issues of co-ordination and negotiation.

- Stability, scalability and performance issues — investigations need to be carried out to establish suitable minimum levels of performance and, clearly, these systems have to be shown to be stable.

- Learning — what are the appropriate learning mechanisms for different types of problems? Would learning not lead to instability? How do you ensure an agent does not spend much of its time learning, instead of participating in its set-up?

- Evaluation of collaborative agent systems — how are they verified and validated to ensure they meet their functional specifications? Are unanticipated events handled properly?

In conclusion, despite the criticisms of collaborative agents, there are many industrial applications which would benefit significantly from them. For example, a potential major role is seen for them in business process management.

5.2   Interface Agents — An Overview

Interface agents (see Fig 1) emphasise autonomy and learning in order to perform tasks for their owners. Maes [23] points out that the key metaphor underlying interface agents is that of a personal assistant who is collaborating with the user in the same work environment. Note the subtle emphasis and distinction between collaborating with the user and collaborating with other agents as is the case with collaborative agents.

Essentially, interface agents support and provide proactive assistance, typically to a user learning to use a particular application such as a spreadsheet or an operating system. The agent observes and monitors the actions taken by the user in the interface (i.e. 'watches over the shoulder of its user'), learns new 'short-cuts', and suggests better ways of doing the task. As for learning, typically, interface agents learn to assist their users in the following four ways:

- by observing and imitating the user;

- through receiving positive and negative feedback from the user;

- by receiving explicit instructions from the user;

- by asking other agents for advice.

Generally, the learning modes are memory-based learning by rote or parametric, though other techniques such as evolutionary learning are also being introduced. Their co-operation with other agents, if any, is limited to asking for advice.

Maes [24] specifies two preconditions to be fulfilled by suitable application programs for interface agents — firstly, that there is substantial repetitive behaviour in using the application (otherwise, the agent will not be able to learn anything), and, secondly, that this repetitive behaviour is potentially different for different users (otherwise, use a knowledge-based approach).

5.2.1 Benefits/Roles

The general benefits of interface agents are threefold. Firstly, they make less work for the end user and application developer. Secondly, the agent can adapt, over time, to its user's preferences and habits. Finally, know-how among the different users in a community may be shared (e.g. when agents learn from their peers). Perhaps these will be understood better by discussing a few of the roles for which Maes and her team at Massachusetts Institute of Technology (MIT) are building interface agents.

Kozierok and Maes [25] describe an interface agent, Calendar Agent, that assists its user in scheduling meetings. It can learn, over time, the preferences and commitments of its user, e.g. does not like to attend meetings on a Friday, prefers meetings in the morning. The learning techniques employed are memory-based learning and reinforcement learning. Dent et al [26] also describe a similar learning apprentice agent, the Calendar Apprentice (CAP).

Liebermann [27] describes Letizia, a keyword and heuristic-based search agent, which assists in Web browsing. Since most browsers encourage depth-first browsing, Letizia conducts a breadth-first search concurrently for other useful locations in which the user may be interested. It does this by 'guessing' the user's intention from their browsing behaviour (e.g. keeps returning to some particular page) and proceeding to search using the search engine. By doing this, it is able to recommend some other useful serendipitous locations.

Maes [23] describes a news filtering agent, NewT, that helps users filter and select articles from a continuous stream of Usenet Netnews. NewT agents are trained by presenting to them positive and negative examples of what should or should not be retrieved. They are message-content and keyword-based but also exploit other information such as the author and source.

5.2.2 Interface Agents — Some Challenges

The key criticism of interface agents is that, so far, they tend to function in stand-alone fashions or, at the most, only engage in restricted and task-specific communication with identical peers [28]. This is not necessarily bad but it would be useful to have interface agents being able to negotiate with their peers as with collaborative agents. Furthermore, as Mitchell et al note:

> "...it remains to be demonstrated that knowledge learned by systems like CAP can be used to significantly reduce their users' workload." [29]

Some other challenges for interface agents include:

- carrying out experiments using various machine learning techniques over several domains to determine which learning techniques are preferable for what domains and why;

- guaranteeing the users' privacy and the legal quagmire which may ensue following the fielding of such agents [23];

- extending the range of applications of interface agents into other areas.

However, having stated these, there is no denying the fact that interface agents can be deployed in real applications in the short term because they are simple, operate in limited domains and require no co-operation.

5.3 Mobile Agents — An Overview

5.3.1 Hypothesis, Motivation and Benefits

Mobile agents are software processes capable of roaming wide area networks (WANs) such as the WWW, interacting with foreign hosts, gathering information on behalf of their owners and coming 'back home' having performed the duties set them. These duties may range from making a flight reservation to managing a telecom-munications network. Mobile agents are agents because they are autonomous and they co-operate, albeit differently from collaborative agents. For example, they may co-operate or communicate by one agent making the location of some of its internal objects and methods known to other agents.

The key hypothesis underlying mobile agents is the idea that, in certain applications, they provide a number of practical, though non-functional, advantages which escape their static counterparts. For example, as BT's Barry Crabtree notes: "Imagine having to download many images just to pick out one. Is it not more natural to get your agent to 'go' to that location, do a local search and only transfer the chosen compressed image back across the network?"

5.3.2 How Mobile Agents Work — A Brief Telescript View

Telescript is an interpreted object-oriented and remote programming language which allows for the development of distributed applications [30]. Figure 3 summarises a part view of the Telescript architecture. The Telescript Development Environment (TDE) comprises, among other things, the engine (interpreter and run-time development environment), browser, debugger and associated libraries.

Telescript applications consist of Telescript agents operating within a 'world' or cyberspace of places and engines; both of which are objects. The top class in Telescript's object hierarchy is the process. A Telescript engine is itself a pre-emptive multi-tasking interpreter which can run multiple processes. Hence, the engine can host multiple agents that share data/information between themselves. Furthermore, a place is a process which can contain an arbitrary number and depth of other places. Agents, unlike places, are objects which cannot contain other processes, but they can 'go' from place to place. An agent requiring a service defined at some given place must go to that place and call the operations there (see Fig 3). Thus, 'go' is the primitive which allows for inter-process communication. Two or more agent processes can meet in a place and make use of each other's services.

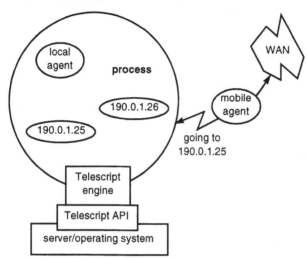

Fig. 3.   Part view of Telescript architecture (adapted from Wayner [31]).

A 'go' requires a destination place and the host engine packages up the agent along with all its data, stack and instruction pointer and ships it off to this destination place which may be across a vast WAN. At its destination, the other Telescript-enabled engine unpacks it, checks its authentication, so that it is then free to resume execution at this new place. When it finishes, it returns to its original host having performed the task required by its owner.

There are other languages which support mobile agent system development, notably Java from Sun Microsystems, though it is not a remote programming language like Telescript. It is also important to point out that mobile agent systems need not only be constructed using a remote programming system like Telescript. Wayner [31] shows examples of how mobile agents can be scripted in Xlisp. Other languages to consider include Agent-Tcl, Safe-Tcl and C/C++. Indeed, Appleby and Steward [32] prototyped an award-winning C/C++ programmed mobile agent-based system for controlling telecommunications networks.

5.3.3   Mobile Agent Applications

Mobile agent applications do not currently abound but are likely to increase in the future. However, the first commercial application was Sony's Magic Link PDA or personal intelligent communicator [33]. Essentially, it assists in managing a user's e-mail, facsimile, telephone and pager as well as linking the user to Telescript-enabled messaging and communications services such as America Online and AT&T PersonaLink Services.

Plu [34] mentions that France Telecom has prototyped some services based on Telescript. In one of their demonstrators, mobile Telescript agents integrate railway ticketing and car renting services. IBM plans to launch their Communication System [35] which uses mobile agents for providing a communications super-service capable of routeing and translating communications from one service and medium to another, e.g. mobile to desktop, PDA to facsimile, speech to text.

5.3.4 Mobile Agents — Some Challenges

Wayner [36] lists the major challenges of mobile agent research and development.

- Transportation — how does an agent pack up and move from place to place?

- Authentication — how do you ensure the agent is who it says it is, and is representing who it claims to be representing?

- Secrecy — how do you ensure that your agents maintain your privacy? How do ensure others do not read your personal agent and execute it for their own gains? How do you ensure your agent is not killed and its contents 'core-dumped'?

- Security — how do you protect against viruses? How do you prevent an incoming agent from entering an endless loop and consuming all the CPU cycles?

- Cash — how will the agent pay for services? How do you ensure that it does not run amok and run up an outrageous bill on your behalf?

In addition to these are the following.

- Performance issues — what would be the effect of having hundreds, thousands or millions of such agents on a WAN?

- Interoperability/communication/brokering services — how do you provide brokering/directory type services for locating engines and/or specific services? How do you execute an agent written in one agent language on an agent engine written in another language? How do you publish or subscribe to services, or support broadcasting necessary for some other co-ordination approaches?

Having listed some of the challenges of mobile agent research, it must be noted that some of them are already being addressed successfully in development environments like TDE using various techniques including the following:

- using ASCII-encoded, Safe-Tcl scripts or MIME-compatible e-mail messages for transportation;

- using public- and private-key digital signature technology for authentication, cash and secrecy;

- providing limited languages that will not allow an agent to write to memory, say, for security.

As a result, much software and hardware which exploit mobile agent-based services are currently in the pipeline.

5.4 Information/Internet Agents — An Overview

5.4.1 Hypothesis, Motivation and Benefits

Information agents perform the role of managing, manipulating or collating information from many distributed sources. The motivation for developing information agents is at least twofold. Firstly, there is simply a need for tools to manage the information explosion of the WWW. Everyone on the WWW would benefit from them in the same way as they are benefiting from search facilitators such as spiders, lycos or webcrawlers. Secondly, there are vast financial benefits to be gained. Recall that Netscape Corporation grew from relative obscurity to a billion dollar company almost overnight and a Netscape or Mosaic client simply offers general browsing capabilities, albeit with a few add-ons. Whoever builds the first usable Netscape equivalent of a proactive, dynamic, adaptive and co-operative WWW information manager is certain to reap enormous financial rewards.

5.4.2 How Information Agents Work

Internet agents could be mobile; however, this is not the norm as yet. Typical static ones are embedded within an Internet browser and use a host of Internet management tools such as spiders and search engines in order to gather the information. Etzioni and Weld [37] describe a state-of-the-art Internet agent called the Internet 'softbot' (software robot). It allows a user to make a high-level menu-based request such as 'send the budget memos to Mitchell at CMU' and 'Get all of Ginsberg's technical reports that aren't stored locally', and the softbot is able to use search and inference knowledge to determine how to satisfy the request in the Internet. In doing so, it is able to tolerate ambiguity, omissions and the inevitable errors in the user's request. Etzioni and Weld use a strong analogy to a real robot in order to describe their softbot's interface to the Internet. For example, they describe the softbot's effectors to include ftp, telnet, mail and numerous file manipulation commands including mv or compress. The sensors provide the softbot with information about the external world and they include Internet facilities such as archie, gopher and netfind.

5.4.3 A Brief Critical Review of Information Agents Work

Information agents are expected to be a major growth area in the next couple of years. At BT Laboratories, Davies and Weeks [38] have designed and implemented the Jasper agent. Jasper agents work on behalf of a user or a community of users, and are able to store, retrieve, summarise and inform other agents of information useful to them found on the WWW. As a user works with their Jasper agent, a profile of their interests is built dynamically, based on keywords. A Jasper agent is able to suggest interesting WWW pages to a user by matching their profile with those of other users in the community. A successful match results in the user being told of other WWW pages that peers find 'interesting'.

The key problem with static information agents is in keeping their indexes up-to-date in the very dynamic WWW environment. For this reason, and for similar reasons mentioned in section 5.3, it is probable that the majority of future information agents will be of the mobile variety. They will be able to navigate the WWW and store its topology in a database, say, at their home site.

As regards the criticisms and challenges of information agents, they are essentially similar to those of either interface or mobile agents, depending on whether the information agent is static or mobile respectively.

5.5 Reactive Software Agents — An Overview

Reactive agents represent a special category of agents which do not possess internal, symbolic models of their environments; instead they respond in a stimulus-response manner to the present state of the environment in which they are embedded. Reactive agents work dates to research such as Brooks [12] and Agre and Chapman [13], but many theories, architectures and languages for these sorts of agents have subsequently been developed.

Maes [39] highlights the three key ideas which underpin reactive agents. Firstly, 'emergent functionality' — reactive agents are relatively simple and they interact with other agents in basic ways. Nevertheless, complex patterns of behaviour emerge from these interactions when the ensemble of agents is viewed globally. Hence, there is no *a priori* specification (or plan) of the behaviour of the set-up of reactive agents. Secondly, 'task decomposition' — a reactive agent is viewed as a collection of modules which operate autonomously and are responsible for specific tasks (e.g. sensing, motor control, computations, etc). Com-munication between the modules is minimised and of quite a low-level nature. No global model exists within any of the agents and, hence, the global behaviour has to emerge. Thirdly, reactive agents tend to operate on representations which are close to raw sensor data, in contrast to the high-level symbolic representations that abound in the other types of agents discussed so far.

5.5.1 Hypothesis, Motivation and Benefits

The essential hypothesis of reactive agent-based systems is a specification of the physical-grounding hypothesis, not to be confused with the physical-symbol system hypothesis. The latter hypothesis holds that for a physical system to demonstrate intelligent action it should be a physical-symbol system. The physical-grounding hypothesis challenges this long-held AI view, arguing it is flawed fundamentally, and that it imposes severe limitations on symbolic AI-based systems. This new hypothesis states that in order to build a system that is intelligent, it is necessary to have representations grounded in the physical world. Brooks [40] argues that this hypothesis obviates the need for symbolic representations or models because the world becomes its own best model. Furthermore, this model is always kept up to date since the system is connected to the world via sensors and/or actuators. Hence, the reactive agents hypothesis may be stated as follows: "Smart agent systems can be developed from simple agents which do not have internal symbolic models, and whose 'smartness' derives from the emergent behaviour of the interactions of the various agents."

The key benefits which motivate reactive agents work is the hope that they would be more robust and fault tolerant than other agent-based systems, e.g. a single agent in an ensemble may be lost without any catastrophic effects. Other benefits include flexibility and adaptability in contrast to the inflexibility, slow response times and brittleness of classical AI systems.

5.5.2   Reactive Agent Applications

There are relatively few reactive software agent-based applications. Partly, due to this reason, there is no standard mode to their operation; rather, they tend to depend on the reactive agent architecture chosen.

Perhaps the most celebrated reactive agent architecture is Brooks' subsumption architecture [41]. The architecture consists of a set of modules, each of which is described in a subsumption language based on augmented finite state machines (AFSM). An AFSM is triggered into action if its input signal exceeds some threshold, though this is also dependent on the values of suppression and inhibition signals into the AFSM. Note that AFSMs represent the only processing units in the architecture, i.e. there are no symbols as in classical AI work. The modules are grouped and placed in layers which work asynchronously, such that modules in a higher level can inhibit those in lower layers (see Fig 4). Each layer has a hard-wired purpose or behaviour, e.g. to avoid obstacles or to enable/control wandering. This architecture has been used to construct at least ten mobile robots at MIT.

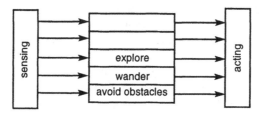

Fig. 4.   Brooks' subsumption architecture.

Arguably, the most basic reactive architecture is that based on situated-action rules. A situated action agent acts essentially in ways which are 'appropriate' to its situation, where 'situation' refers to a potentially complex combination of internal and external events and states [42]. Situated-action 'agents' have been used in PENGI, a video game [13], and to simulate ant societies where each ant is modelled as an agent, and a limited ecosystem composed of biotapes, shoals of fish and fishermen [14].

5.5.3   A Brief Critical Review of Reactive Agents Work

Many criticisms can be levelled against reactive software agents and their architectures. Firstly, as already noted, there are too few applications about based on them. Secondly, the scope of their applicability is currently limited, mainly games and simulations. To be fair, it is still early days for such research — arguably, symbolic AI did not start delivering any useful industrial applications until more than two decades after it was born. So, there is a clear need to expand the range of languages, theories, architectures and applications for reactive agent-based systems. Thirdly, it is not obvious how to design such systems so that your intended behaviour emerges from the set-up of agents. How many of such agents are required for some applications? Currently, since it is not allowable to tell the agents how to achieve some goal, as with genetic algorithms:

"One has to find a 'dynamics', ... involving the system and the environment which will converge towards the desired goal." [43]

This would not only be time-consuming, but it also smacks of 'trial and error' with all its attendant problems. Furthermore, Maes [43] points out that this situated agents work has some important limitations precisely because "of their lack of explicit goals and goal-handling capabilities", requiring the designers of the systems to precompile or hard-wire the action selections. Hence, while a planning approach leaves much to the agent, the situated agents approach leaves much to the designers. Fourthly, how are such systems extended, scaled up or debugged? What happens if the 'environment' is changed?

5.6   Hybrid Agents — An Overview

5.6.1   Hypothesis, Motivation and Benefits

So far, five types of agents have been reviewed — collaborative, interface, mobile, Internet and reactive agents. The debates as to which of them is 'better' are academic, sterile and rather premature. Since each type has or promises its own strengths and deficiencies, the trick as always is to maximise the strengths and minimise the deficiencies of the most relevant technique for your particular purpose. Frequently, one way of doing this is to adopt a hybrid approach, like Maes [43], which brought together some of the strengths of both the deliberative and reactive paradigms. In such a case the reactive component, which would take precedence over the deliberative one, brings about the following benefits — robustness, faster response times and adaptability. The deliberative part of the agent would handle the longer term goal-oriented issues. Hence, hybrid agents refer to those whose constitution is a combination of two or more agent philosophies within a singular agent.

5.6.2   Hybrid Agent Architectures

As is the case with reactive agents, there are few hybrid agent architectures. Typically, however, they have a layered architecture as is evidenced by InteRRaP [44] and TouringMachines [45]. Both are described briefly below.

Muller et al's InteRRaP architecture (Fig 5) comprises three control layers — the behaviour-based layer (BBL), the local planning layer (LPL) and the co-operative planning layer (CPL). The reactive part of the framework is implemented by the BBL which contains a set of situation-action rules. These describe the agent's reactive skills which implement fast situation recognition in order to react to time-critical situations. The intermediate LPL implements local goal-directed behaviour while the topmost CPL enables the agent to plan/co-operate with other agents in order to achieve multi-agent plans, as well as resolve conflicts. LPL and CPL allow for more deliberation. The three layers all work asynchronously with different models in the agent's knowledge base — BBL, LPL and CPL operate with the world, mental and social models respectively. The InteRRaP architecture has been evaluated by constructing a FORKS application which simulates forklift robots working in an automated loading dock environment.

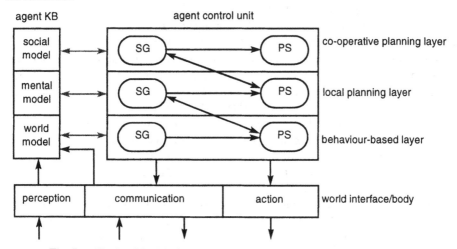

Fig. 5. The InteRRaP hybrid architecture (adopted from Fischer et al [46]).

Ferguson's TouringMachines [45] architecture, which is similar to Brooks' subsumption architecture (see Fig 4), consists of three control layers — the reactive layer, the planning layer and the modelling layer, which all work concurrently. A key distinction between TouringMachines and Brooks' subsumption architecture on the one hand, and InteRRaP on the other is that the former are horizontal architectures while the latter is a vertical architecture. This means that all the layers in TouringMachines and the subsumption architecture have access to the perception data and can contribute to the actions (as shown in Fig 4), while only the bottom layer in InteRRaP receives and acts on the perceptual data (see Fig 5). Therefore, to achieve co-ordination in TouringMachines, Ferguson has control rules capable of suppressing the input to a certain layer, similar to the inhibition mechanisms in the subsumption architecture.

5.6.3   A Brief Critical Review of Hybrid Architectures and Challenges

Hybrid agent architectures are still relatively few in number but the case for having them is overwhelming. There are usually three typical criticisms of hybrid architectures in general. Firstly, hybridism usually translates to *ad hoc* or unprincipled designs. Secondly, many hybrid architectures tend to be very application-specific, and for good reasons too. Thirdly, the theory which underpins hybrid systems is not usually specified. Therefore, the challenges for hybrid agents research would appear to be quite similar to those identified for reactive agents. In addition to these, hybrids of agent philosophies other than reactive/deliberative ones would be expected to appear.

5.7   Heterogeneous Agent Systems — An Overview

5.7.1   Hypothesis, Motivation and Benefits

Heterogeneous agent systems refer to an integrated set-up of at least two or more agents which belong to two or more different agent classes. A heterogeneous agent system may also contain hybrid agents. Genesereth and Ketchpel [47] articulate clearly the motivation for heterogeneous agent systems. The essential argument is that the world abounds with a rich diversity of software products. Though these programs work in isolation, there is an increasing demand to have them interoperate, hopefully in such a manner that they provide greater 'added-value' as an ensemble than they do individually. Indeed, a new domain called agent-based software engineering has been invented in order to facilitate the interoperation of miscellaneous software agents.

A key requirement for interoperation among hetero-geneous agents is having an agent communication language through which the different software 'agents' can communicate with each other. Genesereth and Ketchpel [47] note that agent-based software engineering is often compared to object-oriented programming in that an agent, like an object, provides a message-based interface to its internal data structures and algorithms. However, they note that there is a key distinction — in object-oriented programming, the meaning of a message may differ from object to object, whereas in agent-based software engineering, agents use a common language with agent-independent semantics. They begin to address the particulars of such an agent-independent communication language through ACL, an agent communication language they have been developing.

5.7.2   How Heterogeneous Agent Systems Work

To commence, the rather specific definition is provided of the word 'agent' proffered in agent-based software engineering. It defines a software agent as such 'if and only if it communicates correctly in an agent communication language' [47]. If new agents are constructed such that they abide by this dictum, then putting them together in a heterogeneous set-up is possible, though not trivial. However, with legacy software, they need to be converted into software agents first. Genesereth and Ketchpel [47] note that there are three ways of doing this conversion. Firstly, the legacy software may be rewritten totally — a most costly approach. Secondly, a transducer approach may be used. The transducer is a separate piece of software which acts as an interpreter between the agent communication language and the legacy software's native communications protocol. This is the favoured approach in situations where the legacy code may be too delicate to tamper with or is unavailable. Lastly, there is the wrapper technique in which some code is 'injected' into the legacy program in order to allow it communicate in ACL. The wrapper can access directly and modify the program's data structures. This is clearly a more interventionist approach, but offers greater efficiency than the transduction approach.

Once the agents are available, there are two possible architectures to choose from — one in which all the agents handle their own co-ordination or another in which groups of agents can rely on special system programs to achieve co-ordination. The disadvantage of the former is that the communication overhead does not ensure scalability. As a consequence, the federated approach (see Fig 6) is typically preferred.

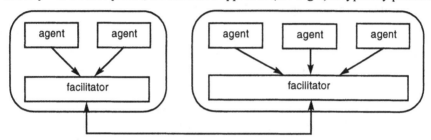

Fig. 6. A federated system (adapted from Genesereth and Ketchpel [47]).

In the federated set-up of Fig 6, there are five agents distributed on two machines. The agents do not communicate directly with one another but do so through intermediaries called facilitators. Essentially, the agents surrender some of their autonomy to the facilitators who are able to locate other agents on the network capable of providing various services. The facilitators also establish the connections across the environments and ensure correct 'conversation' among agents. ARCHON [22] and PACT [48] used such an architecture.

The work on heterogeneous agent systems is ongoing and there is a need for methodologies, tools, techniques and standards for achieving such interoperability among heterogeneous information sources.

6. Some General Issues

An overview of a broad range of work which goes under the banner of 'agents' has been provided, together with their various promises as well as their challenges. We believe, like Greif [49], that agents can have an enormous effect, but that this will appear in everyday products as an evolutionary process. Greif notes, correctly in our view, that agents would initially leverage simpler technologies available in most applications (e.g. word processors, spreadsheets or knowledge-based systems). Then they would gradually be evolved into more complicated applications, doing for example, real work-flow management or controlling real telecommunications networks.

However, apart from the technical issues considered so far, there are also a range of social and ethical problems that are looming, following the large-scale fielding of agent technology, which society would have to grapple with through various legislation.

- Privacy — how do you ensure your agents maintain your privacy when acting on your behalf?

- Responsibility which goes with relinquished authority — when you relinquish some of your responsibility to software agents, be aware of the authority that is being transferred to them. How would you like to come home after a long hard day to find you are the proud owner of a used car negotiated for and bought, courtesy of one of your software agents?

- Legal issues — imagine your agent, which you bought off-the-shelf and customised, offers some bad advice to other peer agents, resulting in liabilities to other people — who is responsible? The company who wrote the agent? You who customised it? Both?

- Ethical issues — already, Eichmann [50] and Etzioni and Weld [37] are concerned enough about the ethics of software agents that they have proposed etiquettes for information service and user agents as they gather information on the WWW.

However, such issues are not that critical immediately, but will become so in the medium to long term.

7. Conclusions

"Smart agents are here to stay. Once unleashed, technologies do not disappear." [51]

This paper has pilfered from a diverse literature in order to overview the rapidly evolving area of software agents. Only Wooldridge and Jennings [6] have attempted a similar extensive review of this area, which they do from a theories, architecture and languages angle. This paper has overviewed the same area from the viewpoint of the clear diversity of agents being researched in universities and research laboratories world-wide. Its aim has been to provide a useful contribution to understanding this exciting field of software agents. A more detailed exposition of this topic is available in Nwana [52].

Acknowledgements

The many informal discussions with Barry Crabtree, Mark Wiegand, Paul O'Brien, Robin Smith and Nader Azarmi, which have shaped some of the views propounded in this paper, are gratefully acknowledged. This work was funded by BT Laboratories.

References

1. Hewitt C: 'Viewing Control Structures as Patterns of Passing Messages', Artificial Intelligence, 8, No 3, pp 323—364 (1977).

2. Huhns M N and Singh M P: 'Distributed Artificial Intelligence for Information Systems', CKBS-94 Tutorial, University of Keele, UK (June 1994).

3. Chaib-draa B, Moulin B, Mandiau R and Millot P: 'Trends in Distributed Artificial Intelligence', Artificial Intelligence Review, 6, pp 35—66 (1992).

4. Bond A H and Gasser L: 'Readings in Distributed Artificial Intelligence', San Mateo, CA, Morgan Kaufmann (1988).

5. Gasser L and Huhns M: 'Distributed Artificial Intelligence 2', San Mateo, CA, Morgan Kaufmann (1989).

6. Wooldridge M and Jennings N: 'Intelligent Agents: Theory and Practice', The Knowledge Engineering Review, 10, No 2, pp 115—152 (1995).

7. Wooldridge M and Jennings N (Eds): 'Intelligent Agents, Lecture Notes in Artificial Intelligence', 890, Heidelberg, Springer Verlag (1995).

8. Wooldridge M, Mueller J P and Tambe M: 'Intelligent Agents II, Lecture Notes in Artificial Intelligence', 1037, Heidelberg, Springer Verlag (1996).

9. Wooldridge M: 'Conceptualising and developing agents', in Proc UNICOM Seminar on Agent Software, London, pp 40—54 (April 1995).

10. Sycara K: 'Intelligent Agents and the Information Revolution', UNICOM Seminar on Intelligent Agents and their Business Applications, London, pp 143—159 (November 1995).

11. Guilfoyle C: 'Vendors of Agent Technology', UNICOM Seminar on Intelligent Agents and their Business Applications, London, pp 135—142 (November 1995).

12. Brooks R A: 'A Robust Layered Control System for a Mobile Robot', IEEE J Robotics and Automation, 2, No 1, pp 14—23 (1986).

13. Agre P E and Chapman D: 'Pengi: An Implementation of a Theory of Activity', Proc 6th National Conf on Artificial Intelligence, San Mateo, CA, Morgan Kaufmann, pp 268—272 (1987).

14. Ferber J: 'Simulating with Reactive Agents', in Hillebrand E and Stender J (Eds): 'Many Agent Simulation and Artificial Life', Amsterdam, IOS Press, pp 8—28 (1994).

15. Bates J: 'The Role of Emotion in Believable Characters', Communications of the ACM, 37, No 7, pp 122—125 (1994).

16. Jennings N R: 'Specification and Implementation of a Belief Desire Joint-Intention Architecture for Collaborative Problem Solving', J Intelligent and Cooperative Information Systems, 2, No 3, pp 289—318 (1993).

17. Rao A S and Georgeff M P: 'BDI Agents: From Theory to Practice', in Proc 1st Int Conf on Multi-Agent Systems (ICMAS-95), San Francisco, USA, pp 312—319 (June 1995).

18. Durfee E H, Lesser V R and Corkill D: 'Coherent Cooperation among Communicating Problem Solvers', IEEE Trans on Computers, C-36, No 11, pp 1275—1291 (1987).

19. URL1: http://www.cs.cmu.edu/afs/cs.cmu.edu/project/theo-5/www/pleiades.html

20. O'Brien P and Wiegand M: 'Agents of Change in Business Process Management', BT Technol J, 14, No 4, pp ... (October 1996)

21. Titmuss R, Crabtree I B and Winter C S: 'Agents, mobility and multimedia information', BT Technol J, 14, No 4, pp 141—148 (October 1996).

22. Wittig T (Ed): 'ARCHON: An Architecture for Multi-Agent Systems', London, Ellis Horwood (1992).

23. Maes P: 'Agents that Reduce Work and Information Overload', Communications of the ACM, 37, No 7, pp 31—40 (1994).

24. Maes P: 'Intelligent Software', Scientific American, 273, No 3, (September 1995).

25. Kozierok R and Maes P: 'A Learning Interface Agent for Scheduling Meetings', Proc ACM-SIGCHI Int Workshop on Intelligent User Interfaces, Florida, pp 81—93 (1993).

26. Dent L, Boticario J, McDermott J, Mitchell T and Zabowski D A: 'A Personal Learning Apprentice', in Proc 10th National Conf on Artificial Intelligence, San Jose, California, AAAI Press, pp 96—103 (1992).

27. Lieberman H: 'Letizia: An Agent that Assists Web Browsing', Proc IJCAI 95, AAAI Press (1995).

28. Lashkari Y, Metral M and Maes P: 'Collaborative Interface Agents', In Proc 12th National Conf on Artificial Intelligence, 1, Seattle, WA, AAAI Press, pp 444—449 (1994).

29. Mitchell T, Caruana R, Freitag D, McDermott J and Zabowski D: 'Experience with a Learning Personal Assistant', Communications of the ACM, 37, No 7, pp 81—91 (1994).

30. URL2: http://www.genmagic.com

31. Wayner P: 'Agents Unleashed: A Public Domain Look at Agent Technology, Boston, MA, AP Professional (1995).

32. Appleby S and Steward S: 'Mobile Software Agents for Control in Telecommunications Networks', BT Technol J, 12, No 2, pp 104—113 (April 1994).

33. URL3: http://www.sel.sony.com

34. Plu M: 'Software Agents in Telecommunications Network Environments', UNICOM Seminar on Intelligent Agents and their Business Applications, London, pp 225—243 (November 1995).

35. Reinhardt A: 'The Network with Smarts', Byte, pp 15—66 (October 1994).

36. Wayner P: 'Free Agents', Byte, 105—114 (March 1995).

37. Etzioni O and Weld D: 'A Softbot-Based Interface to the Internet', Communications of the ACM, 37, No 7, pp 72—76 (1994).

38. Davies N J and Weeks R: 'Jasper: Communicating Information Agents', in Proc 4th Int Conf on the World Wide Web, Boston, USA (December 1995).

39. Maes P (Ed): 'Designing Autonomous Agents: Theory and Practice from Biology to Engineering and Back', London, The MIT Press (1991).

40. Brooks R A: 'Elephants Don't Play Chess', in Maes P (Ed): 'Designing Autonomous Agents: Theory and Practice from Biology to Engineering and Back', London, MIT Press, pp 3—15 (1991).

41. Brooks R A: 'Intelligence without Representation', Artificial Intelligence, 47, pp 139—159 (1991).

42. Connah D: 'The Design of Interacting Agents for Use in Interfaces', in Brouwer-Janse D and Harringdon T L (Eds): 'Human/Machine Communication for Educational Systems Design', NATO ASI Series, Series F, Computer and Systems Sciences, 129, Heidelberg, Springer Verlag (1994).

43. Maes P: 'Situated Agents Can Have Goals', in Maes P (Ed): 'Designing Autonomous Agents: Theory and Practice from Biology to Engineering and Back', London, The MIT Press, pp 49—70 (1991).

44. Muller J P, Pishel M and Thiel M: 'Modelling Reactive Behaviour in Vertically Layered Agent Architectures', in Wooldridge M and Jennings N (Eds): 'Intelligent Agents, Lecture Notes in Artificial Intelligence 890', Heidelberg, Springer Verlag, pp 261—276 (1995).

45. Ferguson I A: 'Towards an Architecture for Adaptive, Rational, Mobile Agents', in Werner E and Demazeau Y (Eds): 'Decentralized AI 3: Proc 3rd European Workshop on Modelling Autonomous Agents and Multi-Agent Worlds (MAAMAW-91)', Amsterdam, Elsevier, pp 249—262 (1992).

46. Fischer K, Muller J P and Pischel M: 'Unifying Control in a Layered Agent Architecture', Technical Report TM-94-05, German Research Center for AI (DFKI GmbH) (1996).

47. Genesereth M R and Ketchpel S P: 'Software Agents', Communications of the ACM, 37, No 7, pp 48—53 (1994).

48. Cutkosky M R, Engelmore R S, Fikes R E, Genesereth M R, Gruber T R, Tenenbaum J M and Weber J C: 'PACT: An Experiment in Integrating Concurrent Engineering Systems', IEEE Computer, 1, pp 28—37 (January 1993).

49. Greif I: 'Desktop Agents in Group-Enabled Products', Com-munications of the ACM, 37, No 7, pp 100—105 (1994).

50. Eichmann D T: 'Ethical Web Agents', HREF = "ethics.html#FN1", http://www.ncsa.uiuc.edu/SDG/IT94/P...ents/eichmann.ethical/eichman.htm (1994).

51. Norman D: 'How might people interact with agents', Communications of the ACM, 37, No 7, 68—76 (1994).

52. Nwana H S: 'Software Agents: an overview', Knowledge Engineering Review, 11, No 3, pp 205—244 (1996).

Artificial Societies and Psychological Agents

S N K Watt

Knowledge Media Institute, The Open University,
Walton Hall, Milton Keynes, MK7 6AA, UK.
E-mail:S.N.K.Watt@open.ac.uk

Agents have for a while been a key concept in artificial intelligence, but often all that the word refers to is a computational process or task with a capability for autonomous action, either alone or in an artificial society of similar agents. However, the artificial nature of these societies restricts the flexibility of agents to a point where social interaction between people and agents is blocked by significant social and psychological factors not usually considered in artificial intelligence research. This paper argues that to overcome these problems it will be necessary to return to the study of human psychology and interaction, and to introduce the concept of 'psychological agents.'

1. Introduction

There are several different kinds of artificial intelligence research. Firstly, there is research on applications — on building a new generation of systems by borrowing problem-solving techniques through analogies with physics, biology, and psychology, and creating a discipline that is mostly intended as an advancement on computer science. Secondly, there is research on artificial intelligence as a methodological tool in psychology, building psychological models and using them to study how the human mind works, and trying to find insights into the nature of human intelligence. There are other kinds of research in this field, but it is the interplay between these two principal themes that is the focus of this paper.

Recently there has been a new link between these two research themes through a joint growth of interest in commonsense — or 'folk' — psychology, particularly as expressed in the form of systems that can reason about explicit goals, intentions and beliefs, either their own or other people's. In psychology, this has led to a dramatic growth of interest in 'theory of mind' [1—3]. In artificial intelligence, much of this research has been driven by distributed artificial intelligence, which also needed to build systems which can reason about each other — systems which are usually called 'agents' [4].

'Agent' is a difficult word for a difficult concept; covering a rag-bag of concepts that span a whole gamut of different kinds of behaviour, including, for example, autonomy, learning and social interaction [5]; but there is a common ground. An agent will set out to do something, and do it; therefore it has competences for intending to act, for action in an environment, and for monitoring and achieving its goals. Of course, for adequate performance of these, other competences, such as learning, negotiation, and planning, may be helpful or even necessary.

This is not the whole story. Agency is a lot more than action in an environment, or, rather, the environment is not just a simple passive system. Often the environment will contain other agents, which is why social interaction and collaboration are so often stressed as a feature of agency. More interestingly, perhaps, the environment may even contain people, leading to the human kind of agency — the kind we talk about in terms like 'estate agent.' Agents are embedded in an environment, but this environment is social as well as physical — social not only in that an agent is working with other agents, but also in that an agent must work with people as well. The environment, therefore, and the social rules that apply, are those of human social behaviour.

Work in artificial intelligence has never really addressed the problems of binding together its agents in human societies to the same degree as has the field of human/ computer interaction. In artificial intelligence, agents are designed to form unrealistic social systems, or, rather, they take valid models of realistic social systems and interpret the models too literally and too strictly. The human components of conflict, morality, and responsibility, for instance, are all simplified out of existence and, therefore, agents have real problems in human societies, except in small niche contexts where people can accept these limitations. The result is that agents are not usually flexible enough to be able to work effectively in human societies.

The true challenge for artificial intelligence is to remove this fault-line separating its agents from human societies. We do not need to do it all at once; we do not necessarily need to do it by making the agents truly intelligent; human societies can adapt to some extent, too; but, at the end of the day, we must make this shift for agents to become more than yet another temporary technological innovation.

In this paper I will argue that this separation can be overcome by drawing on agent ideas from human/computer interaction [6, 7] and using them to create a more psychological and sociological background for agents. In the next section, I will discuss two dimensions against which the concept of an agent can be measured, and in section 3 how agents face up to the pressures of action in human social environments. Section 4 introduces the key theme of the paper — psychological agents — and argues that a new dependence on human psychology is necessary for effective agents. Section 5 follows this up with a case study of how even simple agents can follow this path.

2. On Agents

Before we can look at the fault-line between agents and human societies in more detail, I need to be a bit clearer about what I mean by an agent. People in artificial intelligence use the word 'agent' in several different senses, and it is important to be clear which of these is meant. I will discuss two different dimensions along which the concept can be measured; firstly, the contrast between metaphorical and ideal interpretations of the concept, and, secondly, between internal and external points of view regarding an agent's behaviour. I will look at the interpretation of the concept first.

One possibility is that the concept of an agent is metaphorical. In this sense, the concept of an agent is mainly a tool for thinking with — a paradigm if you like. This certainly seems the intention behind some of the uses of the word [8, 9]. However, I do not think the case is especially clear that the concept of an agent is substantially different from a hybrid of two existing computational concepts, the task and the object. If people are using terms like 'agent-oriented programming' in order to introduce this new paradigm, it should be pointed out explicitly that this is a metaphorical use of the word 'agent.'

The second possibility is that the concept 'agent' is something more of an ideal to which our computer agents are still only an approximation. In this sense, the ideal concept of an agent is the kind of agency that we humans are familiar with — and the technical concept is just the best we have been able to do so far.

As is probably obvious, I want to advocate the second, idealistic, interpretation. If the first, metaphorical, interpretation is to be accepted, then I would suggest that agents are a temporary technological innovation, one to be abandoned in the face of later, more sophisticated ideas at the next paradigm shift in the programming community.

Despite this, there are some real advantages to using agents metaphorically, as characters if you like; they make it possible to develop solutions to problems that are better structured than might otherwise be the case. Watt et al [10] show that there may be many different ways to describe a system as a set of agents — some of which are traditionally rooted in distributed artificial intelligence, where others bring out human perspectives that are often hidden in knowledge-based systems. However, even this human emphasis already leans a little to the second, idealistic, interpretation. We find here that one of the key advantages of the agent approach is that the structure and format of interaction becomes far closer to the structures and formats of human interaction.

So there are advantages to the second, more idealistic, interpretation of the concept; it leaves room for a far more human kind of agency. Taken to the limit this would mean that agents have to be full-blown artificial intelligences, but this does not necessarily inhibit us from making good use of the technology in the meantime. We can still use the concept metaphorically, but explicitly as an interim step to keep our feet on the right path. If we do not make this explicit, the arguments about what constitutes an agent might eventually become a somewhat pointless termino-logical dispute.

There is a second way to cut up the concept of an agent, taking either an internal or an external stance to explaining its behaviour. In artificial intelligence, agents are described principally in terms of the internal states, the desires, beliefs and goals, over which the agent has control. This is appealingly close (perhaps too close) to the commonsense notions of folk psychology, but raises many problems about what these 'desires,' 'beliefs' and 'goals' really are, since they are clearly not the same as human desires, beliefs and goals, at least, they are not in the current state of the field. The question is, is the difference one of degree or of kind? Are they metaphorical or ideal? Most workers in this field sidestep the issue completely by pretending that these words are being used as metaphors, mostly so they do not get attacked by philosophers on what they see as a non-critical issue.

Human/computer interaction, by contrast, uses the word 'agent' for any active entity that will take on a user's goals and act on them. Typically it means '...extending everything we do to be part of a grand collaboration with one's self, one's tools, other humans, and increasingly, with agents' [6]. The human/computer interaction literature avoids describing what is going on inside an agent, falling back to an intuitive definition of agent as something which initiates and performs actions. On one level, they are merely mirrors of a user's goals, and are no more agents than the Eliza program [11] is a psychotherapist. On another level, they are clearly agents; they are capable of acting on their own, or, rather, their users treat them as if they are capable of acting on their own — and this is what really matters. It is the behaviour, the whole behaviour, and nothing but the behaviour that counts.

Of course, the internal and external views cannot be completely separated — neither is an adequate description, and in practice most people prefer to adopt a view somewhere between the two. Besides, they both focus on an individual agent, so there is something missing from both views — society.

3. Getting into the Social Context

No agent is an island. It is the social context that helps to define the boundaries and the behaviour of any agent. Agency is a social and a psychological phenomenon rather than just a biological or physical one. It is the social structure in which an agent participates that shapes its action.

But human society is not constant. Society changes rapidly. Consider the telephone. It is more than just another form of communication, because there is a strong element of presence. 'When you talk on the telephone your face and body still emit expression, even though you know full well that the person at the other end can see none of it' [12]. There is a perceptible difference in people's attitudes to each other using the different media — some people are typically angrier on the telephone than in face-to-face conversation, and others more polite. Why should a new form of communication have such strange and subtle effects on people's attitudes?

Agents can communicate in two different ways — either between themselves or with others outside their immediate group. This distinction is sometimes very clear and sometimes it is cloudy, but it can serve to highlight the distinction between the traditional artificial intelligent approach to agency and the psychological/social approach to agency that I am advocating. In the traditional artificial intelligence approach to agency, agents communicate with each other through a specialised language which is usually designed as a set of different kinds of speech acts [13].

For an agent to communicate with people, it needs to talk a human 'language' — or at least to be able to communicate on human rather than machine terms. That, after all, was the whole point of the Turing test [14]. We can, of course, learn to infer a machine's inner states from its expressions — be they panels of flashing lights or what have you — but this is, for us humans, a fundamentally foreign language; and, instead of forcing people to learn a foreign language, would it not be better to teach the agents our language — after all, it is they who are beginning to participate in our society.

There is a fundamental difference between the ways people communicate by language and the ways that agents communicate by language. Usually agents interact through a formal made-up language, a kind of 'techno-esperanto', perhaps something like KQML [15]; these languages are, of course, pretty hopeless for people. Proper agents must communicate using languages that people can understand. We should design agents which can interact using human natural language, as far as we can get them to understand it. Sure, this is a lot harder for us as designers, but the pay-off, potentially, is a way of binding together human and agent societies far more effectively, as humans and agents begin to communicate through the same language. That does not necessarily mean that agents need to be full natural- language systems to be proper agents, although in the long run that may be required. Instead, it is intended to suggest that agents should communicate with each other using the same channels that people do, and that the communications themselves should be in human forms rather than machine ones. Even a stylised, rigid, but at least human-comprehensible version of plain text, perhaps using forms, is better than an arcane language like KQML.

This focus on language can be misleading; by 'language' I mean something much richer than text — covering the whole range of human communicative acts. Consider this example — when I switch on my Macintosh computer it smiles at me, to tell me that the computer is 'happy'. I recognise this because I know that in my human social context, people smile when they are happy. I have borrowed from my experience of human society to help me understand what the computer is feeling. (This is rather anthropomorphic. The designers of the Macintosh used this anthropomorphism for precisely this purpose — it helps people work with the computer.) I do not need to know anything about computers to 'read' this cue — even a child could do it — I borrow this skill from my natural, human, commonsense psychology [16].

Agents in artificial intelligence need to be more human-like in their behaviour both in the traditional psychological sense as well as in their social context, i.e. they need to be able to 'read' all the expressions of our inner mental states to be able to collaborate and interact with us appropriately. The study of agency in artificial intelligence has so far taken an over-simplified view of the effects of human psychology and society; it has created artificial societies, artificial social contexts in which its own kind of agency has a valid status. In order to create real artificial agents, these assumptions need to be lifted, the gap between these artificial social contexts and the reality of human society needs to be closed.

Artificial intelligence has usually tried to take its models from human behaviour, and when trying to build models of social interaction it was to human social systems that it turned. In practice, the models that were developed all represented more or less plausible models of the ways that agents could interact, but, when turned into formal descriptions which could be implemented, all the elasticity implicit in the original model was lost. Unfortunately, it was this elasticity that enabled the society to work effectively and to adapt to new circumstances, and these formalised models lost all this elasticity because they were all unrealistically rigid compared to human societies and organisations.

For example, even when a human social system is nominally called hierarchical, as a large company sometimes is, there may be many direct links between the members of the structure aside from those that make up the hierarchy. Engineers working on different projects may meet in the corridor over coffee, and the exchange of ideas can benefit all. A production-line worker may meet the managing director when they are in the greengrocer's, and each may gain insight into the problems of the other. The hierarchical structure on its own is too rigid to work effectively when real people are involved, and human social systems of any scale are never as pure and uniform as they are usually represented.

Natural human social structures are more complex than those applied in artificial intelligence because the human kind of intelligence has evolved hand-in-hand with these social systems. If we are to build agents which can live in our human social systems, we need to transfer some of our psychology to them, by one means or another, so they can participate in and see our societies from our point of view. To do this, we need to look at how human psychology affects human interaction — and then use the lessons from this to restructure the concept of an agent to fit into these same psychological principles. This is what I mean by 'psychological agency.'

4. Psychological Agents

The relationship between me and you — and even between me and a computer — is a social and psychological one, and a set of social rules apply which help me to interpret the behaviour of those I interact with, whether they are people or computers. Of course, the social relationships between me and you and between me and a computer are superficially very different, reflecting different sets of social assumptions, but there are all sorts of interplay between them and in many ways they are closely tangled: 'People's expectations about human/computer interaction are often inherited from what they expect from human/human interaction' [17].

This very kinship opens up an immense possibility for conflict when there is a dissonance between these expectations and reality — when the expectations from human/human collaboration conflict with the reality of human/computer interaction. Although people will readily attribute some kind of agency to many computer systems, this is really anthropomorphism. People inevitably anthropomorphise their computer — not because they are told to, but because it is part of the way people relate to each other, and they use this to 'read' the computer. Computers are, after all, social objects rather than just physical ones — and people apply social and psychological principles when interacting with them [18]. 'At the grossest level, people simply attribute agency to the computer itself (I did this, and then the computer did that). They also attribute agency to application programs (My word processor trashed my file)' [19].

Human societies and individuals have a human flexibility which can be added, if needed, to make sense of a situation. This requires at the minimum a kind of 'naive physics' [20] --- an ability to make commonsense predictions about the behaviour of objects, but also, and more importantly, a kind of 'naive' (what Humphrey [21] calls 'natural') psychology.

This natural psychology is not the same as academic psychology, more it is the ability of humans to understand and predict the behaviour and feelings of other humans. It is the psychology of motivation as well as that of cognition, dealing with feelings, emotions, and moods, recognising them and interpreting their effects on people's behaviour. This links back to the origins of agent theory, as it was this commonsense psychology that was the source of the explicit goals, intentions and beliefs that led to the advent of agents in artificial intelligence. The difference is that, from necessity, artificial intelligence has over-formalised these concepts in adopting them, and shut out the human psychology that originally underpinned them. Humans have this natural psychology, this ability to understand their own and other people's essentially human mental states, including their goals, intentions and beliefs. It is part of the glue that holds human society together. For artificial intelligence agents to gain first-class status within our human societies, they must be able to reason with and communicate about these same, essentially human, mental states. 'Alien' or machine kinds of mental state can, and possibly even do, exist, but that is simply not relevant; it is human mental states that are the fabric of human society and for artificial intelligence agents to have a status within our society these agents must have the same kind of human commonsense psychology.

So human psychology has a fundamental effect on what it is to be an agent. Now we can start to reconstruct the concept of an artificial intelligence agent in these terms. To show this most clearly, I will propose a new model for agents which links three different levels, and kinds, of agency (see Fig 1).

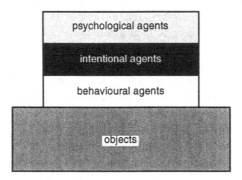

Fig. 1. A three-layer model of agency.

The most primitive level is what we might call 'behavioural' agency. This is the aspect of agency which is most directly concerned with action. At this level, something is an agent because it acts with apparent autonomy. This is the level at which an alarm clock is an agent. There is nothing in this kind of agent which would normally correspond to a 'belief' for example, about another agent. A behavioural agent can act, even act autonomously, but it has no knowledge of or ability to reason about another agent's goals, intentions or beliefs.

The next level is what we might call 'intentional' agency. At this level, agents have intentional states up to an arbitrary number of levels. This means that they cannot only behave as before, they can also have explicit beliefs about other agents, and intentions and goals which involve acting indirectly through other agents, as well as or instead of acting directly for themselves. At this level agents are capable of reasoning about themselves and other agents in their society with the whole gamut of beliefs, desires and intentions, to an arbitrary degree. Intentional agents are capable of shared commitment, negotiation and deception, for example, and all the other behaviours that are associated with the beliefs, desires and intentions model [22, 23].

So far so good. This is the traditional artificial intelligence model. I now want to suggest that a third level is necessary, 'psychological' agency. In part, this is a stopgap, because research does seem to suggest that a 'representational theory of mind' [24], which corresponds to second-level, intentional agency, is not enough, even in principle, to build human agents [25]. The distinction I have in mind here is that at this third level, agents can use commonsense heuristics to guess at, as well as to reason about, human intentional states. They are also capable of ascribing rationality to agents, i.e. distinguishing autonomously between things which are agents and things which are not [26, 27]. Finally, they should be able to perceive and recognise all the 'backchannels' in human interaction, the half-smiles, nods, and frowns that frame and can completely change the meaning of any linguistic interaction they accompany. All this requires changes in an agent's perceptual apparatus as well as its psychology.

There are a number of implicit assumptions here. First and foremost, by asserting that psychological agency is different from intentional agency, I am implicitly asserting that there is something more to human psychology than intentional states. This is a claim that is not certain either way, but the claim that intentional states are sufficient (as opposed to merely being necessary) for psychology is not really supported by the evidence [3, 25]. There does seem to be a gap between intentional states and human psychology.

The fundamental reason for my emphasis on human psychology lies in the claim that true machine intelligence must be isomorphic with true human intelligence. Turing once said of the Turing test [14]: '...might not a machine do something which might be called thinking, but which is unlike what people do?' I think he was wrong about this.

Machines could already be fully conscious beings on that basis — if we accept that people cannot recognise them as intelligent, because they possess some 'alien intelligence.' Computers could already be classed as superintelligent in an alien sense for their exceedingly fast numerical processing, but that is not what I count as intelligent. I want to argue that for intelligence to mean anything, it must be the kind of thing that other **people** recognise and are prepared to call 'intelligence.'

As things stand, then, a useful goal for artificial intelligence research would be to study and to develop models of agency which are truly psychological, not just intentional in level. Of course, this is a long-term project — one which will undoubtedly take at least my lifetime — but that does not mean we should not try. It also does not mean that we cannot reap a useful benefit from systems which are only vague shadows of this in the short term, and I will discuss this, with an example, in the next section.

5. Steps to the Grand Collaboration — Luigi

Agents change the way we work with programs. In the future, neither an individual nor a social, not an internal nor an external, view will be sufficient to describe how agents will work. Agents will work both with people and with other agents, in a form we might call 'heterogeneous groupware'. Agents have ceased to become objects, and have become a medium in their own right — a distinction that Kay [6] describes as the shift from manipulation (of objects) to management (of agents). This offers both problems and opportunities for agent design.

In human/computer interaction an interface agent is often a character living in the computer acting on behalf of someone in a virtual environment, with a degree of autonomy. Sometimes this is taken to extremes, giving the agent a human name, face and voice, making the agent seem like a virtual person. But interface agents are not without their problems. There is a psychological price to be paid for the anthropomorphism that is built into many interface agents. Just because an agent has a human name, looks human, or speaks like a human, it does not mean that people will interact with them as if they are human; the behaviour of the agent has to live up to this expectation, and if it fails there is a kind of 'anthropomorphic dissonance' which undermines the collaboration. (This is another way of seeing the conflict I mentioned earlier between expectations inherited from human/human interaction and the reality of human/computer interaction.) People get frustrated if they have to negotiate work indirectly through an over-anthropomorphised agent ('some dip in a bow tie,' [19]) rather than acting directly when they already know what to do.

In order to study how agents interact with people, we selected a domain where people interacted with each other and with computer programs — diary and meeting management. Meeting management software has been available for many years, and has been the focus of efforts by project management specialists, user interface specialists, workgroup software specialists and artificial intelligence specialists. But despite this interest, diary and meeting management software has never been as successful as the more conventional forms of collaborative communication, such as the telephone or electronic mail.

This kind of system has been permanently a victim to the 'weakest link in the chain' phenomenon — unless everyone in the workgroup plays by the rules and keeps an on-line accessible electronic diary up to date (a diary which is compatible with everybody else's software), the underlying premise of the workgroup software falls apart. This is typical of the failure of much computer-supported co-operative work, in that there are different people in different roles, and the benefits of co-operation fall unequally on the roles and leads to a breakdown in co-operation when co-operative actions cost people in some roles more than they benefit. We can call this 'role conflict' [28].

These observations, together with in-house experience of one of the major commercial packages and observation of the ongoing patterns of electronic mail among human meeting makers led us to investigate a 'least common denominator' approach.

'Luigi' is an agent which embodies this approach. Luigi communicates using a widespread medium, and interacts directly with people, so that they do not need to keep up a diary, or run any special software at all. A proposer can send a message to Luigi requesting a meeting, saying who is invited, how long the meeting will last, and, suggesting a number of possible dates. Luigi then sends mail to the delegates and manages the meeting for the proposer, negotiating the possible dates and keeping the proposer informed on the progress of the meeting, and, when a date has eventually been agreed, it asks the proposer to confirm the meeting for that date. Luigi, then, acts for the proposer but interacts with all the potential participants.

Figure 2 shows how Luigi acts as an intermediary between the meeting's proposer and the invited participants. Luigi takes away some of the administrative burden, but has to be careful to ensure that the proposer does not feel they have lost control of the meeting.

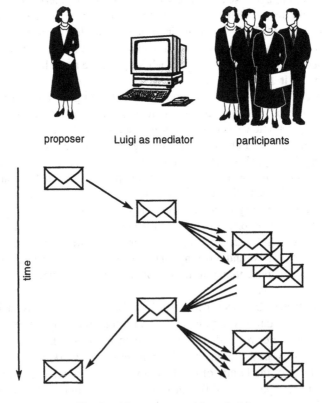

Fig. 2. Messages to and from Luigi.

This strategy means that Luigi, building on a medium with relatively few implicit role biases, such as electronic mail [29], can help, where other meeting systems cause a breakdown between the roles, by assisting some roles (meeting organisers, in this case) without any additional cost to others in keeping electronic diaries up to date, i.e. Luigi avoids role conflict. More agents can be added, each addressing a specific role, and gradually a complex society of human and artificial agents will emerge. Separate agents can be added for each participant to delegate automatic acceptance of certain meeting requests — these agents can then negotiate directly with Luigi without having to bother the meeting's proposer.

Luigi is a complete prototype system. It can successfully plan meetings using a forms interface, either with simple textual forms in mail messages or using forms on the World Wide Web. But the prototype is more a sketch to let us try out ideas for this kind of agent, and to explore the psychological effects of different media and different message content on the collaborative processes.

How does Luigi fit into our model of psychological agency? Luigi clearly is not anything remotely resembling a full-blown artificial intelligence — rather, it shows a greater attention to the psychology of the human proposer and participants than it does to fancy reasoning with beliefs, desires and intentions. This is, though, an area where we expect Luigi to develop substantially in the future.

But even so Luigi is a lot more than a naive scheduler. Luigi has to accept real responsibility for a sensitive kind of discussion — that involved in planning a meeting. The texts that it uses for its messages have to be very carefully toned to avoid invoking feelings (such as those of alienation or frustration) in those it is bringing together. It is a system which must interact with people and with agents, and where it has to use well-phrased natural language for com-munication and for negotiation. With this in place, we can work to make Luigi gradually better at dealing with the human psychological processes which make real meeting planning and negotiation so hard.

The important part of the approach for us is that we do not regard the successes and failures of Luigi as 'bugs' but as hints about how people, psychologically and socially, respond to agents. These hints can then be used in turn to refine the designs of future agents to work better with people.

Luigi shares some features with other interface agents for meeting scheduling, such as those of Kozierok and Maes [30] and Sycara and Zeng [31], but there are important differences. Maes' approach to interface agents [7] stresses collaboration with an individual user in a single human/computer interface, where Luigi collaborates with a group rather than an individual. Secondly, Maes' agents operate within the user's work environment, where Luigi takes on a task to the extent that it passes partly outside that single work environment. Sycara and Zeng's agent is primarily an agent-oriented implementation of a solution to the problem of planning a visit with collaborating information agents; there is no strong connection with the user. On both scores, the fundamental difference between Luigi and similar agents is that Luigi is situated, in the sense of Suchman [32], but in the human social world of collaborating to set up meetings.

The fundamental principles of this approach — heterogeneous groupware mixing people and agents, careful avoidance of any extra work burden on any participant, and a wide variety of forms of interaction — seem both theoretically sound and practically useful in both the short term and the long term. Luigi shows the immediate practical utility of agency in a modified form, in a safe middle ground between the Scylla of anthropomorphic agency and the Charybdis of pure manipulation. It allows us to explore the psychology of interaction between humans and agents in a relatively controlled environment. As such, I believe that this is where research on intelligent agents should be focused in the near future.

6. Conclusions

There are some themes which vaguely resemble the hype in the current interest on agent technologies. At the core, however, there are some very deep psychological issues, some of which are old and some new. All potentially offer a way to a new generation of systems which are designed to collaborate with each other and with people, and which are better able to cope with the social systems in which they have to operate.

Firstly, I have suggested that agents should collaborate with people on human terms, even human psychological and social terms, rather than on formal abstract mathematical or logical ones. This is clearly a lot harder for us as researchers now, but I believe that gradually elevating agents to our human level is going to be necessary, eventually.

By advocating a three-layer model of agency, I intend to throw new emphasis on the psychology of agent interaction, namely on the issues of how people recognise something as an agent, and how people ascribe new mental states to these agents. This is in contrast to the previous, intentional-states model, which mainly focuses on the logical procedures which can be used to make inference about existing mental states.

As a research programme, this is, fundamentally, as hard as true artificial intelligence — indeed, it can be argued that this is the key to true artificial intelligence [33]. It should not be regarded as the kind of problem that we can crack in a matter of a few years.

In the interim, then, I suggest that we just take the ideas and not be too worried about the purity of the psychological principles that underpin them. Artificial intelligence has got on very well borrowing ideas from psychology without feeling that it has to adhere to them too closely. We can already build systems which fit into human societies, which take on responsibilities, and which interact autonomously with each other and with people. We can already use psychological principles in the design of these systems, and, furthermore, by looking at the successes and failures, the strong and the weak points of these systems, we can indirectly discover the pure psychological principles that are necessary for true agency.

This approach to agency is fundamentally quite radical. Instead of building progressively more complex agents, I propose building progressively more **human** agents. At first we will not succeed; the agents will both be and appear to be quite mechanical, but that must not put us off our long- term goal. We must not get distracted into designing more and more artificial societies in which our agents can act and interact; instead we must remember that we are human, and begin to design more and more human agents. Even now, in the short term, we must start to see our agents less as tools, and more as assistants — assistants that respond to our needs as people and talk to us in our language, without expecting us to talk to them in their language. Underneath all that hype, there still lurks the glimmer of true psychological agency — we must not let it get buried under technology or caged in artificial societies.

Acknowledgements

Luigi was designed collaboratively by Marc Eisenstadt, Zdenek Zdrahal, and the author. The author is especially indebted to Marc Eisenstadt for moral and textual support, to Tamara Sumner and Hyacinth Nwana for reviewing the paper, and to all the participants in BT's 1995 agents workshop for an exciting exchange of ideas and perspectives.

References

1. Baron-Cohen S, Tager-Flusberg H and Cohen D J: 'Understanding Other Minds: Perspectives From Autism', Oxford, Oxford University Press (1993).

2. Davies M: 'The Mental Simulation Debate', in Peacocke C (Ed): 'Objectivity, Simulation and the Unity of Consciousness', pp 99—128 (1994).

3. Perner J: 'Understanding the Representational Mind', Cambridge, Massachusetts, MIT Press (1991).

4. Bond A H and Gasser L: 'An Analysis of Problems and Research in DAI', in Bond A H and Gasser L (Eds): 'Readings in Distributed Artificial Intelligence', San Mateo, Morgan Kaufmann, pp 3—35 (1998).

5. Nwana H S: 'Software Agents: An Overview', Knowledge Engineering Review, 11, No 3, pp 205—244 (1996).

6. Kay A: 'User Interface: A Personal View', in Laurel B and Mountford S J (Eds): 'The Art of Human-Computer Interface Design', Addison-Wesley, pp 191—207 (1990).

7. Maes P: 'Agents that Reduce Work and Information Overload', Communications of the ACM, 37, pp 31—40 (1994).

8. Genesereth M R and Ketchpel S P: 'Software Agents', Communications of the ACM, 37, pp 48—53 (1994).

9. Shoham Y: 'Agent Oriented Programming', Artificial Intelligence, 60, pp 51—92 (1992).

10. Watt S N K, Zdrahal Z and Brayshaw M: 'Multiple Agent Systems for Configuration Design', in Hallam J (Ed): 'Frontiers in artificial intelligence and applications', IOS Press, pp 217—228 (1995).

11. Weizenbaum J: 'ELIZA: A Computer Program for the Study of Natural Language Communication between man and machine', in Communications of the ACM, 9, pp 36—45 (1966).

12. Negroponte N: 'Hospital Corners', in Laurel B and Mountford S J (Eds): 'The Art of Human/Computer Interface Design', Addison-Wesley, pp 191—207 (1990).

13. Searle J R: 'Speech Acts', Cambridge, Cambridge University Press (1969).

14. Turing A M: 'Computing Machinery and Intelligence,' Mind, 59, pp 433—460 (1950).

15. Finin T, McKay D, Fritzson R and McEntire R: 'KQML — an information and knowledge exchange protocol', in Fuchi K and Yokoi T (Eds): 'Knowledge building and knowledge sharing', Ohmsha and IOS Press (1994).

16. McCarthy J: 'The Little Thoughts of Thinking Machines', Psychology Today, 17 (1983).

17. Brennan S E: 'Conversation as Direct Manipulation,' in Laurel B and Mountford S J (Eds): 'The Art of Human/Computer Interface Design', Addison-Wesley (1990).

18. Nass C, Steuer J and Tauber E R: 'Computers are Social Actors', in the Proceedings of CHI'94 (1994).

19. Laurel B: 'Computers as Theatre', Reading, Massachusetts, Addison-Wesley (1991).

20. Hayes P J: 'The Naive Physics Manifesto', in Michie D (Ed): 'Expert Systems in the Microelectronic Age', Edinburgh, Edinburgh University Press, pp 242—270 (1979).

21. Humphrey N K: 'The Social Function of Intellect', in Bateson P P G and Hinde R A (Eds): 'Growing Points in Ethology', Cambridge, Cambridge University Press (1976).

22. Cohen P R and Levesque H J: 'Intention Is Choice with Commitment', Artificial Intelligence, 42, pp 213—261 (1990).

23. Rao A S and Georgeff M P: 'BDI agents: from theory to practice', in the Proceedings of the First International Conference on Multi-Agent Systems, ICMAS'95, San Fransisco, USA (1995).

24. Fodor J A: 'Fodor's Guide to Mental Representation: The Intelligent Auntie's Vade-Mecum', Mind, No 94, pp 55—97 (1985).

25. Samet J: 'Autism and Theory of Mind: Some Philosophical Perspectives', in Baron-Cohen S, Tager-Flusberg H and Cohen D J (Eds): 'Understanding Other Minds: Perspectives from Autism', Oxford, Oxford University Press, pp 427—449 (1993).

26. Dennett D C: 'The Intentional Stance', Cambridge, Massachusetts, MIT Press (1987).

27. Shultz T R: 'From Agency to Intention: A Rule-Based Computational Approach', in Whiten A (Ed): 'Natural Theories of Mind: Evolution, Development and Simulation of Everyday Mindreading', Oxford, Basil Blackwell, pp 79—95 (1991).

28. Watt S N K: 'Role conflict in groupware', in the Proceedings of First International Conference on Intelligent Cooperative Information Systems, Rotterdam, Netherlands (1993).

29. Grudin J: 'Groupware and Cooperative Work: Problems and Prospects', in Laurel B and Mountford S J (Eds): 'The Art of Human-Computer Interface Design', Addison-Wesley (1990).

30. Kozierok R and Maes P: 'A Learning Interface Agent for Scheduling Meetings', in the Proceedings of the ACM SIGCHI International Workshop on Intelligent User Interfaces, Orlando, Florida (1993).

31. Sycara K and Zeng D: 'Visitor-Hoster: Towards an Intelligent Electronic Secretary', in the Proceedings of the CIKM-94 (International Conference on Information and Knowledge Management) workshop on Intelligent Information Agents (1994).

32. Suchman L A: 'Plans and Situated Actions: The Problem of Human/Machine Communication', Cambridge, Cambridge University Press (1987).

33. Watt S N K: 'A Brief Naive Psychology Manifesto', Informatica, 19, pp 495—500 (1995).

Co-ordination in Multi-Agent Systems

H S Nwana[1], L Lee[1] and N R Jennings[2]

[1] Intelligent System Research, Advanced Applications & Technology Department,
BT Laboratories, Martlesham Heath, Ipswich, Suffolk, IP5 7RE, UK.
E-mail: hyacinth/leelc@info.bt.co.uk

[2] Department of Electronic Engineering, Queen Mary and Westfield College
(University of London), Mile End Road, London E1 4NS, UK.
E-mail: n.r.jennings@qmw.ac.uk

The objective of this paper is to examine the crucial area of co-ordination in multi-agent systems. It does not attempt to provide a comprehensive overview of the co-ordination literature; rather, it highlights the necessity for co-ordination in agent systems and overviews briefly various co-ordination techniques. It critiques these techniques and presents some conclusions and challenges drawn from this literature.

1. Introduction

Co-ordination is a central issue in software agent systems in particular, and in distributed artificial intelligence (DAI) in general. However, it has also been studied by researchers in diverse disciplines in the social sciences, including organisation theory, political science, social psychology, anthropology, law and sociology. For example, organisation theorists have investigated the co-ordination of systems of human beings, from small groups to large formal organisations [1, 2]. Economists have studied co-ordination in markets of separate profit-maximising firms [3]. Even biological systems appear to be co-ordinated though individual cells or 'agents' act independently and in a seemingly non-purposeful fashion. Human brains exhibit co-ordinated behaviour from apparently 'random' behaviours of very simple neurones. Essentially, co-ordination is a process in which agents engage in order to ensure a community of individual agents acts in a coherent manner.

The scope of this paper is limited mainly to software multi-agent systems (MAS). The breakdown of the paper is as follows. Section 2 argues more cogently why co-ordination is vital, not only in DAI and agent-based systems, but also to open distributed systems. Section 3 overviews briefly various co-ordination techniques. Negotiation, overviewed in section 4, is one of the techniques used to achieve co-ordination in agent-based systems. It is overviewed separately because it has an extensive literature in its own right. Section 5 presents some lessons learned and some heuristics on co-ordination, and section 6 concludes the paper.

2. The Necessity for Co-ordination

What is co-ordination? Why is it necessary or desir-able? Co-ordination has already been defined, in section 1, as a process in which agents engage in order to ensure their community acts in a coherent manner. Coherence means that the agents' actions gel well, and that they do not conflict with one another. In other words, coherence refers to how well a system of agents behaves as a unit [4]. There are several reasons why multiple agents need to be co-ordinated [5, 6].

- Preventing anarchy or chaos — co-ordination is necessary or desirable because, with the decentralisation in agent-based systems, anarchy can set in easily. No longer does any agent possess a global view of the entire agency to which it belongs. This is simply not feasible in any community of reasonable complexity. The chairman of BT, for example, cannot possibly be aware of the detailed activities of all his 130 000 employees. Consequently, agents only have local views, goals and knowledge which may conflict with others. They can enter into all sorts of arrangements with other agents or agencies. Like in any society, such haphazard arrangements are prone to anarchy; to achieve common goals, which is a *raison d'être* for having multiple agents in the first place, a group of agents need to be co-ordinated.

- Meeting global constraints — there usually exist global constraints which a group of agents must satisfy if they are to be deemed successful. For example, a system of agents constructing a design may have to work within the constraints of a pre-specified budget. Similarly, agents doing network management may have to respond to certain failures within seconds and others within hours. Agents need to co-ordinate their behaviour if they are to meet such global constraints.

- Distributed expertise, resources or information — agents may have different capabilities and specialised knowledge in a similar manner to paediatricians, neurologists and cardiologists. Alternatively, they may have different sources of information, resources (e.g. processing power, memory), reliability levels, responsibilities, limitations, charges for services, etc. In such scenarios, agents have to be co-ordinated in just the same way that different medical specialists including anaesthetists, surgeons, ambulance personnel, nurses, etc, work together to treat someone who has been in a near-fatal accident. In this example, none of these experts working in isolation possesses all the necessary expertise, information, or the casualty and medical resources (e.g. equipment).

- Dependencies between agents' actions — agents' goals are frequently interdependent. Consider two agents solving the trivial blocks world problem shown in Fig 1.

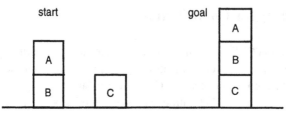

Fig. 1   A blocks world problem.

The easiest way to solve it would be for the first agent to take on the sub-goal of stacking B on C while the second stacks A on top of the stack B-C in order to achieve A-B-C. Clearly, the sub-goals are interdependent; the second agent has to wait for the first agent to complete its sub-goal before it can perform its own. Where such interdependencies exist, and they invariably do in MAS, the activities of the agents must be co-ordinated .

- Efficiency — even when individuals can function independently, thereby obviating the need for co-ordination, information discovered by one agent can be of sufficient use to another agent that both agents can solve the problem twice as fast.

Co-ordination, in turn, may require co-operation; but it is important to emphasise that co-operation among a set of agents would not necessarily result in co-ordination; indeed, it may result in incoherent behaviour. This is because for agents to co-operate successfully, typically, they must maintain models of each other as well as develop and maintain models of future interactions. If agents' beliefs about each other are wrong, for example, incoherent behaviour may well result. Co-ordination may occur without co-operation. For example, if a person is running towards you, and you get out of his way, you have co-ordinated your actions with his. However, you have not entered into co-operation with him. Likewise, non-co-operation among agents does not necessarily lead to incoherent behaviour (it may just happen to end up co-ordinated); however, it is likely to do so. Competition is a form of co-ordination involving antagonistic agents. To achieve co-ordination, agents may have to communicate with one another. However, as Huhns and Singh [7] point out, agents may achieve co-ordination without communication, provided they possess models of each others' behaviours. In such a situation, co-ordination can be achieved mainly via organisation. However, to facilitate co-ordination, where agents have to co-operate through communication, it is vital that they make known their goals, intentions, results and state to other agents. The literature on co-ordination abounds because it is used to address several DAI and distributed computing issues, including:

- network coherence — maximising how well a distributed system of agents work together;

- task and resource allocation among agents;

- recognising and resolving disparities or conflicts in goals, facts, beliefs, viewpoints and behaviour of agents;

- determining the organisational structure (i.e. architecture) of an agent set-up, i.e. defining the roles, responsibilities and chains of authority between agents.

The above list is not exhaustive. The outcome of a co-ordination process is, hopefully, a coherent set-up of agents — a set-up in which deadlock and livelock are avoided. Deadlock refers to a state of affairs in which further action between two or more agents is impossible; on the contrary, livelock refers to a scenario where agents continuously act (e.g. exchange tasks), but no progress is made. A co-ordinated set-up also maximally exploits the capabilities of individual agents and minimises conflicts and resource contentions between them. A coherent system will minimise or avoid conflicting and redundant efforts among agents. Clearly then, co-ordination is a necessary and desirable property of agent systems.

Co-ordination is not only a concern to agent researchers. With emerging technologies such as open systems, client-server computing, the World Wide Web (WWW) and the Internet, there is an unmistakable trend towards distributed computing systems, and this trend is set to continue well into the next millennium. The autonomous components or parts of such open distributed systems, which are analogous to agents in agent-based systems, need to be co-ordinated.

3. An Overview of Co-ordination Techniques

There are many approaches which have been devised to achieve co-ordination in agent systems. Co-ordination techniques are classified here in the following four broad categories:

- organisational structuring;

- contracting;

- multi-agent planning;

- negotiation.

There follows an overview and brief critique of each category separately.

3.1 Organisational Structuring

This is the simplest co-ordination scenario which exploits the *a priori* organisational structure. This is because the organisation defines implicitly the agent's responsibilities, capabilities, connectivity and control flow. It provides a framework for activity and interaction through the definition of roles, communication paths and authority relationships. Durfee et al define this as the pre-defined long-term relationships between agents [8]. Hierarchical organisations abound, yielding the classic master/slave or client/server co-ordination technique, used typically for task and resource allocation among slave agents by some master agent. This technique is implemented in a couple of ways.

- The master agent plans and distributes fragments of the plan to the slaves. The slaves may or may not communicate among themselves, but must ultimately report their results to the master agent.

  In this case, while the master has full autonomy with respect to the slaves, the slaves have only partial autonomy with respect to their master.

- Blackboard negotiation exploits the classic blackboard architecture [9] to provide a co-ordinating base. In this scheme the blackboard's knowledge sources are replaced by agents who post to and read from the general blackboard. The scheduling agent (or master agent) schedules the agents' reads/writes to/from the blackboard. This scheme is employed by Werkman in his DFI system [10]. This approach may be used when the problem is distributed, a central scheduling agent is present or when tasks have already been assigned, *a priori*, to agents. Sharp Multi-Agent Kernel (SMAK) also adopts a blackboard strategy [11].

The latter point highlights the fact that organisational work ought not to be solely associated with hierarchies. For example, in the DVMT system [12] which also exploits a blackboard, co-ordination occurs among peer agents.

Other organisational structures exist, of course, including the centralised and decentralised market structures. The centralised market structure employs a master/ slave co-ordination approach while a contracting technique, described in the next section, is more suitable for a decentralised market structure.

Critique

These strategies are useful where there are master/slave relationships in the MAS being modelled. Much control is exerted over the slaves' actions, and hence the problem-solving process. However, such control, in its extremes, mitigate against all the benefits of DAI — speed (due to parallelism) reliability, concurrency, robustness, graceful degradation, minimal bottlenecks, etc. In the blackboard co-ordination scheme, with no direct agent-to-agent communication, a severe bottle-neck may result if there are many agents, even in the case of multi-partitioned blackboards. Furthermore, all agents would need to have a common domain understanding (i.e. semantics). For this latter reason, most blackboard systems tend to have homogeneous and rather small-grained agents as is the case in the DVMT prototype [12]. Durfee et al [13] point out that such centralised control as in the master/slave technique is contrary to the basic assumptions of DAI. It presumes that at least one agent has a global view of the entire agency — in many domains, this is an unrealistic assumption. Even when a master/slave co-ordination technique is used, the designer should ensure that the slaves are of sufficient granularity to compensate for the overheads which result from goal distribution.

Distributing trivial or small tasks can be more expensive than performing them in one location [8].

3.2 Contracting

A, now classic, co-ordination technique for task and resource allocation among agents and determining organisational structure is the contract net protocol [14, 15]. In this approach, which assumes a decentralised market structure, agents can assume two roles:

- a manager who breaks a problem into sub-problems and searches for contractors to do them, as well as to monitor the problem's overall solution;

- a contractor who does a sub-task — however, contractors may recursively become managers and further decompose the sub-task and sub-contract them to other agents.

Managers locate contractors via a process of bidding which proceeds as follows:

- a manager announces a task;

- contractors evaluate the task with respect to their abilities and commitments;

- contractors table bids to the manager;

- the manager evaluates received bids, chooses a contractor and awards the contract to it;

- the manager waits for the result of the contract.

This is a completely distributed scheme where a node can both simultaneously be manager and contractor. This approach has been used in many applications, e.g. Parunak [16]. It has also been further generalised in other projects like the multistage negotiation in Conry et al [17].

Critique

Huhns and Singh [7] note that the contract net is a high-level co-ordination strategy which also provides a way of distributing tasks, and a means for self-organising a group of agents. It is best used when:

- the application task has a well-defined hierarchical nature;

- the problem has a coarse-grained decomposition;

- there is minimal coupling among sub-tasks.

The advantages of the contract net include the following — dynamic task allocation via self-bidding which leads to better agreements, agents can be introduced and removed dynamically, it provides natural load-balancing (as busy agents need not bid), and it is a reliable mechanism for distributed control and failure recovery [7].

Its limitations include the fact that it does not presume agents with contradictory demands; hence, the approach neither detects nor resolves conflicts, which is one key reason why co-ordination is needed in the first place. The agents in the contract net are rather passive, benevolent and non-antagonistic which for many real-world problems is unrealistic. Conry et al's generalisation of the contract net approach [17] essentially introduces an iterative mechanism for getting agents with conflicting goals to arrive at a consensus. Lastly, the contract net approach is rather communication-intensive, the costs of which may outweigh some of its advantages in real-world applications.

3.3   Multi-agent Planning

Another approach to co-ordination in agent-based systems is to engage the agents in multi-agent planning. In order to avoid inconsistent or conflicting actions and interactions, agents build a multi-agent plan that details all the future actions and interactions required to achieve their goals, and interleave execution with more planning and re-planning. There are two types of multi-agent planning:

- centralised multi-agent planning;

- distributed multi-agent planning.

In centralised multi-agent planning, there is usually a co-ordinating agent who, on receipt of all partial or local plans from individual agents, analyses them in order to identify potential inconsistencies and conflicting interactions (e.g. conflict between agents over limited resources). The co-ordinating agent then attempts to modify these partial plans and combines them into a multi-agent plan where conflicting interactions are eliminated. Georgeff [18, 19] exemplifies such an approach where conflicting interactions are identified and grouped into critical regions. In the final multi-agent plan, communication commands are inserted to synchronise agents' interactions appropriately. Cammarata et al [20] also employ centralised multi-agent planning in a simulated air-traffic control domain. In this demonstrator, agents (i.e. aeroplanes) in a potential conflict scenario, e.g. two aeroplanes are heading for collision, decide on one of their number to act as co-ordinating agent to whom the plans of the other agent are sent. This co-ordinating agent will then attempt to modify its own flight plan in order to resolve the conflict. Jin and Koyama [21] propose their MATPEN model for co-ordinating autonomous and distributed agents based on centralised planning. Their approach exploits an 'expectation-based negotiation protocol' which draws from the roles of agents in the organisational structure. When two agents share a conflict, they form a conflict group and initiate a negotiation process. The exchange 'expectations' (which represent the expected behaviour of other agents in order to resolve the conflict) in order to decide who should play what role in the negotiation process. Eventually, they generate a multi-agent plan to resolve the conflict. They have constructed a collision avoidance system for ships using MATPEN.

In distributed multi-agent planning, the idea is to provide each agent with a model of other agents' plans [22]. Agents communicate in order to build and update their individual plans and their models of others' until all conflicts are removed. An exemplification of this approach is Lesser and Corkill's functionally accurate and co-operative (FA/C) protocol [23]. In this approach, loosely-coupled agents form high-level (but possibly incomplete) plans, results and hypotheses which they exchange with each other. Next, they refine these until they all converge on some global complete plan. Local inconsistencies are detected and only the part of each agents' results that are consistent with local information are integrated into the local databases. This approach has been used in Lesser and Corkill's Distributed Vehicle Monitoring Testbed (DVMT) — a system for testing co-ordination strategies [12]. Another exemplification of distributed multi-agent planning is Durfee's partial global planning (PGP) approach [24]. In this technique, agents execute their local plans with each other, which, in turn, are modified continuously based on partial global plans (built by exchanging local plans). Therefore, agents are always looking out for potential improvements to group co-ordination.

Critique

Generally, multi-agent planning of whatever form requires that agents share and process substantial amounts of information; hence, it is likely to require more computing and communication resources than other approaches. The centralised multi-agent planning technique shares many of the limitations of the master/slave co-ordination technique. Naturally, the co-ordination in distributed multi-agent planning is much more complex than in the centralised form as there may not be any agent who possesses a global view of the distributed system. Furthermore, since co-ordination in some existing multi-agent planning techniques, such as PGP, is a gradual process, the scopes of their applicability may be better for some domains than others [7].

4. Negotiation

A significant part of the co-ordination work which has been done or is being done world-wide goes under the heading 'negotiation'. This is because most co-ordination schemes involve some sort of negotiation. For this reason, it has merited a section on its own in this paper. The literature abounds because negotiation is a key co-ordination technique used to address several DAI issues such as those listed in section 2. However, there are probably as many similar definitions of negotiation as there are negotiation researchers. Perhaps, a more succinct and basic one is that of Bussman and Muller [25]:

"...negotiation is the communication process of a group of agents in order to reach a mutually accepted agreement on some matter."

Sycara further points out that to negotiate effectively, agents must reason about beliefs, desires and intentions of other agents [4], and this has led to the development of techniques for the following:

- representing and maintaining belief models;

- reasoning about the other agents' beliefs;

- influencing other agents' intentions and beliefs.

These latter topics lead to the usage of all sorts of artificial intelligence (AI) and mathematical techniques including logic, case-based reasoning (CBR), belief revisions, distributed truth maintenance, multi-agent planning, model-based reasoning (MBR), optimisation and game theory. Furthermore, there is literature which proposes and reports on multi-agent test-beds, languages, protocols and interlinguas. In addition, there are also the purely social, cognitive and sociologically based papers. Thus, it is not difficult to explain the huge and varied literature on this subject of negotiation.

It is also conceded that the distinction made between negotiation and the other co-ordination approaches discussed in section 3 is quite fuzzy. Indeed, another paper, which overviews negotiation strategies [5], covers many of the aforementioned co-ordination techniques. This overview is not meant to be so exhaustive as to provide a road map through the more important literature on negotiation. Negotiation techniques are classified in the following three broad categories:

- game theory-based negotiation;

- plan-based negotiation;

- human-inspired and miscellaneous AI-based nego-tiation approaches.

4.1   Game Theory-based Negotiation

There is now a growing body of work on negotiation which is based on game theory [26]; perhaps the origins of such work can be traced back to Rosenschein's doctoral thesis [27]. With the help of one of his former students, Rosenschein has since refined, synthesised and collated his earlier work in one volume [28]. Using the tools of game theory, this book outlines an approach which shows how to achieve co-ordination among a set of rational and autonomous agents without an explicit co-ordination mechanism built into these agents *a priori*. In other words, it does not presume the 'benevolent agent assumption'.

The key concepts in this game theory approach to negotiation are the following — utility functions, a space of deals, strategies and negotiation protocols. Utility is defined as the difference between the worth of achieving a goal and the price paid in achieving it. A deal is an action an agent can take which has an attached utility. The negotiation protocol defines the rules which govern the negotiation, including how and when it ends (e.g. by agreement or no deal). In the book [28], several protocols and strategies for negotiation are outlined.

The actual negotiation proceeds as follows. Utility values for each outcome of some interaction for each agent are built into a pay-off matrix, which is common knowledge to both (typically) parties involved in the negotiation. The negotiation process involves an interactive process of offers and counter-offers in which each agent chooses a deal which maximises its expected utility value. There is an implicit assumption that each agent in the negotiation is an expected utility maximiser. At each step in the negotiation, an agent evaluates the other's offer in terms of its own negotiation strategy.

Zlotkin and Rosenschein [29] have also extended work to cover agents that are not truthful, i.e. they can be deceptive; interestingly, using some simple demonstrators, they show that if an agent withholds certain information or deliberately misinforms other agents, this may result in better negotiation deals for the agent. In this work they view negotiation as a two-stage process — the actual negotiating and the execution of the joint plans. In their recent work, they are working on a general theory of automated negotiation in which they classify complex domains into three — task-oriented domains, state-oriented domains and worth-oriented domains [28].

Kraus and Wilkenfield also examine negotiation using game-theory techniques with appropriate modification [30]. In this paper, they propose a strategic model that claims to take time into consideration during the negotiation process. Time influences the outcome of the negotiations and avoids delays in reaching agreements.

Critique

Game theory-based negotiation fails to address some crucial issues [31]. Firstly, agents are presumed to be fully rational and acting as utility maximisers using predefined strategies. Secondly, all agents have knowledge of the pay-off matrix, and therefore full knowledge of the other agent's preferences — this is certainly unlike the real world where agents only have partial or incomplete knowledge of their own domains, let alone those of others. Therefore, this is unrealistic for truly non-benevolent and loosely-coupled agencies. Furthermore, the pay-off matrix could become very large and intractable for a negotiation involving many agents and outcomes. Thirdly, agents only consider the current state when deciding on their deal — past interactions and future implications are simply ignored. Fourthly, agents are considered to have identical internal models and capabilities. Fifthly, much of the work presumes two agents negotiating, though some later work is addressing n-agent negotiation [32]. Sixthly, and consequently, despite Zlotkin and Rosenschien's provision of mathematical proof of their ideas [32], it is unlikely that game theory-based negotiation will suffice for real-life, industrial agent-based applications for the reasons already offered. In brief, its assumptions are untenable in real applications.

4.2 Plan-Based Negotiation

Alder et al [33] investigate negotiated agreements and discuss methods of conflict detection and resolution in the domain of telephone network traffic control. They imbue their agents with planning knowledge as they strongly maintain that negotiation and planning are very tightly intertwined due to the fact that agents need information from others to function effectively and efficiently.

Kreifelt and von Martial propose a negotiation strategy for autonomous agents [34]; they view negotiation as a two- stage process — firstly, agents plan their activities separately, and then, secondly, they co-ordinate their plans. The co-ordination of all the agents' plans is done by a separate co-ordination agent, though they note that this role may be played by any of the agents. They then proceed to present a negotiation protocol in terms of agents' states, message types and conversation rules between agents. This proposal also has many limitations. As Bussman and Muller [25] rightly point out, it does not really present a negotiation model but just prescribes one, and it is really left to the agents how they really achieve consensus. The protocol itself also needs some further clarification. In general, plan-based negotiation suffers from the limitations of centralised or distributed multi-agent planning (see section 3.3), depending on which of these two types is used.

4.3   Human-Inspired and Miscellaneous AI-based Negotiation Approaches

It appears that almost every form of human interaction requires some degree of explicit or implicit negotiation [10]. Hence, it is not very surprising that many negotiation researchers draw from human negotiation strategies. As noted earlier, these often lead to the usage of miscellaneous AI techniques including logic, CBR, constraint-directed search, etc, as is evidenced by the following. However, some of the examples below just provide AI-based negotiation approaches which do not necessarily borrow from human interactions.

Sycara's work [4], which sees negotiation as an iterative activity, proposes a general negotiation model that attempts to handle multi-agent, multiple-issue, single and repeated type negotiations. Her view of negotiation leads her to exploit CBR and multi-attribute utility theory. She argues for a case-based approach based on her belief that human negotiators draw from the past negotiation experiences to guide present and future ones. In the absence of past cases, she resorts to preference analysis based on multi-attribute theory. In the latter case, issues involved in negotiation are represented by utility curves. By combining these curves in additive and multiplicative fashions, a proposal is chosen which maximises the utility. Sycara has constructed a system called PERSUADER that resolves adversarial conflicts in labour relations with the aid of two practising negotiators. Agents can modify others' beliefs, behaviours and intentions via persuasion. Sycara strongly believes that the latter is a necessity in order to create co-operative interactions.

Sathi and Fox [35] argue that negotiation may be viewed as a constraint-directed search of a problem space using negotiation operators. They see negotiation as composed of two phases — a communications phase, where all information is communicated to participating agents, and a bargaining phase, where deals are made between individuals or in a group. In their approach, agents negotiate via relaxing various conflicts and constraints until agreement is reached. Alternatively, the solutions may be modified. Initially, preferences of negotiation are modelled as constraints. The negotiation operators are drawn from human negotiation studies [36] and include operators which simulate relaxation, reconfiguration and composition, which are used to generate new constraints. This approach has been used to build a system for resource allocation which 'performs marginally better than experts'.

The main limitation of this iterative approach stems from the fact that selecting relaxations to achieve a compromise is a major problem as no criteria are provided, and hence agents easily get caught in an infinite loop of exchanging offers (i.e. livelock).

Werkman proposes a knowledge-based model of an incremental form of negotiation [10]. Werkman's Designer Fabricator Interpreter (DFI) model, it is claimed, is based largely on various human models of negotiation. This scheme uses a shared-knowledge representation, called shareable agent perspectives, which:

"...allows agents to perform negotiation in a manner similar to co-operating (or competing) experts who share a common background of domain knowledge."

Essentially, it exploits a blackboard with partitions for requested proposals, rejected proposals, accepted proposals, a communications partition and shared knowledge. Such rich detail and knowledge of the perspectives of other agents provide invaluable information for agents to make better proposals in the future.

Werkman [10] sees negotiation as a three-phase cycle. The first phase involves some proposing agent announcing a proposal which is received and evaluated by the receiving agent. The second phase involves generating a counter proposal if the latter is not happy with the initial proposal, or it may be simply accepted. Phase three involves the submission of the counter proposal for review by other agents. An arbitrator agent assists when two agents get into deadlock by reviewing the negotiation dialogue and uses their mutual information network to generate alternative proposals. This is done using issue relaxation techniques or some intelligent proposal generator. This may fail, in which case the arbitrator may set time limits or use other techniques.

This proposal is interesting and definitely worth studying in greater detail. The use of arbitration is relatively novel. His agents communicate via the blackboard through a speech-act based language. The centralised blackboard could be a bottle-neck, and, without an explicit scheduler, reading and posting to the blackboard seems chaotic. However, this proposal does seem to have a good understanding of the negotiating process. It has also been implemented in the DFI system.

Conry et al [37] specifically concerned themselves with negotiation strategies for distributed constraint satisfaction problems where a network of agents have a goal, but each node or agent has only limited resources. The local constraints give rise to a complex set of global and inter-dependent constraints. This investigation was done in the context of the long-haul transmission and more complex communication networks which they were researching. Their implementation involved developing algorithms for multi-agent planning while taking the inevitable conflicts into consideration. This piece of work is interesting because it begins the investigation of whether specific generic tasks may be linked with specific negotiation strategies. Researchers on negotiation will need to identify such links if the literature is to be made less *ad hoc*.

Bussmann and Muller's negotiating framework for co-operating agents [25] is, arguably, one of the most useful papers on negotiation in the literature. Drawing from socio-psychological theories of negotiation, particularly Gulliver's eight phases of the negotiation process [38], they evolve a cyclic negotiation model which is both general and simple. They attempt to address many of the limitations of other negotiation proposals/models. The cyclic nature of the model addresses the thorny issue of conflict resolution.

The general strategy is that negotiation begins with one, some or every agent making a proposal. Then agents evaluate and check the proposals against their preferences, and criticise them by listing their preferences which are violated by the proposals. The agents then update their knowledge about other agents' preferences and the negotiation cycle resumes with a new proposal or proposals in the light of the newly gleaned information. Conflicts between agents are handled in a concurrent conflict resolution cycle.

Bussmann and Muller's suggestion is untested but it does seem to draw from and address the limitations of many others. In this respect, it is an interesting proposal.

Finally, other researchers have proposed negotiation protocols including Kuwabara and Lesser's extended protocol for multistage negotiation [39] and Durfee and Montgomery's hierarchical protocol for co-ordinating multi-agent behaviour [40]. Naturally, protocols of this nature implicitly implement some negotiation strategy (e.g. Kuwabara and Lesser's implements the multistage negotiation strategy of Lesser's group at the University of Massachusetts), and, if it is suitable for some particular task, then it may as well be reused.

5. Lessons Learned and Some Heuristics on Co-ordination/Negotiation

This section synthesises some of the key lessons culled from this review of the co-ordination literature, and presents some conclusions which have been drawn from the literature on co-ordination.

- One-off co-ordination strategies (or combination of strategies) are devised and used in one-off projects. Hence, solid conclusions as to their scope, applicability, usability, etc, have not been established.

- There is little empirical or theoretical support for any strategy or strategies. Not enough studies have been done to validate many of the proposals.

- It is not very clear when, where, how and why various negotiation and co-ordination strategies or combinations of them are used in various applications or proposals.

- The contract net and the master/slave models and variations of them appear to be the most used strategies due to their simplicity. Various AI, mathematical and operational research techniques are being used to realise co-ordination. This paper has highlighted some, e.g. including viewing negotiation as constraint-directed search [35]. Most of them seem to be either problem-dependent or were just used because the researchers had experience using those techniques; hence, their choice seem rather *ad hoc*. However, the problem-dependent issues cannot be ignored as they are crucial to the success of individual applications.

- Various techniques make fundamental assumptions about agents which must be understood. For example, the contract net approach presumes truly benevolent, trustful, non-conflicting and helpful agents.

- Most co-ordination or negotiation strategies do not involve any complex meta-reasoning required of most domains. For example, few take into consideration the time aspects, and the fact that agents' goals, beliefs, intentions, etc, change with time. Hence, in real life, something an agent is currently doing may no longer matter because, say, the deadline is past, in which case it is best that it stops or forgets about that particular task/sub-task. Alternatively, the resources may not be available at the times required by the agents. These introduce non-trivial dimensions to co-ordination.

- There is a lack of fundamental analysis of the process of co-ordination and negotiation. Jennings [6] is a step in this direction.

6. Conclusions

This paper has overviewed the diverse literature on co-ordination in agent-based systems. Successful co-ordination is a key design objective for most multi-agent system builders. Without good co-ordination mechanisms, many of the benefits of the multi-agent paradigm simply disappear. For this reason, researchers have invested significant resources in devising, implementing, and evaluating a large array of co-ordination techniques. As discussed in this paper, the various approaches have their relative advantages and disadvantages. At this time, there is no universally best method. In general, the theoretical methods produce good results in well-constrained environments, but many of their underpinning assumptions are not suited to developing real-world systems. Extant implementation-oriented work, on the other hand, operates well in limited domains but suffers from a lack of grounding and rigorous evaluation.

Based on our experiences and observations, it is possible to identify four major components which must be present in any comprehensive co-ordination technique [6]. Firstly, there must be structures which enable the agents to interact in predictable ways. Secondly, there must be flexibility so that agents can operate in dynamic environments and can cope with their inherently partial and imprecise viewpoint of the community. Thirdly, there must be social structures which describe how agents should behave towards one another when engaged in the co-ordination process. Finally, the agents must have sufficient knowledge and reasoning capabilities to exploit both the available structure (individual and social) and the flexibility.

For the future, further theoretical work is needed to develop adequate, and appropriately broad, models of co-ordination which address all of the four major components identified above. This should then lead to better specified implementations of co-ordination algorithms which have clearly delimited ranges of applicability. This approach will also enable more systematic evaluation of the different algorithms to be undertaken so that system builders can base their design decisions on empirical evidence (rather than on their *ad hoc* preconceptions).

Acknowledgements

This paper has drawn extensively from some of the work done by the first author as part of a short-term fellowship at BT Laboratories in the summer of 1994 while he was an academic. The help, in particular, of Mark Wiegand and Robin Smith, who both initiated the fellowship, is acknowledged.

References

1. Galbraith J R: 'Organization design', Addison-Wesley (1977).

2. Thompson G, Frances J, Levacic R and Mitchell J (Eds): 'Market, Hierarchies and Networks — The Coordination of Social Life', Sage Publications (1991).

3. Malone T W: 'Modeling Coordination in Organizations and Markets', Management Science, 33, No 10, pp 1317—1332 (1987).

4. Sycara K: 'Multi-agent Compromise via Negotiation', in Gasser L and Huhns M (Eds): 'Distributed Artificial Intelligence 2', Morgan Kaufmann (1989).

5. Nwana H S: 'Negotiation Strategies: An Overview', BT Laboratories internal report (1994).

6. Jennings N R: 'Coordination Techniques for Distributed Artificial Intelligence', in O'Hare G M P and Jennings N R (Eds): 'Foundations of Distributed Artificial Intelligence', London, Wiley pp 187—210 (1990).

7. Huhns M and Singh M P: 'CKBS-94 Tutorial: Distributed Artificial Intelligence for Information Systems', Dake Centre, University of Keele (1994).

8. Durfee E H, Lesser V R and Corkill D D: 'Coherent Cooperation among Communicating Problem Solvers', IEEE Trans Comput, 11, pp 1275—1291 (1987).

9. Hayes-Roth B: 'A Blackboard Architecture for Control', Artificial Intelligence, No 25, pp 251—321 (1985).

10. Werkman K J: 'Knowledge-based model of negotiation using shareable perspectives', Proc of the 10th Int Workshop on DAI, Texas (1990).

11. Kearney P, Sehmi A and Smith R: 'Emergent behaviour in a multi-agent economics simulation', in Cohn A G (Ed): 'Proceedings of the 11th European Conference on Artificial Intelligence', London, John Wiley (1994).

12. Lesser V and Corkill D: 'The Distributed Vehicle Monitoring Testbed: A Tool for Investigating Distributed Problem-Solving Networks', AI Magazine, 4, No 3, pp 15—33 (1983).

13. Durfee E H, Lesser V R and Corkill D D: 'Trends in Cooperative Distributed Problem Solving', IEEE Knowledge and Data engineering, 1, No 1, pp 63—83 (1989).

14. Davis R and Smith R G: 'Negotiation as a metaphor for distributed problem solving', Artificial Intelligence, No 20, pp 63—109 (1983).

15. Smith R G: 'The Contract Net Protocol: High-Level Communication and Control in a Distributed Problem Solver', IEEE Trans on Comput, 29, No 12 (December 1980).

16. Parunak H V-D: 'Manufacturing Experience with the Contract Net', in Gasser L and Huhns M (Eds): 'Distributed Artificial Intelligence 2', Morgan Kaufmann (1989).

17. Conry S E, Meyer R A and Lesser V R: 'Multistage Negotiation in Distributed Planning', COINS Technical Report, University of Massachusetts, Amherst, Boston (1986).

18. Georgeff M: 'Communication and Interaction in Multi-Agent Planning Proc 1983 National Conf Artificial Intell, pp 125—129 (August 1983).

19. Georgeff M: 'A Theory of Action for Multi-Agent Planning', Proc 1984 National Conf Artificial Intell, pp 121—125 (August 1984).

20. Cammarata S, McArthur D and Steeb R: 'Strategies of Cooperation in Distributed Problem Solving', Proc of the Eighth Int Joint Conf on Artificial Intell, pp 767—770 (1983).

21. Jin Y and Koyama T: 'Multi-agent planning through expectation-based negotiation', Proc of the 10th Int Workshop on DAI, Texas (1990).

22. Corkill D D: 'Hierarchical Planning in a Distributed Environment', Proc 6th Int Joint Conf Artificial Intell, pp 168—179 (August 1979).

23. Lesser V and Corkill D: 'Functionally accurate, cooperative distributed systems, IEEE Trans on Systems, Man and Cybernetics, 11, No 1, pp 81—96 (1981).

24. Durfee E H and Lesser V R: 'Using Partial Global Plans to Co-ordinate Distributed Problem Solvers', Proc of the 1987 Int Joint Conf on Artificial Intell, pp 875—883 (1987).

25. Bussmann S and Muller J: 'A Negotiation Framework for Co-operating Agents', in Deen S M (Ed): 'Proc CKBS-SIG', Dake Centre, University of Keele, pp 1—17 (1992).

26. Luce R D and Raiffa H: 'Games and Decisions', John Wiley & Sons (1957).

27. Rosenschein J S: 'Rational Interaction: Cooperation Among Intelligent Agents', PhD Thesis, Stanford University (1985).

28. Rosenschein J S and Zlotkin G: 'Rules of Encounter: Designing Conventions for Automated Negotiation among Computers', MIT Press (1994).

29. Zlotkin G and Rosenschein J S: 'Blocks, Lies, and Postal Freight: The Nature of Deception in Behaviour', Proc of the 10th Int Workshop on DAI (1990).

30. Kraus S and Wilkenfield J: 'The Function of Time in Cooperative Negotiations: Preliminary Report', Department of Computer Science, University of Maryland (1991).

31. Busuioc M and Winter C: 'Negotiation and Intelligent Agents', Project NOMADS-001, BT Laboratories internal report (1995).

32. Zlotkin G and Rosenschein J S: 'One, Two, Many: Coalitions in Multi-Agent Systems', Proc of the 5th European Workshop on Modelling Autonomous Agents in a Multi-Agent World (August 1993).

33. Alder M R, Davis A B, Weihmayer R and Forest R W: 'Conflict-resolution strategies for non-hierarchical distributed agents', in Gasser L and Huhns M N (Eds): 'Distributed Artificial Intelligence 2', Morgan Kaufmann (1989).

34. Kreifelt T and von Martial F: 'A negotiation framework for autonomous agents', in Demazeau Y and Muller J P (Eds): 'Decentralized AI2', Elsevier Science (1991).

35. Sathi A and Fox M: 'Constraint-directed negotiation of resource allocations', in Gasser L and Huhns M (Eds): 'Distributed Artificial Intelligence 2', Morgan Kaufmann (1989).

36. Pruitt D G: 'Negotiation Behaviour', Academic Press (1981).

37. Conry S E, Meyer R A and Lesser V R: 'Multistage Negotiation in Distributed Planning', in Bond A H and Gasser L (Eds): 'Readings in Distributed Artificial Intelligence', San Mateo, Morgan Kaufmann (1988).

38. Gulliver P H: 'Disputes and Negotiations — A cross-cultural perspective', Academic Press (1979).

39. Kuwabara K and Lesser V R: 'Extended Protocol for Multistage Negotiation', Proc of the 9th Workshop on Distributed Artificial Intell (1989).

40. Durfee E H and Montgomery T A: 'A hierarchical protocol for coordinating multi-agent behaviour', Proc of the 8th National Conf on Artificial Intell, Boston, MA, pp 86—93 (1990).

Software Agent Technologies

H S Nwana[1] and M Wooldridge[2]

[1] Intelligent System Research, Advanced Applications & Technology Department,
BT Laboratories, Martlesham Heath, Ipswich, Suffolk, IP5 7RE, UK.
E-mail: hyacinth@info.bt.co.uk
[2] Mitsubishi Electric Digital Library Group,
18th Floor, Centre Point, 103 New Oxford Street, London, WC1A 1EB, UK.
E-mail: mjw@dlib.com

It is by now a cliché that there is no one, universally accepted, definition of intelligent agent technology, but a number of loosely related techniques. Yet there are certain themes that appear common to agent-based systems, and, correspondingly, certain problems that must be addressed and overcome by all agent system builders. The aim of this paper is to briefly survey the tools and techniques that can be used to address these common issues, and that hence form a substrate for software agent systems. This paper begins with a review of agent communication languages, focusing particularly on the emerging standard known as KQML. Then a thumbnail sketch of various programming languages for building agent-based systems is presented, and there follows a discussion on support for ontologies, which allow agents to communicate using commonly defined terms and concepts. Then other computing infrastructure support for agent-based systems is considered, in particular, the use of client/server architectures and distributed object frameworks. Finally, some general comments and conclusions are presented.

1. Introduction

At the time of writing, intelligent agents and multi-agent systems are among the most rapidly growing areas of research and development in computer science. Unfortunately, as with object technology a decade ago, there is great confusion about agents — hardly anyone agrees on even the basic question of what an agent is, still less on more contentious issues. New definitions and systems seem to appear one week, and disappear the next. Journalists and practitioners, ever eager to keep abreast of new technologies, attend conferences and seminars only to be presented with a collection of apparently unrelated concepts and terms; and, of course, experience with all things object-oriented indicates that this situation is here to stay, at least for the foreseeable future.

Given this state of affairs, it would be naive to make predictions about how agent technology will develop, and, in particular, about the exact form or structure of future agent applications. Yet there are certain themes that appear common to most agent-based systems, and, correspondingly, certain problems that must be addressed and overcome by all agent system builders. In brief, the purpose of this paper is to survey the various technologies that are capable of providing (or which currently provide) this substrate for building agent-based applications. It should be noted that, for the reasons mentioned above, no attempt is made to survey actual agent architectures or applications. Rather, the aim is to focus on what might be called the 'enabling technologies' for agent-based systems.

In order to facilitate such an overview, an abstraction of some current or future technologies involved is helpful. Figure 1 shows one classification of some of the technologies involved. It is emphasised that this represents an abstract organisation of the technologies that facilitate the implementation of agent-based applications [1]. The hierarchy depicted may be considered by some to be contentious and arbitrary. Nevertheless, it represents a useful classification device, around which the remainder of the paper is structured.

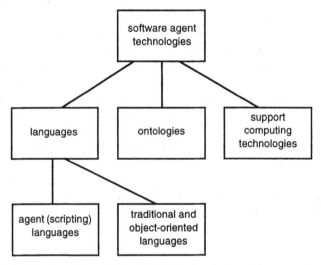

Fig. 1.   A classification of some technologies for developing software agent applications.

Typically, applications containing multiple agents make use of an agent communication language (ACL); the idea is similar to a human society using a common language (such as English). A couple of categories of agent communication languages are reviewed in section 2. In section 3, languages that facilitate the construction of agent applications are briefly listed. However, it is noted that agent-based applications can be (and have been) developed using traditional third-generation languages like Lisp, C, or Prolog, and object-oriented (OO) languages such as C++ or Smalltalk. Next, agents working together need to share a certain amount of foundational, 'common' knowledge, in just the same way that humans do. When one agent tells another agent to buy a widget, they must agree both on what a 'widget' is, and what 'buy' means. Section 4 reviews the techniques available for representing such foundational knowledge. In section 5, some current and emerging computing technologies that lend themselves to supporting agent-based applications are briefly discussed, and section 6 provides a discussion and conclusion to the paper.

2. Agent Communication Languages

A key rationale for having multiple agent systems (MAS) is that the ensemble of agents provide 'added value', beyond that which would otherwise be obtained from any single agent [2, 3]. This added value is typically achieved via co-operation. If every agent had perfect information about the state of the entire system — if every agent knew what every other agent knew, what every other agent intended to do, and how everything in the system stood in relation to everything else in the system — then co-operation could proceed without any communication at all [4]. The agents could work together as a perfectly co-ordinated team, without ever having to communicate. Of course, except in the most trivial systems, such perfect knowledge is impossible to achieve. Agents have at best partial, possibly incorrect information about the state of their environment. Thus, in order to co-operate effectively in any moderately realistic system, agents are required to communicate with one another. Where agents need to communicate, they must individually 'understand' some agent communication language (ACL). Indeed, Genesereth and Ketchpel [5] maintain that some piece of software:

> "...is a software agent if, and only if, it communicates correctly in an agent communication language."

Although this statement is arguable because it fails to mention other attributes that are considered germane to agenthood, the importance of having an ACL is acknowledged — imagine a society without some lingua franca.

ACLs are designed specifically to facilitate communication between two or more agents. Agents need to communicate information, intentions, goals, etc, to other agents. As Cohen and Levesque [6] also note, an ACL should allow agents to enlist the support of others to achieve goals, to monitor their execution, to report progress, success, failure, to acknowledge receipt of messages, to refuse task allocations, and to commit to performing tasks for other agents.

Most ACLs, both 'standard' and *ad hoc*, derive their inspiration from speech act theory [7, 8] which was developed by linguists in an attempt to understand how humans use language in everyday situations, to achieve everyday ends. In speech act theory, human utterances are viewed as actions, in the same sense as actions performed in the everyday physical world (e.g. picking up a block from a table). The theory considers three aspects of utterances. Locution refers to the act of utterance itself — simply uttering an acceptable sentence of some language. Illocution refers to the 'type' of utterance, for example, an utterance may be a request to turn on the heater or an assertion about the temperature. There are many different illocutionary verbs (or performatives) in English — examples include 'request', 'warn', 'inform'. Perlocution refers to the effect of an utterance — how it influences the recipient. In the context of agent-based applications, researchers have proposed ACLs based on speech act theory, or more specifically, on illocutionary speech acts.

The illocutionary verbs (such as request, inform, warn) in a natural language like English typically correspond to performatives in some ACL. There is an implicit assumption that the illocutionary performative utterance of some agent succeeds because the sending agent is communicating some attitude(s) of itself such as beliefs, goals, or assertions. It is illocutionary because the agent expects that its utterance will be understood (as it intends it to be) by the receiving agent, even though it has no control over how the utterance influences this receiving agent, i.e. it is not perlocutionary. The aspect of locution, in the context of ACLs, is trivial because it is usually implicit in the explicitly encoded performative. In other words the type and structure of the message, for example:

accept [to: agent_2, from: agent_3, reference: contract_4, cost: £40]

is implicitly an instance of a locutionary act. More importantly, it is assumed that by virtue of being sent, it will effect some illocutionary action (in this example, agent_2 updates its belief set to reflect the fact that agent_3 has accepted to do contract_4 at the cost of £40).

For the purposes of this paper, ACLs will be classified into two categories — 'standard' ones and *ad hoc* ones.

2.1 A Standard ACL — KQML

The Knowledge Query and Manipulation Language (KQML) is an evolving standard ACL, being developed as part of the DARPA knowledge-sharing effort (KSE) [9, 10]. The KSE is a distributed research program that is investigating and constructing software tools for co-ordination and knowledge sharing among information systems, i.e. between separate knowledge-based modules, as well as between knowledge-based systems and databases [11]. As Finin [12] notes, the KSE research program:

> "...focuses on the ability of such agents to effectively interoperate by communicating information and knowledge in spite of problems introduced by heterogeneity of platforms, implementation technol-ogy, operating environments and development. This communication requires a common language or language framework which involves syntactic, semantic and pragmatic components."

The KSE programme consists of four separate but inter-working groups. One major product so far from one of these groups, the External Interfaces Working Group (EIWG), is KQML — a high-level communication language and protocol for exchanging information and knowledge. KQML has been implemented in several research groups across North America.

At the heart of KQML are more than three dozen performatives that define the allowed 'speech acts' that agents may use, and which provide the substrate for constructing more complex co-ordination and negotiation strategies (as discussed in

Nwana et al [4]). These performatives are grouped into nine categories, as shown in Table 1.

Table 1. KQML performatives [13].

Category	Reserved performative names
Basic informational performatives	tell, deny, untell, cancel,
Basic query performatives	evaluate, reply, ask-if, ask-about, ask-one, ask-all, sorry
Multi-response query performatives	stream-about, stream-all
Basic effector performatives	achieve, unachieve
Generator performatives	standby, ready, next, rest, discard, generator
Capability definition performatives	advertise
Notification performatives	subscribe, monitor
Networking performatives	register, unregister, forward, broadcast, pipe, break
Facilitation performatives	broker-one, broker-all, recommend-one, recommend-all, recruit-one, recruit-all

The KQML language can be viewed as consisting of three layers — the content, message and communication layers, as shown in Fig 2.

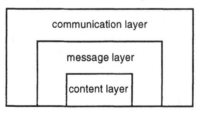

Fig. 2. An abstract view of the KQML language.

The content layer specifies the actual content of the message, and the KQML standard itself has nothing to say about this. A KQML-conforming message could contain Prolog code, C code, natural-language expressions, or whatever, as long as it is ASCII-representable. The set of performatives provided by the language, and shown in Table 1, constitute the message layer, which in turn forms the core of the language. This layer of abstraction provides the performative and specifies the protocol for delivering the message that subsumes the content.

Protocol is defined as the rules that agents must use when initiating and maintaining an exchange. KQML specifies several protocols, including synchronous (where a blocking query waits for an expected reply) and asynchronous (which involves non-blocking messages).

The chosen performative specifies that the content is a query, an assertion or any of the other categories of performatives. The set of KQML performatives is extensible, but EIWG has tried to strike a balance between providing a small set (thereby requiring overloading at the content layer), and providing a large set (where they are likely to overlap with one another, or else the distinctions between them become very fine). These performatives are neither necessary nor sufficient for all agent applications; however, agent application developers are encouraged to use them as specified in order to increase interoperability across applications. If some application does not support the correct usage of any of the performatives, then it would not be KQML-compliant.

The communication layer encodes low-level com-munication parameters, such as the identities of the sender and the recipient, and unique identifiers for the particular speech act. It should be noted that the provision of a secure and reliable communications medium (essentially, the lower five layers of the seven-layer OSI model) tends to be taken for granted in most agent-related research. Only the upper two layers (presentation and application) are considered an issue.

For a flavour of KQML, here is an example of an instantiated performative:

```
(tell
            : content "cost(bt, service-4, £5677)"
            : language standard prolog
            : ontology bt-services-domain
            : in-reply-to quote service-4
            : receiver customer-2
            : sender bt-customer-services)
```

The KQML performative in this message is tell, and the agent that is sending it seeks to inform some customer, customer-2, of a quote for performing some service, service-4, in reply to an earlier request from customer-2, to BT customer services. The content of the message is expressed in standard Prolog, and the ontology for BT's services domain is assumed.

KQML has a number of shortcomings. Cohen and Levesque [6] identify three general difficulties with it. Firstly, the actual specification of KQML is ambiguous and vague. KQML does not, in fact, have a precise, formal semantics, as is normal of programming languages. Cohen and Levesque believe this is a real problem:

"Without [a precise semantics], agent designers cannot be certain that the interpretation they are giving to a 'performative' is in fact the same as the one some other designer intended it to have. Moreover, the lack of a semantics for communication acts leads to a number of confusions in the set of reserved 'performatives' supplied." [6]

In KQML's defence, its inventors emphasise that it:

"...is concerned primarily with pragmatics (and secondarily with semantics)." [10]

Pragmatics, as Huhns [14] explains, is about knowing with whom to communicate and how to find them, knowing how to initiate and maintain an exchange (i.e. protocol), and knowing the effect of the communication on the recipient.

More troubling, it is not at all clear how one could go about giving the language a precise semantics, in such a way that it is possible to determine whether any given application is or is not KQML-conformant. Also, if it is impossible to determine, accurately and unambiguously, whether or not a system that claims to conform to some standard actually does conform to the standard, one must ask what the point of the so-called standard is. Secondly and thirdly, Cohen and Levesque also argue [6] that KQML suffers from mis-identified and missing performatives respectively, i.e. they suggest that some KQML performatives are not what they claim to be, and that, in addition, KQML is missing an entire class of performatives (commissives, which commit the utterer to a course of action).

Mayfield et al [1] also attempt an evaluation of KQML, and highlight some of its other merits and demerits. On the positive side, many prototype applications have already been constructed in North America and Europe that are KQML-compliant. It may be that, in the absence of any serious competition, KQML is becoming the *de facto* ACL standard.

2.2   Ad Hoc ACLs

To date, many agent-based applications with collaborative agents use an *ad hoc* set of performatives within *ad hoc* agent communication languages. Many others, strictly speaking, do not have explicit ACLs — they communicate by depositing information in some shared data structure. Applications with their own ACLs are mostly speech act-based. They possess a limited subset of performatives, similar to KQML's, but they are usually specified differently to their KQML equivalents, and they have different protocols. For example, SRI's Open Agent Architecture [15] has an ACL called the Inter-agent Communication Language (ICL). It possesses only three speech act types — solve (i.e. a question), do (a request) and post (an assertion to a shared data structure).

Naturally, the shortcoming of such *ad hoc* approaches is that it makes it non-trivial, if not impossible, for interoperation to occur between agent applications built by different developers. The case for having an ACL standard like KQML therefore seems compelling.

3.   Languages for Constructing Agent Applications

There are many languages currently available to prototype agent-based applications. However, these do not warrant them being referred to as agent languages, as many do. Wooldridge and Jennings [16] write:

"... by an agent language, we mean a system that allows one to program hardware or software computer systems in terms of some of the concepts developed by agent theorists. At the very least, we expect such a language to include some structure corresponding to an agent."

This is fine, but it begs the polemical question: "What is an agent?" As there is no consensus yet (indeed, there may never be) with respect to this question, it is axiomatic that a language which some researchers may refer to as an agent language will not be referred to as such by others. What is true is that there are a whole range of languages which lend themselves, to varying degrees, to different types of agent applications and definitions. It has been argued in Nwana [2] and Nwana and Ndumu [3] that the word 'agent' is really a banner word for a heterogeneous body of on-going research and development, and a typology for software agents was provided. This typology is now used to classify the languages covered in this section. The typology includes the following agent types — collaborative, interface, mobile, information and reactive. More detailed information is available in Nwana [2] or Nwana and Ndumu [3].

3.1 Some Languages that Facilitate the Building of Agent Applications

Table 2, which provides a list of some available languages, is by no means exhaustive; moreover, a significant number of these languages are research demonstrators only.

It should also be noted that Table 2 does not show many languages as suitable for developing collaborative (multi-) agent systems. This is because, in general, collaborative agents are much more complex than interface, information or mobile agents. They tend to require not only languages for their development, but architectures or platforms, e.g. DVMT [24] or ARCHON [25]. Alternatively, they are constructed 'from scratch' using some third-generation language like C++, Smalltalk, or Prolog. The languages from Table 2 are not discussed in any detail here.

3.2 Traditional Languages Used to Construct Agent Applications

It is perfectly possible to implement, say, an Ada compiler in machine code. However, machine code would not generally be used for such a task, because there are better tools for the job — high-level languages like Pascal or C. In just the same way, it is possible to implement agent-based systems in languages like Pascal, C, Lisp, or Prolog. As a rule, however, one would not choose to do so because such languages are not particularly well-suited to the job. A poor choice of language will necessitate the re-implementation of what other languages offer for free. For example, it is probably not very wise to develop mobile agent applications in standard C, which allows the user to write and manipulate memory with impunity. Many people would agree that mobile agents could be malicious, and allowing arbitrary, erred access to memory is a sure way to allow trouble. Hence, writing such an application in C would require the implementation of a 'safe' layer on top of C, which disallows direct memory access; but doing this will involve replicating the functionality that you get with the scripting language Safe-TCL. In summary, it makes sense to use the 'right' (i.e. minimum cost, whatever the definition of 'cost' is) tool for the job. Table 2 provides a 'first-cut' set of several heuristics for making such choices.

Table 2.   Some languages for developing different agent-based applications.

Agent type(s)	Language Class	Example(s)	Major reference(s)
Collaborative agents	Actor Languages	Actors	Agha [17]
	Agent-oriented programming languages	Agent-0	Shoham [18]
		Placa	Thomas [19]
Interface agents	Scripting lanaguages	TCL/TK	Oustershout [20] http://www.smli.com/research/tct/
Information agents		Safe-TCL, Safe-Tk	
Mobile agents			
		Java	http://java.sun.com/
		Telescript	http://www.genmagic.com/
		Active Web tools	
		Python	http://www.python.org
		Obliq	http://www.research.digital/com.SRC/Obliq/
		April	McCabe [21] McCabe and Clark [22]
		Scheme-48	http://photo.net/~jar/s48.html
Reactive agents	Reactive language	RTA/ABLE	Wavish and Graham [23]

Typically, object-oriented languages such as Smalltalk, Java, or C++ lend themselves more easily to the construction of agent systems. This is because the concept of an 'agent' is not too distant from that of an 'object' —agents share some properties with objects such as encapsulation, and, frequently, inheritance and message passing. However, agents differ distinctly from objects *vis-à-vis* polymorphism.

Objects respond to messages by invoking certain functions within them —
polymorphism ensures that they do not necessarily 'understand' the same messages in
the same way. In contrast, agents must have a common ACL that they all understand.

4. Ontologies for Agent Applications

Any specific agent application is grounded in some domain ontology or ontologies.
Ontology, here, means the:

> "...physical study of what exists. In the AI context, ontology is concerned with
> which categories we can usefully quantify over and how those categories relate to
> each other." [26]

In other words, it is the foundational knowledge that agents need to share enough to
communicate meaningfully. Consider the scenario, borrowed from Guha and Lenat
[27], of a teacher, walking into a physics class, presuming that at least the following are
shared with the students:

- most of the important vocabulary to be used (e.g. time, space, causality, friction);

- most of the knowledge involving these terms in the vocabulary.

These constitute the required shared ontology between the teacher and the students
for any meaningful instruction to proceed. In other specific contexts, we (as humans)
also bring different ontologies to bear, e.g. when we go into restaurants; in this case, the
menu lists a number of important additions to the required ontology.

Similarly, for computational agents, the common ontology contains the terms that
will be used in communication between agents, and the knowledge relating to these
terms. This knowledge includes their definitions, their attributes, and relationships
between terms and constraints. Such a shared ontology is a *sine qua non* for any useful
agent-to-agent communication using an ACL like KQML, because without it, the ACL
is just syntax — much of the semantics derives from the domain ontology.

Work on ontologies in the context of agents is classified here in three different
categories — *ad hoc*, 'standard', and global ontologies.

4.1 Ad Hoc Ontologies

As with *ad hoc* ACLs, most current agent-based prototypes have some implicitly
defined ontology. It is implicit in the sense that it is imposed by the designer 'from the
outside' — i.e. an exo-strategy is employed [27]. Therefore, an agent application in the
domain of business process management, e.g. BT's ADEPT demonstrator [28], builds
the vocabulary of the business process domain into the task structures of the individual
agents from the outside. Furthermore, the knowledge involving these terms is usually
linked, implicitly, with the purpose (i.e. the task structures) and the co-ordination
mechanisms of the agents in the demonstrator.

Naturally, there are problems with such an approach.

- Every demonstrator or application defines their own limited ontologies for their limited applications. There is little or no possibility for agent-based demonstrators based on the same domain, say business process management, to interoperate — even if they used a standard ACL. This is because the ontologies of the two different systems would almost certainly be different.

- The approach is not scalable. For example, if the prototype is required to be extended beyond the business process management domain, say to include the domain of network management, it would require a total reconstruction of the original demonstrator in order to accommodate the two sets of ontologies.

4.2   'Standard' Ontologies

To counter the sort of limitations mentioned in the preceding section, there are currently efforts to develop ontologies that can be shared across disparate software developers. Perhaps the best known, most advanced work in this area is the ARPA knowledge-sharing effort (KSE), which includes the ontology-sharing project — this section focuses on this work.

The ARPA KSE program has argued for a while that a common ontology is a requirement if two or more heterogeneous agents or knowledge-based systems are to interoperate by communicating information. An ontology is required in order to counter the lack of consistency between separate knowledge bases, in terms of their different vocabulary, underlying assumptions, and, most importantly, the problem of semantics.

KIF, an acronym for Knowledge Interchange Format [29], is an ongoing effort to address such issues as semantics. Essentially, it provides an *interlingua* for knowledge bases to interoperate. In other words, for two agents with different legacy knowledge bases to interoperate, both knowledge bases could be translated into KIF, which will be the shared representation language. Given n knowledge base formats, the use of an *interlingua* such as KIF necessitates at most $2n$ format converters, as opposed to the $n(n-1)$ converters that would otherwise be required.

KIF is essentially the first-order predicate calculus, recast into a Lisp-like notation. The following example depicts the content slot of an 'untell' KQML performative expressed in KIF; this example is borrowed from Finin et al [10]:

```
(untell
        : language KIF
        : ontology motors
        : in-reply-to S1
        : content (= (val (torque motor1) (sim-time 5))
                    (scalar 12kgf)))
```

The content slot of this message says that the torque of object motor1 at simulation time (sim-time) 5 is 12 kgf. It is assumed that the ontology motors (mentioned in the ontology slot of the message) defines the terms torque, sim-time, kgf and so on. Note that KIF is not an implemented knowledge representation language. Rather, it is an implementation-independent *interlingua* that allows for precise and unambiguous knowledge representation. For more details, see Genesereth and Fikes [29].

Ontolingua is another ARPA-sponsored effort towards reusable ontologies. Figure 3 depicts its mode of operation.

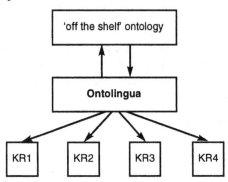

Fig. 3.   Ontolingua's mode of usage (abstracted from Gruber [30]).

Thus, Ontolingua is a domain-independent translation tool, which has nothing to do with the intellectual task of defining ontologies. Like KIF, it is also not an implemented language; rather, it allows for the 'explicit specification of a conceptualisation', which is how Gruber defines an ontology [30].

Ontolingua is a declarative and formal language that can be used to capture and represent ontologies at the knowledge level [31], but which acts as a mediating representation for translating from 'off-the-shelf' ontolo-gies into several bespoke symbol-level knowledge- representation (KR) languages, e.g. Loom [32].

The knowledge sharing arises because the same Ontolingua specification, e.g. some generic knowledge-based planning program, can be translated into different symbol-level languages. The ontology of such a planner would include descriptions such as objects, events, resources, constraints, etc, and the planner assigns resources and times to objects and events [30]. Reuse occurs when the same ontology is used in different applications or by different developers.

Ontolingua statements and axioms are written in an extended KIF notation and natural language sentences, though the latter are not parsed. The Ontolingua system includes a KIF parser and syntax checker, a consistency checker, a hypertext editor and several translators from KIF to other bespoke languages. For more details, consult Gruber [30] and Ontolingua's Web page [33].

4.3   Global Ontologies

There are also several efforts aimed at defining and generating more global ontologies, i.e. rather than being directed at specific domains, global ontologies are intended to be in some sense general. Such ontologies may provide invaluable substrates for agent-based applications. Two notable ones are the WordNet and the CYC projects. These are discussed briefly below.

WordNet [34] is an on-line lexical database with more than 166 000 word form and sense pairs. For example, the word form 'back' is interpreted as a noun in some linguistic context, as a verb in another, and even as an adjective or adverb in yet others. Each of these contexts are entered separately into WordNet. WordNet also includes many semantic relationships between words and word senses, and it also contains several semantic relations including synonymy, antonymy, hyponymy, meronymy, troponymy and entailment. It must be emphasised that WordNet is not really designed for agent applications; clearly, it is of much relevance to natural language understanding applications. However, it is possible to use it to complement further the ontology defined for some agent applications.

CYC [27, 35] is a project that began in 1984 with the ambitious goal of capturing and representing commonsense knowledge. The original motivation for CYC was to address the brittleness problem of expert systems. In brief, the point is that while a medical expert system might in some sense be an expert in, say, blood diseases, it will typically be unable to address any questions outside this narrow domain. CYC's inventors believe that the way to solve this problem is to build a system that has broad (though not necessarily deep) knowledge — the kind of knowledge that would be required by anyone attempting to understand an encyclopaedia article. Examples of such knowledge are:

- you have to be awake to eat;

- you can usually see people's noses but not their hearts;

- you cannot remember events that have not yet hap-pened;

- if you cut a lump of peanut butter in half, each half is also a lump of peanut butter — but if you cut a table in half, neither half is a table.

CYC currently contains 10^5 concepts, and 10^6 commonsense axioms that have been hand-crafted into it; millions more have been inferred and cached by CYC [35]. Today, CYC's inventors believe that the first real applications of CYC will be into mainstream computing, particularly in the domain of information management [27]. Lenat [35] posits that CYC could form the standard ontology underlying the World Wide Web (WWW) and electronic commerce. In such contexts, CYC-enabled applications which may (or may not) be agent-based, could facilitate interoperability. If the CYC dream comes true, it will obviate the need for most knowledge representation languages and current efforts including KIF and Ontolingua. For example, the content of a KQML expression could be specified in CYCL, the language in which CYC's concepts and axioms are encoded. It is unlikely that such a global ontology as CYC will be needed or available (it is currently too costly) for relatively small-scale agent demonstrators and applications in the short term. However, if CYC even approaches the functionality predicted by its inventors, it will revolutionise not just agent applications, but much of computing beyond.

5. Support Computing Technologies

In tandem with some developments in languages, ontologies and protocols, there are also several developments in the supporting computing technologies that facilitate the design and implementation of agent applications. Some of these are briefly highlighted below. However, to get a better appreciation of this section, perhaps a brief historical diversion is required.

Up until the mid-1980s, computing was dominated by big, monolithic mainframe applications. Such applications still exist in many large organisations. The costs that have been invested in such systems over the years, and their criticality to the smooth, everyday functioning of the organisation, ensure that their replacement — no matter how persuasive the arguments for such moves are — is anathema to the senior management of these organisations. This is the legacy software problem and, literally, it gets worse by the day.

The idea of client/server computing was proposed as an alternative to the centralised computing model more than two decades ago. Since then, client/server computing has prompted a Kuhnian paradigm shift in the computing industry. However, the idea only began to really change computing in the 1980s, with the development of better hardware, and the demand for applications that matched this hardware. The new hardware included personal computers (PCs) and local area networks (LANs) such as Ethernet. Client/server computing changed computing by replacing monolithic mainframe applications, which were typically accessed via green-screen terminals attached directly to these mainframes.

Today, clients, which are typically PCs with sophisticated graphical user interfaces (GUIs), interact with server programs that manage shared resources; server applications typically manage databases.

5.1 Agents and Client/Server Computing

The key point here is that the client/server model naturally lends itself to the implementation of software agent systems. To see why, first note that there are several motivations for having multiple agent systems. They include [2]:

- to solve problems that are too large for a centralised single agent to do due to resource limitations or the sheer risk of having one centralised system;

- to allow for the interconnecting and interoperation of multiple existing legacy systems such as expert systems and decision-support systems;

- to provide solutions to inherently distributed problems such as distributed sensor networks [24] or air-traffic control;

- to enhance modularity (which reduces complexity), speed (due to parallelism), reliability (due to redundancy), flexibility (i.e. new tasks are composed more easily from the more modular organisation) and reusability at the knowledge level (hence shareability of resources).

These points all relate to the merits of decentralised computing over monolithic systems — agent-based systems are decentralised systems. The client/server model thus closely matches the decentralisation associated with agent technology. To summarise, there is a synergistic relationship between agent technology and client/server computing, and hence client/server architectures provide a natural environment within which to develop agent applications.

5.2   Agents and Distributed Objects

Although we are yet to see the full impact of the first client/server revolution, advances in hardware are already fuelling a second client/server revolution [36]. This second revolution is being driven by wide area networks (WANs) and object-oriented technology. The integration of these two relatively old technologies yields a powerful new approach for achieving large-scale client/server computing — distributed objects. As Orfali et al write:

"...by and large, today's client/server applications remain difficult to build, manage, and extend. Distributed objects change this. With the proper packaging and infrastructure, objects will help subdivide today's monolithic client/server applications into self-managing components that can play together and roam across networks and operating systems. Component-like objects allow us to create client/server systems by assembling 'live blobs of intelligence and data' in an infinite number of lego-like arrangements. These components represent the ultimate form of client/server distribution and prepare us for the near future when millions of machines — mostly desktops — will be both clients and servers." [36]

Distributed objects allow for the packaging of software into components with well-defined interfaces which, in turn, offers other advantages. Firstly, new information systems can be built by assembling various components, lego-like, as long as the interfaces are consistent with one another. Secondly, components or objects are portable — they can run on different operating systems such as OS/2, Macintosh or Unix. In 1989, a consortium of object vendors grouped together to form the Object Management Group (OMG).

Since then, they have been defining standards and an architecture (shown in Fig 4), which allows object components written by different vendors to interoperate across networks and operating systems. Hence, interoperability is a third advantage of distributed objects. The key to interoperability is the object bus, or Object Request Broker (ORB). The ORB allows clients (objects) to make requests and receive responses, statically or dynamically, to other local objects, which act as servers. Clients are totally unaware of the lower-level communication mechanisms involved. The specification of the architecture is referred to as the Common Object Request Broker Architecture (CORBA), and the first set of specifications, CORBA 1.1, were agreed in 1991. In December 1994, the CORBA 2.0 standard was agreed, which allows for interoperability across ORBs from different vendors.

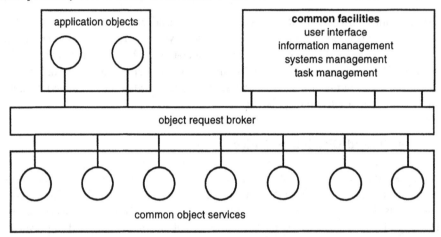

Fig. 4. The OMG object management architecture (adapted from Orfali et al [36]).

The key to CORBA is its Interface Definition Language (IDL). The IDL is a declarative language, which allows for the definition of application program interfaces (APIs). The IDL definition language allows for the definition of the objects, their attributes, the methods they export and the parameters of these methods. IDL has no control structures or variables, and, together with the ORB, constitutes the object bus.

Objects written in different programming languages, packaged as binaries, and running on different operating systems, can have IDL interfaces so that they can interoperate, and invoke each others' methods. The point of this is that objects written in, say, Cobol, Lisp, or C++ linked to an ORB, can now interoperate in various client/server modes across different operating systems. Clients do not therefore need to care about where the distributed objects reside nor on what operating systems they are running.

This is a significant development, even within client/server computing. For example, it would allow work-flow objects on some server in Amsterdam to interoperate with some customer's business process objects in Ipswich. Therefore, a fourth advantage of distributed objects is that new objects may co-exist with legacy applications, if the latter are provided with IDL interfaces. OMG's ultimate goal is to create a collaborative client/server component-based environment.

What has all these got do with agents? Simply that such emerging technologies and standards ensure that computing will continue to be increasingly decentralised. Such decentralised architectures, as noted earlier, provide natural substrates for the construction of an agent layer. This agent layer will provide many of the core services required to build agent applications. This is already happening — the ADEPT demonstrator [28] has essentially built such an agent layer on top of a CORBA-compliant implementation.

6. Discussion and Conclusions

This closing section briefly discusses some of the issues that have emerged in this survey. As indicated at several points in this paper, standards play an important role in agent-based systems, for exactly the same reason that they are important in distributed systems and telecommunications generally — agents need to be able to talk to, and understand one another. Yet while the importance of standards seems clear, there are also a number of dangers associated with standardisation. It is worth pausing to consider what these dangers are, and how they might adversely affect the development of agent systems.

Firstly, there is the danger of standardising too early, or, equivalently, of picking the wrong standard. Arguably, standards are most successful in stable domains, or domains where the future development of the technology is easy and safe to predict. This is not the case with the agent field. To see why, consider the World Wide Web. This enormously popular service did not exist before 1993; nor could its enormous success have been predicted. If anyone attempted to standardise information services for WANs in 1992, they were almost certainly wasting their time. Unfortunately, the agent field is developing at a similarly rapid pace. This makes standardisation a particularly difficult problem for agent researchers. It could be argued that KQML (the agent communication language discussed in detail in section 2.1) is an attempt to standardise too early, as the requirements for ACLs are not sufficiently understood — there are too few real multi-agent systems in existence to know what features an ACL must support.

Just as it is possible to standardise too early, so it is possible to standardise too late. A good example here is the X.400 e-mail standard, which was widely expected to take over from the Internet's Simple Mail Transfer Protocol (SMTP). This did not happen, despite the technical superiority of X.400 over the cruder (and comparatively ancient) SMTP standard. One reason for this failure was simply that by the time X.400 had passed through the time- consuming international standardisation process, and working X.400 systems became available, SMTP was already established as the *de facto* standard. So, although X.400 was technically right (in that it provided for many sophisticated and powerful services) it arrived too late to have the impact it perhaps deserved. A similar situation within the agent field may be occuring with Telescript [37] a programming language and development environment for mobile agent applications. Telescript was eagerly awaited within the Internet agent community, but by the time it was made available to the public, the Java programming language had already been released, and was supported within the popular Netscape World Wide Web browser. As a result, Java had a very large end-user base, making it much more attractive to software developers than Telescript. Java does not, however, provide facilities for building mobile agent applications in the way that Telescript does. In this sense, the two languages are not really competing — but Java appears to be winning the race anyway.

Standards will be essential if agent technology is to realise its potential; but, as it is hoped has been made clear, standardisation is as much about timing and judgement as it is about technical issues.

In summary, no firm predictions can be made about exactly what form future agent-based systems will take, but it is certain that agents have much to offer. It is hoped that this paper has illustrated some of the technologies that are likely to underpin this promising new software industry.

Acknowledgements

Discussions with Divine Ndumu and Mark Wiegand, that have shaped some of the ideas propounded in this paper, are gratefully acknowledged.

References

1. Mayfield M, Labrou Y and Finin T: 'Evaluation of KQML as an Agent Communication Language', in Wooldridge M, Mueller J P amd Tambe M (Eds): 'Intelligent Agents II', Lecture Notes in Artificial Intelligence 1037, Heidelberg, Springer Verlag (1996).

2. Nwana H S: 'Software Agents: An Overview', The Knowledge Engineering Review, 11, No 3 (1996).

3. Nwana H S and Ndumu D T: 'An introduction to agent technology', BT Technol J, 14, No 4, pp 55—67 (October 1996).

4. Nwana H S, Lee L, and Jennings N R: 'Co-ordination in software agent systems', BT Technol J, 14, No 4, pp 79—88 (October 1996).

5. Genesereth M R and Ketchpel S P: 'Software Agents', Communications of the ACM, 37, No 7, pp 48—53 (1994).

6. Cohen P R and Levesque H J: 'Communicative Actions for Artificial Agents', in Proceedings of the First International Conference on Multi-Agent Systems, San Francisco, Cambridge, AAAI Press, pp 65—72 (1995).

7. Austin J L: 'How to Do Things with Words', Cambridge, MA, Harvard University Press (1962).

8. Searle J R: 'Speech Acts', Cambridge, MA, Cambridge University Press (1969).

9. Neches R: 'Overview of the DARPA Knowledge Sharing Effort', on http://www-ksl.stanford.edu/knowledge-sharing/papers/kse-overview.html (1994).

10. Finin T, Fritzson R, McKay D and McEntire R: 'KQML as an agent communication language', in Proceedings of the 3rd International Conference on Information and Knowledge Management (CIKM), New York, ACM Press, also available from http://www.cs.umbc.edu/kqml/papers/ (November 1994).

11. Labrou Y and Finin T: 'A Semantics Approach for KQML — a general purpose communication language for software agents', in Proceedings of the 3rd International Conference on Information and Knowledge Management (CIKM), New York, ACM Press, also available from http://www.cs.umbc.edu/kqml/papers/ (November 1994),

12. Finin T: 'Agent Communication Languages: KQML and the Knowledge Sharing Effort', abstract, http://umbc.edu/~finin (1995).

13. Finin T, Weber J, Wiederhold G, Genesereth M, Fritzon R, McKay D, McGuire J, Pelavin R, Shapiro S and Beck C: 'Specification of the KQML Agent-Communication Language', Draft (February 1994).

14. Huhns M M: 'KQML', Tutorial Notes, Tutorial F, Multi-Agent Systems Tools & Research Methods, International Conference on Multi-Agent Systems, San Francisco (1995).

15. Cohen P R, Cheyer A, Wang M and Baeg S C: 'An Open Agent Architecture', in Proceedings of AAAI Spring Symposium, California, AAAI Press (March 1994).

16. Wooldridge M and Jennings N: 'Intelligent Agents: Theory and Practice', The Knowledge Engineering Review, 10, No 2, pp 115—152 (1995).

17. Agha G: (1986), Actors: 'A Model of Concurrent Computation in Distributed Systems', London, MIT Press (1986).

18. Shoham Y: 'Agent-Oriented Programming', Artificial Intelligence, 60, No 1, pp 51—92 (1993).

19. Thomas S R: 'The PLACA Agent Programming Language', in Wooldridge M and Jennings N R (Eds): 'Intelligent Agents — Theories, Architectures, and Languages', Lecture Notes in Artificial Intelligence 890, Heidelberg, Springer Verlag (1995).

20. Oustershout J K: 'Tcl and the Tk Toolkit', New York, Addison Wesley (1994).

21. McCabe F G: 'APRIL Reference Manual', Version 2.1, Department of Computer Science, Imperial College, London (1995).

22. McCabe F G and Clark K L: 'APRIL — Agent PRocess Interaction Language', in Wooldridge M and Jennings N R (Eds): 'Intelligent Agents — Theories, Architectures, and Languages', Lecture Notes in Artificial Intelligence 890, Heidelberg, Springer Verlag (1995).

23. Wavish P and Graham M: 'A Situated Action Approach to Implementing Characters in Computer Games', Applied AI Journal, 10, No 1, pp 53—74 (1996).

24. Durfee E H, Lesser V R and Corkill D: 'Coherent Cooperation among Communicating Problem Solvers', IEEE Transactions on Computers, C-36 No 11, pp 1275—1291 (1987).

25. Jennings N, Corera J M, Laresgoiti L, Mamdani E, Perriollat F, Skarek P amd Varga L: 'Using ARCHON to Develop Real-World DAI Applications for Electricity Transportation and Particle Accelerator Control', IEEE Expert, Special Issue on Real-World Applications of DAI systems (1995).

26. Rich, E and Knight, K. 'Artificial Intelligence (Second Edition)', New York, McGraw Hill (1991).

27. Guha R V and Lenat D B: 'Enabling Agents to Work Together', Communications of the ACM, 37 , No 7, pp 127—142 (1994).

28. O'Brien P D and Wiegand M E : 'Agents of Change in Business Process Management', BT Technol J, 14, No 4, pp 133—140 (1996).

29. Genesereth M R and Fikes R E (Eds): 'Knowledge Interchange Format', Version 3.0 Reference Manual, Computer Science Department, Stanford University, Technical Report Logic-92-1, also available from http://www-ksl.stanford.edu/knowledge-sharing/kif/ (March 1992).

30. Gruber T R: 'A Translation Approach to Portable Ontology Specifications', Knowledge Acquisition, 5, No 2, pp 199—220 (1993).

31. Newell A: 'The Knowledge Level', Artificial Intelligence, 18, pp 87—127 (1982).

32. MacGregor R: 'The Evolving Technology of Classification-Based Knowledge Representation Systems', in Sowa J (Ed): 'Principles of Semantic Networks: Explorations in the Representation of Knowledge', San Mateo, CA, Morgan Kaufmann (1991).

33. Ontolingua: http://www-ksl.stanford.edu/knowledge-sharing/ontolingua/

34. Miller G A: 'WordNet: A Lexical Database for English', Communications of the ACM, 38 No 11, pp 39—41 (1995).

35. Lenat D B: 'CYC: A Large-Scale Investment in Knowledge Infrastructure', Communications of the ACM, 38 , No 11, pp 33—38 (1995).

36. Orfali R, Harkey D and Edwards J: 'The Essential Distributed Object Survival Guide', New York, John Wiley & Sons (1996).

37. White J E: 'Telescript Technology: The Foundation for the Electronic Market-place', White Paper, General Magic Inc, 2465 Latham Street, Mountain View, CA 94040 (1994).

Section 2

Software Agents — Applications

Information Agents for the World Wide Web

N J Davies, R Weeks and M C Revett

Information Management Systems, Advanced Applications & Technology
Department,
BT Laboratories, Martlesham Heath, Ipswich. Suffolk, IP5 7RE, UK
E-mail: John.Davies@bt-sys.bt.co.uk

This paper describes a distributed system of intelligent agents, Jasper, for performing information tasks over the Internet World Wide Web (WWW) on behalf of a community of users. Jasper can summarise and extract keywords from WWW pages and can share information among users with similar interests automatically. Jasper provides agents which can retrieve relevant WWW pages quickly and easily. A Jasper agent holds a profile of its user, based on observing their behaviour and learning more about their interests as the system is used.

A novel three-dimensional front end on to the Jasper system has been created using VRML (virtual reality modelling language), a language for 3-D graphical spaces or virtual worlds networked via the global Internet and hyperlinked within WWW. This and other ongoing research using keyword and document clustering techniques are described.

1. Introduction

In 1982, the volume of scientific, corporate and technical information was doubling every five years. By 1988, it was doubling every 2.2 years and by 1992 every 1.6 years. With the expansion of the Internet and other networks this rate of increase will continue. Key to the viability of such networks will be the ability to manage the information and provide users with what they want, when they want it.

This paper discusses a distributed system of intelligent agents for performing information tasks over the Internet World Wide Web (WWW) on behalf of a user or community of users, describing how agents are used to store, retrieve, summarise and inform other agents about information found on WWW in a system called Jasper (joint access to stored pages with easy retrieval). In certain circumstances, Jasper agents will also identify an opportunity for performance improvement — by observing its user, an agent will attempt to enhance the profile it holds on that user.

The approach here is not motivated by any perceived requirement for another tool for searching WWW — there are already many of these [1, 2] and they are being added to frequently with ever-increasing coverage of the Web and sophistication of search engines. The motivation behind this project is different but related — having found useful information on WWW, how can it be stored for easy retrieval and how can other users, likely to be interested in the information, be identified and informed?

Given the vast amount of information available on WWW, it is preferable to avoid the copying of information from its original location to a local server. Indeed, it could be argued that approach is contrary to the whole ethos of the Web. Rather than copying information, therefore, Jasper agents store only relevant meta-information. As will be shown below, this includes keywords, a summary, document title, universal resource locator (URL) and date and time of access. This meta-information is then used to index on the actual information when a retrieval request is made.

Most current WWW clients (Mosaic, Netscape, and so on) provide some means of storing pages of interest to the user. Typically, this is done by allowing the user to create a hierarchical menu of names associated with particular URLs. While this menu facility is useful, it quickly becomes unwieldy when a reasonably large number of WWW pages are involved. Essentially, the representation provided is not sufficiently rich to permit a useful index of the information stored — the user can only provide a string naming the page. As well as the fact that useful meta-information such as the date of access of the page is lost, a single phrase (the name) may not be enough to accurately index a page in all contexts. Consider, as a simple example, information about the use of knowledge-based systems (KBS) in information retrieval of pharmacological data — in different contexts, it may be KBS, information retrieval or pharmacology which are of interest. Unless a name is carefully chosen to mention all three aspects, the information will be missed in one or more of its useful contexts. This problem is analogous to the problem of finding files containing desired information in a Unix (or other) file system [3], although in most filing systems one at least has the facility to sort files by creation date.

The solution adopted for this problem was to allow the user to access information by a much richer set of meta-information. How Jasper agents achieve this and how the resulting meta-information is exploited is the subject of the next section.

2. Agent Architecture

This section discusses the facilities which Jasper agents offer the user in managing information. These can be grouped in two categories — storage and retrieval.

2.1 Storage

Figure 1 shows the actions taken when Jasper stores information in its page store (JPS). The user first finds a WWW page of sufficient interest to be stored by Jasper in their JPS and sends a 'store' request to Jasper via a menu option on their favourite WWW client (Mosaic and Netscape versions are currently available on all platforms). Jasper then invites the user to supply an annotation to be stored with the page. Typically, this might be the reason the page was stored and can be very useful for other users in deciding which pages retrieved from JPS to visit. Information sharing is discussed further below.

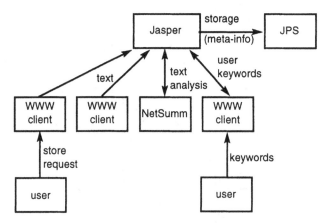

Fig. 1. Jasper's storage process.

Jasper next extracts the source text from the page in question, first stripping out html (Hypertext Mark-up Language) tags. Jasper then summarises the text using NetSumm, BT's automatic text summariser [4]. Jasper also extracts and counts the words occurring in the text, first filtering out a standard 'stop-list' of commonly occurring terms.

At the end of this process, Jasper has the following meta-information about the WWW page of interest:

- a set of keywords (indexing terms);

- the user's annotations;

- a summary of the page's content;

- the document title;

- universal resource locator (URL);

- date and time of storage.

Jasper then adds the page to the JPS. In the JPS, the keywords (of both types) are then used to index on files containing the other meta-information, as shown in Fig 2.

2.2 Retrieval

There are three modes in which information can be retrieved from JPS using Jasper. One is a standard keyword retrieval facility, while the other two are concerned with information sharing between a community of agents and their users. Each is described below.

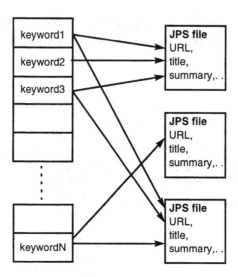

Fig. 2. JPS Structure.

When a Jasper agent is installed on a user's machine, the user provides a personal profile — a set of keywords which describe information the user is interested in obtaining via WWW. This profile is held by the agent in order to determine which pages are potentially of interest to its user.

Keyword Retrieval

As is shown in Fig 3, for straightforward keyword retrieval the user supplies a set of keywords to their Jasper agent via an html form provided by Jasper. The Jasper agent then retrieves the ten most closely matching pages held in JPS, using a simple keyword matching and scoring algorithm. The user can specify in advance a retrieval threshold below which pages will not be displayed. The agent then dynamically constructs an html page with a ranked list of links to the pages retrieved and their summaries. Any annotation made by the original user is also shown, along with the scores of each retrieved page. This page is then presented to the user on their WWW client.

'What's new?' Facility

Any user can ask his Jasper agent 'What's new?' The agent then interrogates the JPS and retrieves the most recently stored pages. It then determines which of these pages best match the user's profile based on the same keyword matching algorithm as that mentioned above. An html page is then presented to the user showing a ranked list of links to the recently stored pages which best match the user's profile and the other pages most recently stored in JPS, with annotations where provided. In this way users are provided with a view both of the pages recently stored of most interest to themselves and of a more general selection of recently stored pages.

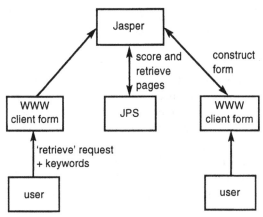

Fig. 3. Jasper's keyword retrieval process.

A user can update the profile which their Jasper agent holds at any time via an html form which allows the addition and/or deletion of keywords from the profile. In this way, the user can effectively select different contexts in which to work. A context is defined by a set of keywords (those making up the profile or, indeed, those specified in a retrieval query) and can be thought of as those types of information in which a user is interested at a given time.

The idea of applying human memory models to the filing of information was explored by Jones [3] in the context of computer filing systems. As he pointed out in the context of a conventional filing system, there is an analogy between a directory in a file system and a set of pages retrieved by a Jasper agent. The set of pages can be thought of as a dynamically-constructed directory, defined by the context in which it was retrieved. This is a highly flexible notion of 'directory' in two senses — firstly, pages which occur in this retrieval can of course occur in others, depending on the context, and, secondly, there is no sharp boundary to the directory, since pages are 'in' the directory to a greater or lesser extent depending on their match to the current context. In this approach, the number of ways of partitioning the information on the pages is thus only limited by the diversity and richness of the information itself.

Communication with Other Interested Agents

Jasper agents are currently being tested by a group of users on a WWW server at BT Laboratories. When a page is stored in JPS by a Jasper agent, the agent checks the profiles of other agents' users in its 'local community' (here the agents in the trial, although this could be any predefined community). If the page matches a user's profile with a score above a certain threshold, an e-mail message is automatically generated by the agent and sent to the user concerned, informing him of the discovery of the page. The e-mail header is in the format:

JASPER KW: $keyword_1$ ... $keyword_n$

This allows the user (before reading the body of the message) to identify it as being one from Jasper and since a list of keywords is provided the user can assess the relative importance of the information to which the message refers. The keywords in the message header vary from user to user, depending on the keywords from the page which match the keywords in their user profile, thus personalising the message to each user's interests. The message body itself informs the user of the page title and URL, who stored the page, and any annotation to the page which the storer provided. Other forms of automatic notification (e.g. via dynamically constructed WWW pages) are also being studied.

As argued in section 4 below, the ability to share relevant WWW information with other users quickly and easily is a key part of the original vision of WWW. A Jasper agent can automate this information task for a user to some extent.

2.3   Learning from Feedback

In certain circumstances, Jasper agents will identify an opportunity for performance improvement and will seek user feedback in order to achieve the desired performance enhancement.

Jasper agents can modify users' profiles if a Jasper agent identifies that the profile does not reflect the pages which the user is storing. When a page is stored (see section 2.1), the agent compares the content of the page with the user's profile. If the profile does not match the page content above a given threshold, Jasper informs the user and invites the user to modify their profile by adding some keywords suggested by the agent based on the page's content. The user can then add these keywords to the profile or add some new keywords of their own to the profile.

3.   Clustering in Jasper

It has been shown that the Jasper store is essentially what would be called a 'collection' in information retrieval (IR) terminology — it is a set of documents indexed by keywords. It differs from a 'traditional' collection in that the documents are typically located remotely from the index — the index actually points to a URL which specifies the location of the document on the Internet. Furthermore, various additional pieces of meta-information are attached to documents in Jasper, such as the user who stored the page, when it was stored, any annotation the user may have provided, and so on.

One additional important area where Jasper differs from most document collections is that all documents in the Jasper store have been entered by users who have made a conscious decision to mark it as a piece of information which they and their peers would be likely to find useful in the future. This, along with the meta-information held, makes a Jasper store a very rich source of information.

Given the similarity between a Jasper store and a standard document collection mentioned earlier, it is sensible to examine whether IR techniques can be applied beneficially to the Jasper store. Accordingly, the use in Jasper of one such technique, clustering, has recently been under investigation.

3.1   Clustering Documents

Jasper's page store (see Fig 2) can be viewed as an example of a term-document matrix, where each element of the matrix m_{ij} represents the number of times term (keyword) j occurs in document (page) i. Jasper's term-document matrix is used to calculate a similarity matrix for the documents in the Jasper store. The similarity matrix gives a measure of the similarity of documents in the store. For each pair of documents, the 'Dice coefficient' is calculated. For two documents D_i and D_j, the Dice coefficient is given by:

$$2 \times |D_i \cap D_j| / |D_i| + |D_j|$$

where $| D_i |$ is the number of terms in document D_i and $| D_i \cap D_j |$ is the number of terms co-occurring in documents D_i and D_j. This coefficient yields a number between 0 and 1. A coefficient of zero implies two documents have no terms in common, while a coefficient of 1 implies that the sets of terms occurring in each document are identical. The similarity matrix, Sim say, represents the similarity of each pair of documents in the store as calculated by the Dice coefficient, so that for each pair of documents i and j:

$$\text{Sim}(i,j) = 2 \times |D_i \cap D_j| / |D_i| + |D_j|$$

This matrix is used to create clusters of related documents automatically using the hierarchical ag-glomerative clustering process [5—7], whereby each document is initially placed in a cluster by itself and the two most similar such clusters are then combined into a larger cluster, for which similarities with each of the other clusters must then be computed. This combination process is continued until only a single cluster of documents remains at the highest level. The way in which similarity between clusters (as opposed to individual documents) is calculated can be varied. The details are of no concern here other than to say that for the Jasper store complete-link clustering has been employed. In complete-link clustering, the similarity between the least similar pair of documents from the two clusters is used as the cluster similarity.

3-D interfaces to Document Collections

The resulting cluster structures of the Jasper store are being used to create a novel three-dimensional (3-D) front- end on to the Jasper system, using VRML (virtual reality modelling language) [8]. VRML is a language for 3-D graphical spaces or virtual worlds networked via the global Internet and hyperlinked within the World Wide Web (WWW).

A major consequence of the introduction of WWW to the Internet has been an increase in the usability of the information within it. This is directly attributable to the navigability of the information — in other words, the Internet is useful (and will be used) to the degree it is capable of conforming to requests made of it. Furthermore, it has added a universal structure to the information within it; through WWW, all four million Internet hosts can be treated as a single, unified data source, and all of the information can be treated as a single, albeit highly complex, document.

Navigability in a purely symbolic domain has limits. The amount of 'depth' present in a subject before it exceeds human capacity for comprehension (and hence, navigation) is finite and relatively limited. However, humans have a sophisticated visual system and the ability to navigate in three dimensions. It thus seems reasonable to propose that the WWW should be extended, increasing its navigation model from two to three dimensions.

It is proposed to exploit these insights within the Jasper system by constructing a shared 3-D space, dubbed the 'Information Garden', through and over which users can fly and wherein information is arranged in a logical, intuitive and accessible way. This arrangement of information is achieved by using the meta-information in the Jasper store and results from the clustering process (described above). Figure 4 shows an early version of the Information Garden. It should be stressed that the current interface is a tentative early design. The Information Garden is a VRML 3-D representation of the Jasper store with documents clustered into various groups. However, it is also viewed as a shared virtual space, in which users (represented by Avatars) can meet, communicate and exchange information.

Figure 4 is a screenshot from a working prototype shared space where avatars can meet, access information via the Information Garden, and communicate via a number of media including text, audio and video. Shared electronic whiteboards are also provided. As the user navigates towards a particular sector, more detail becomes visible, as shown in Fig 5.

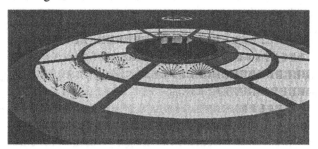

Fig. 4.   Shared information space.

In Fig 5 can be seen clustered groups of documents. Each document is represented by a stalk with a coloured circle at its end. Figure 6 shows a smaller part of the same garden in more detail. The colour coding of the circles on the stalks represents the status of the particular document — red circles indicate that a document has been updated since it was stored in Jasper, black that the link is 'dead' (that is, the URL associated with this document is no longer valid), while a blue circle indicates that neither of these conditions apply. The smaller circles half-way up the document stalk represent a locally held summary of the information, as generated by Jasper.

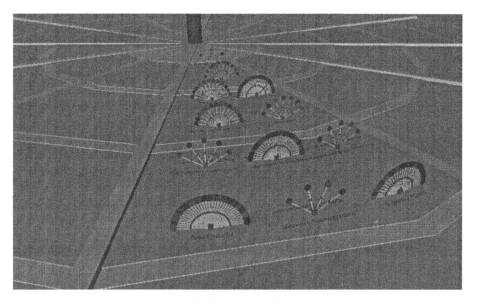

Fig. 5. Information garden — view 1.

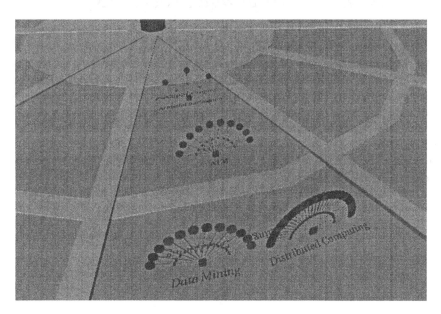

Fig. 6. Information garden — view 2.

At some point, it makes sense to drop down from a 3-D to a 2-D view of the information and by clicking on the large or small circles, the user is shown a WWW page of the original information or the summary respectively. Alternatively, the user can click on the base of the cluster. The system will then present the user with a view of a single cluster, as shown in Fig 7. At this viewpoint, each stalk of the cluster is annotated with the title of the document it represents. As before, the document or its summary can be accessed from here by clicking on the relevant circle.

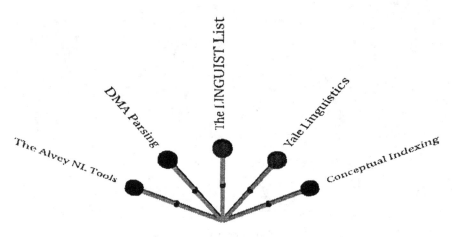

Fig. 7.   Information garden document cluster.

As mentioned above, the preceding paragraphs describe 'work in progress'. A number of issues remain to be resolved, including how to generate clusters of reasonable size for this type of representation and how best to label such clusters. One possibility is to label a cluster with the most commonly occurring terms [9]. Furthermore, it may prove that other metaphors are more appropriate for visualisation of information.

Evaluation of such an interface is also a key issue which has not yet been addressed to any great extent. The shared space is currently being used by a few expert users and is not yet sufficiently robust for a wider trial. Early feedback from those users is encouraging. Features to which they have reacted positively include:

- the 'organic' nature of the garden metaphor, which encourages the idea of information which will grow (and be pruned);

- the ability to represent visually a reasonably large collection of documents at different levels of detail;

- the meta-information about the collection provided by clustering and colour coding of the documents, particularly when viewed at relatively long distance — examples of the information provided include the amount of information available on a given topic and clusters where many links have 'died' or need updating;

- the tendency to get 'lost in hyperspace' is reduced, since the user can stay in the same 3-D space and yet have access to a range of information and meta-information.

Work is continuing in experimenting with this and other metaphors. One current investigation involves the use of spatial information — for example, given that Jasper holds a profile of a user, the document clusters shown in the Information Garden could be spatially arranged such that those likely to be of most interest are closest to the user's entry point to the 3-D space.

Clustering Keywords

Keywords (terms) occurring in a particular collection can also be clustered in a way which mirrors exactly the document clustering technique described above: a similarity matrix for the keywords in the Jasper store can be constructed which gives a measure of the 'similarity' of keywords in the store. For each pair of documents, the Dice coefficient is calculated. Using the same notation as for document clustering, for two keywords K_i and K_j, the Dice coefficient is given by:

$$2 \times |K_i \cap K_j| / |K_i| + |K_j|$$

Once the similarity matrix for a Jasper store is calculated, however, the keywords are not clustered as the documents were, but instead the matrix itself is exploited in two ways.

The first way is profile enhancement. A user's profile is enhanced by adding those keywords most similar to the keywords explicitly represented in the user's profile in a way reminiscent of query reformulation techniques, such as the use of spreading activation networks [10, 11] and other techniques based on the use of semantic nets [12, 13].

In Chakravarthy and Haase [12], for example, the use of semantic knowledge from WordNet [14] in a program called NetSerf for finding information archives on the Internet is reported. Based on a set of 75 queries, NetSerf was reported to have performed significantly better than the Smart [15] information retrieval system. Interestingly, local experiments with WordNet for profile enhancement have found that WordNet did not perform well with respect to the very technical vocabulary which constitutes the terms in the Jasper store. It was this technical bias that led to looking to the store itself for a network of related terms — in effect, the clustered terms constitute a simple spreading activation network. In Wettler and Rapp [11], some results from cognitive psychology research are analysed to explain why it is difficult for people to think of related terms. This difficulty is ameliorated to a degree by the automatic (hidden) enhancement of a user's profile by the system.

Figure 8 shows an example network of keywords which have been built from the keyword similarity matrix extracted from a current Jasper store. The algorithm is straightforward — given an initial starting keyword, find the four words most similar to it from the similarity matrix. Link these four to the original word and repeat the process for each of the four new words. This can be repeated a number of times (in Fig 8, three times). One could of course attach the particular similarity coefficients to each link for finer-grained information concerning the degree of similarity between words.

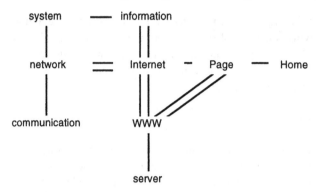

Fig. 8. Clustered keywords from the Jasper store.

Thus, for example, if the words 'virtual', 'reality' and 'Internet' are part of a user's profile but 'VRML' is not, an enhanced profile might add VRML to the original profile (assuming VRML is clustered close to 'virtual', 'reality' and 'Internet'). In this way, documents containing 'VRML' but not 'virtual', 'reality' and 'Internet' may be retrieved whereas they would not have been with the unenhanced profile.

The second way keyword clustering is exploited is proactive searching. The keywords comprising a user's profile can be used by Jasper to search proactively for new WWW pages relevant to their interests, which can then present a list of new pages in which the user may be interested without them having to explicitly carry out a search. These proactive searches can be carried out by Jasper at some given interval, perhaps weekly or fortnightly. Clustering is useful here because a profile may reflect more than one interest. Consider, for example, the following user profile:

{internet, WWW, html, http, football, Manchester, United, linguistics, parsing, pragmatics}

Clearly, three separate interests are represented in the above profile and searching on each separately is likely to yield far superior results than merely entering the whole profile as a query for the given user. It is hoped that clustering keywords from the document collection will automate the process of query generation for proactive searching by a user's Jasper agent. A typical profile is:

{internet, information, retrieval, SMART, clustering, agent, intelligent, corba, idl, dce}

These keywords can be clustered as described above, using the Jasper store, to which the user whose profile this is belongs, as the document collection. The similarity matrix shown in Table 1 is then obtained (the upper right half of the matrix is of course a mirror image of the bottom left). If complete-link clustering is used [5, 7], whereby the similarity between the least similar pair of items from two clusters is taken as the similarity between the clusters, the cluster dendogram shown in Fig 9 is obtained. Note that the vertical axis in Fig 9 represents difference rather than similarity. If a similarity threshold of 0.3 is set, beneath which any clusters are disregarded, the following clusters are obtained:

{dce corba idl}
{SMART clustering}
{internet information}
{intelligent agent}
{retrieval}

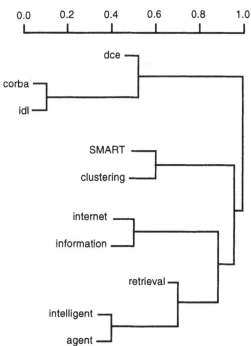

Fig. 9. Dendogram 1.

Similarly, the profile:

{java, corba, agent, internet, information, golf, vrml, realaudio, vrml, http, html}

yields the matrix shown in Table 2, which, when clustered using the complete-link method, gives the clusters shown overleaf:

{internet information}
{http html}
{agent}
{java}
{corba}
{golf}
{realaudio}
{vrml}

Table 1. Term similarity — Matrix 1.

	corba	dce	idl	internet	information	retrieval	intelligent	agent	SMART	clustering
corba	1									
dce	0.62	1								
idl	0.92	0.50	1							
internet	0.03	0.03	0.03	1						
information	0.04	0.04	0.03	0.51	1					
retrieval	0.04	0.08	0.00	0.21	0.27	1				
intelligent	0.00	0.03	0.00	0.21	0.30	0.30	1			
agent	0.07	0.11	0.04	0.16	0.29	0.38	0.53	1		
SMART	0.00	0.00	0.00	0.07	0.07	0.19	0.10	0.14	1	
clustering	0.00	0.00	0.00	0.01	0.03	0.17	0.04	0.12	0.43	1

Table 2. Term similarity — Matrix 2.

	http	html	java	corba	realaudio	vrml	internet	golf	agent	information
http	1									
html	0.044	1								
java	0.10	0.21	1							
corba	0.30	0.06	0.10	1						
realaudio	0.00	0.00	0.00	0.00	1					
vrml	0.13	0.12	0.07	0.00	0.00	1				
internet	0.16	0.26	0.20	0.03	0.03	0.09	1			
golf	0.00	0.00	0.00	0.00	0.00	0.00	0.00	1		
agent	0.05	0.11	0.07	0.07	0.00	0.00	0.16	0.00	1	
information	0.14	0.26	0.12	0.04	0.01	0.09	0.51	0.00	0.29	1

Inspection of the results of clustering these and other profiles indicates that clustering is able to subdivide a Jasper profile into sets of keywords which may prove valid for use as queries. More work remains to be done, however, to determine the best clustering technique (single-link, complete-link or group average) and the most appropriate clustering threshold for a wider range of profiles. It may prove necessary to attempt to tune dynamically the threshold (and indeed perhaps the clustering technique) based on the similarity matrix for a given profile. Consideration is also being given to a semi-automatic technique, whereby the set of queries created by Jasper from the user's profile is presented to the user for confirmation or adjustment before any queries are actually submitted.

Because queries based on profile clusters are made off-line by Jasper, rather than interactively by the user, there is an opportunity to analyse the results before presenting them to the user. For example, when the search results are obtained by Jasper, they can be summarised and matched against the user's profile in the usual way to give a prioritised list of new URLs along with locally held summaries. In addition, a log can be held of the pages which Jasper has found for each user. By checking against this log, only new pages (those the user has not been shown by Jasper previously) will be presented. It is anticipated that the pages will be presented to the user on a dynamically constructed WWW page with the facility to store pages of particular interest in the Jasper store easily. Those pages accepted for storage in Jasper by this mechanism (and indeed those rejected) may additionally afford new opportunities for user-profile adaptation.

4. Related Work

Jasper is an example of a static information agent — its goal is to help the user manage the 'information overload' problem often encountered when using the WWW. However, it does not traverse the WWW on behalf of its user but rather acts as an aid to the user at the user's point of interaction with the WWW. In this sense, it is an interface agent in the sense of Maes [16] — it is acting as an assistant to reduce the information overload of a user (by supplying good quality WWW pages as pre-filtered by other users), and, by observing user actions, it will adapt its own behaviour to better reflect its user's needs (by modifying users' profiles based on the pages they store).

The services provided by existing Internet information- retrieval tools can be divided into four main functions — search, storage, access and organisation.

There are many systems which offer some or all of these to the WWW user, including WAIS [17], Archie [18] and the Harvest system [19]. Harvest is one of the most sophisticated of these types of system and it is briefly described here, and compared with Jasper. All the systems mentioned above can be characterised as 'off-line' systems in the sense that their indexes and stores are not built incrementally, as in Jasper, but are rather constructed off-line for later use. The key elements of the Harvest approach are gatherers and brokers. Gatherers collect indexing data from a given collection of information (http, ftp and gopher protocols are supported). Brokers provide query interfaces to the gathered information. Brokers can access more than one gatherer, as well as other brokers. Experiments indicate that Harvest reduces load on servers and networks. This is due to efficient gathering software and the sharing of information among indexes that need it, in contrast to other comparable information retrievers which use expensive object-retrieval protocols and fail to co-ordinate information gathering among themselves.

Harvest queries on WWW brokers return references to relevant information sources, an indication of the degree of match to the query and a content summary. The summarisation performed on text files is simply to extract the first 100 lines plus the first sentence of each remaining paragraph. Keywords seem to be an alphabetical list of this summary. It is possible in principle to write and plug in a personalised summariser. Harvest also 'summarises' other formats of information, albeit in a fairly simple way. The summary of an audio file, for example, is the file name, while the summary of a perl script is the procedure names and comments therein.

Harvest and Jasper thus differ in several ways — firstly, Harvest is inherently 'off-line' as discussed above while Jasper is 'incremental', and, secondly, Harvest summaries are more simplistic than those attempted by Jasper, although Harvest provides 'summaries' of a wider range of information types.

More similar to Jasper than off-line indexers of information is 'Warmlist' [20], a tool for caching, searching and sharing WWW documents. Like Jasper, Warmlist extends the idea of the hotlist. WWW documents in the Warmlist are automatically cached on the local server, along with the original links to other information. This gives much quicker access to Warmlist pages. A useful feature of a Warmlist is the ability to include other Warmlists as part of one's own Warmlist. The Glimpse indexing and searching package [21] is used to search cached pages.

In Jasper, a different approach is adopted by not storing whole pages but rather storing meta-information about a page. As described above, this allows much enhanced, richer indexing on pages of interest without the necessity of copying remote information to local servers. It is possible that with many users on a WWW server using Warmlist, the server would rapidly fill up with cached pages. Also the concept of a page being copied and stored in many different places (i.e. on multiple Warmlists) seems somewhat against the ethos of the Web. Given that Warmlist caches entire pages, it is unsurprising that it provides no facilities for information summarisation.

WWW documents in a Warmlist can be organised in a hierarchical way with nested directories. As argued above, however, a more flexible way to access information is via a set of keywords describing the contents of the page. This removes the necessity to remember where documents have been stored (e.g. 'Did I store the letter to Smith about the Internet in letters/smith/Internet or Internet/letters or smith/letters or ...?')

As mentioned above, there are four main functions (search, storage, access and organisation) common to many Internet information tools. In the Jasper system, the first steps have been taken towards adding a fifth function — automated information sharing, as described in section 2.2. It is not thought that this functionality is provided by any other Internet tool at the current time.

5. Conclusions

In his seminal article, Bush [22] describes a tool to aid the human mind in dealing with information. He states that previous scientific advances have helped humans in their interactions with the physical world but have not assisted humans in dealing with large amounts of knowledge and information. Bush proposed a tool called a 'memex' which could augment human memory through associative memory, where related pieces of information are linked. Trails through these links could then be stored and shared by others. WWW itself fulfils Bush's vision in some respects — Bush's associative memory can be seen in the hyperlinks of WWW. What is lacking is a way of organising this vast 'memory' of WWW pages into coherent 'trails' which can be saved and communicated to others. Currently, only relatively simplistic hotlists and menus are available.

Jasper goes some way to addressing these problems by providing agents which, as has been shown, can store meta-information about WWW pages which can then be used to retrieve relevant pages quickly and easily and share the information contained in those pages with other users with the same interests. Jasper leaves aside the issue of how best to search WWW for information (many other researchers are working on this) and is an attempt to address the complementary problem of how best to store information once it has been found and how to share information with others with the same interests. As described in sections 3 and 5, much remains to be done — in particular, the exploitation of more of the meta-information obtained by Jasper agents and the provision of adaptive agents which can infer context from users' actions will be a useful enhancement to the current system. However, Jasper is a step along the road towards the original vision for WWW [23] as a network which supports co-operative working and the sharing of information.

References

1.   http://lycos.cs.cmu.edu/

2.   http://www.infoseek.com/

3.   Jones WP: 'On the applied use of human memory models: the memory extender personal filing system', Int J Man-Machine Studies, 25, pp 191—228 (1986).

4.   http://www.labs.bt.com/innovate/informat/netsumm/index.htm

5.   Rasmussen E: 'Clustering Algorithms', in Frakes W B and Baeza-Yates R (Eds): 'Information Retrieval: Data structures and Algorithms', Prentice-Hall, London (1992).

6.   Frakes W B and Baeza-Yates R (Eds): 'Information Retrieval: Data Structures and Algorithms', Prentice-Hall, London (1992).

7. Griffiths A, Robinson L A and Willett P: 'Hierarchic Agglomerative Clustering Methods for Automatic Document Classification', J of Documentation, 40, No 3, pp 175—205 (1984).

8. Raggett D: 'Extending WWW to support Platform Independent Virtual Reality', http://vrml.wired.com/concepts/raggett.html

9. van Rijsbergen C J: 'Information Retrieval', Butterworths, London (1979).

10. Ruge G: 'Human Memory Models and Term Association', Proc 18th Annual International ACM SIGIR Conference, Washington, USA (1995).

11. Wettler M and Rapp R: 'A Connectionist System to Simulate Lexical Decisions in Information Retrieval', in Pfeifer R, Schreter Z, Fogelman F and Steels L (Eds): 'Connectionism in Perspective', Elsevier, Amsterdam (1989).

12. Chakravarthy A S and Haase K B: 'NetSerf: Using Semantic Knowledge to Find Internet Information Archives', Proc 18th Annual International ACM SIGIR Conference, Washington, USA (1995).

13. Rada R and Bicknell E: 'Ranking Documents Based on a Thesaurus', Journal of the American Society for Information Science, 40, No 5, pp 304—310 (1989)

14. Miller GA: 'WordNet: An Online Lexical Database', International Journal of Lexicography, 3, No 4, (1990).

15. Salton G: 'The SMART Retrieval System', Englewood Cliffs, NJ, USA, Prentice-Hall (1971).

16. Maes P: 'Agents that Reduce Work and Information Overload', Comm ACM, 37, No 7 (1994).

17. Brewster K and Medlar A: 'An Information System for Corporate Users: Wide Area Information Servers', Connections — The Interoperability Report, 5, No 11 (November 1991), also available from ftp://think.com/wais/wais-corporate-paper.text

18. Emtage A and Deutsch P: 'Archie: an electronic directory service for the Internet', Proc Usenix Winter Conference (January 1992).

19. Bowman C M, Danzig P B, Hardy D, Manber U and Schwartz M: 'The Harvest Information Discovery and Access System', Proc 2nd Intl WWW Conf, Chicago, Illinois, US (October 1994).

20. Klark P and Manber U: 'Developing a Personal Internet Assistant', http://glimpse.cs.arizona.edu:1994/~paul/warmlist/paper.html

21. Manber U and Wu S: 'GLIMPSE: A Tool to Search through Entire File Systems', Usenix Winter Technical Conference, San Fransisco, US (January 1994).

22. Bush V: 'As We May Think', The Atlantic Monthly (July 1945), also available as http://www.csi.uottawa.ca/~dduchier/misc/vbush/as-we-may-think.html

23. Berners-Lee T: http://www.w3.org/pub/WWW/

Multi-Agent Matchmaking

L Foner[1] and I B Crabtree[2]

[1] Massachusetts Institute of Technology, Media Lab,
20 Ames Street, Cambridge, Massachusetts, USA.
E-mail: foner@media.mit.edu

[2] Intelligent Systems Research, Advanced Applications & Technology Department,
BT Laboratories, Martlesham Heath, Ipswich, Suffolk, IP5 7RE, UK.
E-mail: baz@info.bt.co.uk

Many important and useful applications for software agents require multiple agents on a network that communicate with each other. Such agents must find each other and perform a useful joint computation without having to know about every other such agent on the network. This paper describes Yenta, a matchmaker system designed to find people with similar interests and introduce them to each other. It describes how the agents that make up the matchmaking system can function in a decentralised fashion, yet can group themselves into clusters which reflect their users' interests. These clusters are then used to make introductions or allow users to send messages to others who share their interests. The algorithm uses referrals from one agent to another in the same fashion that word-of-mouth is used when people are looking for an expert. A prototype of the system has been implemented, and the results of its use are presented.

1. Introduction

Software agents are computer programs which attempt to perform some set of tasks autonomously for their users in a trustworthy, personalised fashion. They can be either manually programmed by the user, or use techniques from machine learning to discover how the user does some task and gradually automate it. Examples include mail filtering programs, which learn or are told whose mail is valued and whose is not [1, 2], meeting-scheduling programs, which learn or are told when and with whom to schedule meetings and how flexible to be in negotiating (with other agents) for times depending on who else is in the meeting [3], and so forth. Many software agents are even designed to be primarily entertaining, perhaps with ancillary practical or informative goals [4, 5].

Other agents take more initiative; they actively inform the user when they find items that match the user's known interests. Often, such agents may not understand the domain of interest directly, but are instead facilitators that can find other people who understand the domain better who can advise. Automated collaborative filtering, in which users with similar tastes are matched up, is used in systems such as Webhound [1] or MORSE [6].

While the two agents above match up users' tastes to make recommendations, their focus is not explicitly to matchmaking users and introducing them to each other. The research described in this paper is focused on introducing users who are interested in similar topics. There are a number of reasons why one might want to do this:

- people are often working on similar projects without realising it — be it two people down the hall from each other re-inventing the same wheel, or two doctors both doing research on similar cases but having no idea that both of them are studying the same domain;

- it is often the case that people need to find an expert in some field, but finding such an expert can be difficult and time-consuming — those who are not well 'plugged-in' via word-of-mouth can find this even more difficult;

- in a large organisation, there are likely to be many initiatives that make use of the same underlying methods and techniques — project directories and job titles will be of no use in identifying them but knowledge of people with similar background would be very useful.

1.1   Why Having Multi-agent Systems Helps

Many currently implemented agents use a centralised architecture, in which one agent serves either one or many users. A centralised architecture has its advantages; for example, if there is no effective way for peers to find each other, a centralised solution may be the only workable solution. Unfortunately, there are problems with a centralised architecture:

- scaling such an architecture to large numbers of users is difficult — in systems which must correlate user interests (for example, Shardanand and Maes [7]), straightforward approaches to this problem generally require a quadratic-order complexity;

- if the system requires either high availability (due to constant demand for its services) or high trustability (because it handles potentially sensitive information, such as personal data), a centralised server provides a single point where either accidental failure or deliberate compromise can have catastrophic consequences.

For these reasons and others, many foreseeable future applications for software agents will involve large numbers of agents interacting with each other. Users may have a number of agents operating on their behalf, and agents of any particular user may have to communicate with other agents elsewhere on the network in order to share information.

1.2 Why Multi-agent Systems are Hard to Build

While decentralised, multi-agent systems have several important advantages, one of the largest problems with them is how agents are supposed to find each other. Each agent should not have to know about (and, indeed, probably cannot know about) every other agent, user or resource on the network. Instead, some mechanism by which agents may locate only the useful agents on the network must be arranged.

There are several relatively straightforward approaches that have been used in other networked systems. For example, hierarchical organisation of the entities, as is done with resource records in the Internet domain-name system [8] or with newsgroup topics in the Usenet [9], can help to reduce the inherently quadratic problem into a logarithmic one. However, such approaches depend on some inherent organisational principle that is established in advance, which is neither always optimal nor always convenient; for example, consider the number of crossposted Usenet articles, a clear indication that single-inheritance hierarchies are not necessarily a good match to the underlying topic space.

This research focuses on the problems of a matchmaking service, one designed to find groups of people with similar interests and bring them together to form coalitions and interest groups. This paper does not explicitly deal in romantic matchmaking between users, for many reasons — the most obvious being that shared interests do not necessarily mean that two people are romantically compatible. The intended scale of the matchmaking is that of the entire Internet, an environment in which there are potentially millions of users and millions of agents corresponding to them. The domain and the large number of agents present difficult co-ordination problems, such as:

- there is no obvious *a priori* hierarchy by which to organise the agents (Why would any one person's interests be at the top of any hierarchy? How would we know whom to pick, anyway?);

- asking other agents at random resembles diffusion in a gas and is extremely slow — it means each agent could be required to ask every agent on the network, guaranteeing a solution that scales poorly;

- a centralised approach runs into the problems mentioned above of quadratic complexity, and also is subject to single-point-of-failure problems if the central system either fails or is compromised — an important point for an application handling potentially sensitive data.

1.3 Finding the Right Cluster of Peer Agents — The Core Idea

To address these problems, this research considers an overall organisation which borrows ideas from computational ecology [10], in which agents have only local knowledge, but self-organise into larger units. The core ideas in the approach taken here are to:

- compare the agents' information in a peer-to-peer, decentralised fashion;

- use referrals from one agent to another and an algorithm resembling hill-climbing to find other, more appropriate agents when searching for relevant peers;

- build clusters or clumps of like-minded agents;

- use these clusters of similar or like-minded agents (whose users therefore share similar interests) to introduce users to each other and enable cluster-wide, messaging between users whose interests match;

- use a persistent agent that runs most of the time, for long periods; the user does not start up the agent, get an immediate result, and shut it down, but instead runs it in the background for hours or weeks, while it uses 'word-of-mouth' to find and join appropriate groups of agents whose users share the same interests.

1.4   How the Resulting Clusters can be Used

Once agents have formed clusters — an ongoing and continuous process for real agents on the Internet, due to the scale and constantly-changing environment involved — how can these clusters be used? There are many applications — this is a short summary.

- Messaging into the group — a user whose agent is in some particular group can send a message into the group, either to those other agents known directly by the user's agent to be in the same cluster, or transitively through all other agents in the cluster by following cluster-cache information in a flooding algorithm. Thus, given some particular interest (represented by a local cluster of text files, and referred to as a granule later in this paper) on the user's local agent, the user could ask their agent to send a message to all other agents in the clump of which this interest is a member.

- Introductions — the chain of referrals themselves can be useful information, and can be exposed to the user under certain circumstances. Not only can the user send messages to particular individuals (whether pseudonymously or not), but the agent itself can facilitate a 'flirtatious' sort of introduction in which information can be symmetrically and gradually revealed, via cryptographic protocols.

Users could ask for an explicit introduction to particular members of the cluster, or could instruct their agent to accept or solicit introductions when it looked like there was a particularly good match available.

- Finding an expert — by using a combination of messaging into the group and introductions, the clusters in which a user's agent finds itself can potentially be used to find experts on the subject, since presumably such experts (if they, too, are represented by a Yenta agent) will have their interests reflected in the clustering. Here, a user could prepare a small piece of prose, or find some existing message, which talks about the subject for which the user wants an expert; the clustering algorithm could then generate a granule for this grain and attempt to find a suitable cluster. Once found, it could start the introduction process to acquaint the questioner and the expert.

1.5   What is Described in this Paper

The following sections describe the algorithm used in a prototype of the clustering system, the testing used to evaluate its performance, and how this work is integrated into the larger goal of automatically building interest groups and coalitions on the Internet.

2.   The Approach

The overall goal is to form clusters of agents whose users share similar interests. The details of the approach are covered in Foner [11] but essentially involve answering the following questions:

- What does it mean to have an interest, and how do agents know about these interests?

- How is similarity of interests determined?

- How does a particular agent know which other agents to contact?

- How are clusters of similar agents formed?

2.1   User Interests

When an agent first starts running, it must determine what interests its user possesses and then update this from time-to-time to reflect changing interests. This could be achieved in a number of ways ranging from asking the user for keywords or phrases from time to time in order to gather the interests, or semi-automatically by analysis of the user's e-mail, documents or text files. The second approach has been used here for a number of reasons:

- the agent should be as unobtrusive as possible, therefore asking for keywords is not in line with this approach;

- users' interests could be defined in terms of a few keywords, but this would probably not give the right granularity of information — keywords such as agents, computing, music, etc, which would probably be adequate to give an overview of someone's interest areas would not be useful in the matchmaking sense of Yenta;

- using personal e-mail and documents provides a much richer set of words that can be used to refine different interest sets, and e-mail especially should reflect the gradually changing interests of a user;

- using personal information brings to the forefront issues of privacy and security which will rightly be an issue for the user.

Having taken this second approach of using personal data, specifically e-mail messages, the results of pre-clustering these messages into groups that represent distinct interests, as described in Foner [11], needs to be accurate. Although e-mails have been used to determine users' interests in this case, other information sources, such as documents or Web pages visited by the user, may provide additional information to determine more accurately the user's interests; however, these have not yet been explored. The following section describes some of the results and issues with pre-clustering of e-mail messages.

2.2   Effective Pre-clustering

A number of users were asked to submit quite large tracts of personal e-mail messages (between 1 and 20 megabytes worth each). These were clustered based on the contents of each message and the users were asked to mark the clusters using the following criteria:

- too specific;
- spot on;
- too general;
- garbage.

The initial clustering algorithm based on the whole e-mail message tended to produce a few very large clusters containing 50 to 100 e-mail messages, then many clusters with few messages — about 5, which had been specified as the minimum number of messages (grains) needed to form a cluster. In all, the algorithm would tend to produce 10 to 20 clusters from this data. Overall the results were quite poor, with only about 5 to 10% of the clusters being marked spot on and most of them being marked either garbage or too general.

Looking more closely at the resulting clusters, it became apparent that there were a number of flaws with this approach for the following reasons:

- some clusters were forming because words that formed part of a person's signature became dominant, and therefore, regardless of the content of the message, the signature became the clustering point;
- some long messages would cover a number of topics and would therefore get included in one cluster on the basis of one dominant paragraph;
- many e-mails were in the form of discussions covering a number of viewpoints and would therefore get included repeatedly.

To get round these problems some stringent pre-processing of e-mail messages was undertaken. This included partitioning long e-mail messages into paragraph- sized chunks. Removing any signatures, and removing any parts of 'included' messages. All of this was done automatically by a filter program.

Re-running the clustering on the preprocessed versions of the e-mails improved the markings of the spot-on clusters to between 20 to 25% from the previous 10% and produced many more clusters to mark — typically clustering would produce about 50 clusters to mark.

Users were then asked to rank the spot-on clusters into the following categories:

- considered to be an expert in that area;

- would be interested in that area;

- would like to steer well clear of that area.

An interesting outcome of these markings was that most of the spot-on clusters that were marked 'steer-well-clear' were those clusters that contained meeting agendas or invitations!

2.3   Data Structures Used in Finding Referrals and Clusters

The next step was where the various spot-on clusters (granules) in agents form clusters with other granules. For the sake of concreteness, assume that there are two agents, named A and B, which each have a few granules in them, e.g. $GA0$, $GA1$, etc. Each agent also contains several other data structures:

- a cluster cache (CC) which contains the names of all other agents currently known by some particular agent as being in the same cluster;

- a rumour cache (RC) which contains the names and other information (described below) of the last r agents with whom this agent has communicated;

- a pending-contact list (PC) which is a priority-ordered list of other agents that have been discovered but which the local agent has not yet contacted.

The rumour cache contains more than just the names of other agents encountered on the network. It also contains some subset, perhaps complete, of the text of each granule corresponding to those agents.

2.4   Getting Referrals and Doing Clustering

Now that all this mechanism is in place, performing referrals and clustering is relatively uncomplicated [12, 13].

The process starts when some agent (call it A) has finished preclustering and has found at least one other agent (call it B). Agent A then performs a comparison of its local granules with those of agent B. When this comparison of granules from A with granules from B is complete, agent A may have found some acceptably close matches. Such matches are entered, one pair of granules at a time, in A's cluster cache. B is likewise doing a comparison of its granules with A and is entering items in its own cluster cache.

Whether or not any matches were found that were good enough to justify entering them in a cluster cache, the next step is to acquire referrals to agents that might be better matches. In the example here, agent A asks agent B for the entire contents of its rumour cache, and runs the same sort of comparison on those contents that it did on agent B's own local granules. Good matches are added to A's cluster cache, the rest of the data is added to A's rumour cache, and A's namelist is updated by adding to it those other agents which showed good matches to A, i.e. those agents which had granules that went into A's cluster cache. These agents will be contacted next, after A finishes with B and any other entries in its namelist. The various caches belonging to B that A has been consulting were gathered by B in a similar way; every agent participating in this protocol is thus building up a collection of data for its own use and for the use of other agents.

This procedure acts somewhat like human word-of- mouth. If Sally asks Joe: "What should I look for in a new stereo?" Joe may respond: "I have no idea, but Alyson was talking to me recently about stereos and may know better." In effect, this has put Alyson into Sally's rumour cache (and, if Joe could quote something Alyson said that Sally found appropriate, perhaps into Sally's cluster cache as well). Sally now repeats the process with Alyson, essentially hill-climbing her way towards someone with the expertise to answer her question.

3. Experimental evaluation of the algorithm

The effectiveness of the algorithm has been explored in two ways. Firstly, an early simulation was run on a small number of agents (20) to see if it would work at all, and judge the overall efficiency of the algorithm. The results of this are reported in Foner [11].

There are a number of questions that needed answers to be sure the proposed algorithm would scale appropriately which were not addressed in the earlier experimental work. This section reports on a number of simulations that explore some of the issues with scalability and with tuning the various cache sizes.

Firstly, the earlier work only looked at 20 Yentas. With the intention of using this multi-agent system on a large scale, covering a whole organisation, or indeed the whole of the Internet population, probably the minimum grouping would be in the order of hundreds of Yentas. For smaller groups — say a few tens of Yentas — the matchmaking problems that Yenta is intended to address would probably not arise to make the system worthwhile. Clearly then the system must be tested with hundreds or thousands of Yentas.

There are a number of tuneable parameters with each Yenta such as the size of the rumour cache (i.e. the number of entries it can hold), the frequency at which Yentas will talk to others, the amount of data held from another Yenta, etc, which need to be set appropriately for the whole community of Yentas to work properly.

Clearly the frequency of Yentas talking to each other will be directly proportional to the time it will take to find all the other Yentas with similar interests (given that this approach works). A compromise therefore has to be reached on this level of 'chatter' between Yentas so that it is frequent enough for the Yentas to find out about all others with similar interests, but is not too frequent as to impair overall network traffic or CPU usage on the user's machine. It can probably be assumed that a person's interest is likely to be persistent for a few weeks, and certainly that their area of expertise would be likely to remain persistent for some extended time covering a few months. Given these time-scales, the Yentas can afford to be able to take some time over finding all the other Yentas with the same interest, and there would not be too much concern if it took a number of days of low-level communication for the Yentas to update fully their cluster caches.

The size of the rumour cache will have an impact on the way Yentas will find others with similar interests; the rumour cache holds information about other Yentas which are known about and some indication of their interests as a basis for deciding which Yentas to contact. A rumour cache that is very small would not give a Yenta any view as to which other ones to visit and would correspond to a very limited 'memory' which could cause the Yenta to repeatedly visit certain others. An unbounded or very large rumour cache on the other hand defeats the aim of the system, as every Yenta would get global (if not out-of-date) knowledge of all the others, which is counter-productive and probably unnecessary, as the view is that increasing the rumour cache above a particular size would probably give little benefit.

A final issue to be considered is how the interests are spread between Yentas. If the interests are spread very thinly between users, i.e. in the collection of Yentas only a very small percentage share the same (or similar) interest, it may take longer to cluster them rather than if there were few interests spread between the Yentas, as the cluster caches and rumour caches would contain many links to the others. Therefore it is important to determine what impact this would have on the effectiveness of the Yenta system.

3.1 Scope of the Simulation

To explore these issues a number of simulations were run on a very simplified model of the Yenta system where each Yenta was randomly given one interest out of those available. The impact of this was that the rumour cache and pending contact list were essentially the same thing. The simulations varied the following parameters:

- the number of Yentas in the simulation — this was varied between 200 and 1000;

- the size of the rumour cache, which varied between 2 and 50 entries;

- the number of different interests spread between Yentas, which varied between 5 and 30.

In all the simulations, each Yenta was allowed 500 message exchanges with other Yentas. After every 10 message exchanges, data was collected on the size of each Yenta's cluster cache. This information was then processed to produce a number of animations which were then analysed. The following 3-D graphs (Figs 1—3) are the mid and final frame of each of these animations. In all the graphs, the height of the columns shows the overall effectiveness of the Yenta system as a percentage — 100% indicates that all of the Yentas have found all their counterparts with the same interest[1]. The back walls on the graphs depict the minimum, average and maximum values for the corresponding row of columns.

3.2   Does It Scale Up?

One of the first questions to be answered was does it scale up to hundreds or thousands of Yentas. The answer to that is certainly yes. Taking Fig 1 which shows the coverage of Yentas after 500 iterations where the number of Yentas is varied from 200 to 1000, and the number of distinct interests is varied from 5 to 30, it is seen that, in almost all cases, greater than 90% coverage has been achieved, and, for low number of interests, 100% coverage. Also, from that figure, there can be a reasonable level of confidence that it will scale to greater numbers of Yentas, because as the number of Yentas is increased, the coverage does not get appreciably worse. However, there is an interesting dependency as the number of distinct interests is increased, which deserves more exploration.

3.3   How Long Does It Take?

These simulations were limited to 500 message exchanges between Yentas. This figure of 500 came about from some preliminary experiments to determine how many exchanges were needed; however, it can be seen from the graphs that, as not all Yentas have converged by this time, for larger number of Yentas more time will probably be necessary. As discussed earlier, it is important to get the balance right to ensure the Yentas find each other yet do not cripple their hosts in the process. Therefore, if a moderate communications scheme is suggested where a Yenta communicates every 10 minutes, that gives 500 exchanges in 83 hours or about three and a half days. This is well within the expected window of a user having an area of expertise for a minimum of weeks or months. As before, Fig 1 shows that the majority of Yentas have found all their peers in this time.

---

[1]The percentage is the average of each of the Yenta's coverage. As the standard deviation was also measured but in all cases was very low (no more than four percent), it has been omitted.

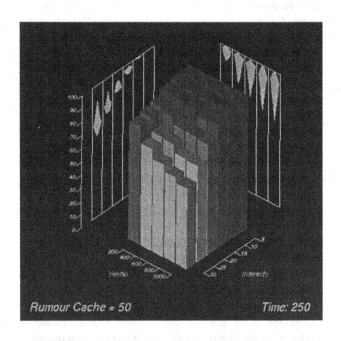

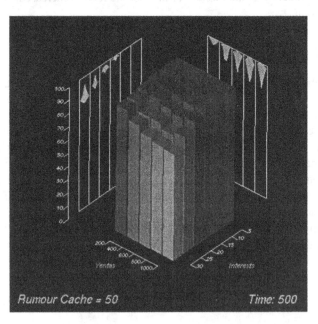

Fig. 1. Varying the number of interests and number of Yentas.

3.4 What is the Impact of the Rumour Cache Size?

It was suggested that there might be minimum and maximum useful rumour cache sizes and the rumour cache size was varied in the experiments to see if this was borne out. Figure 2 shows quite clearly that as the size of the rumour cache is increased, much better results for the system as a whole are obtained when the cache is 30 or above, while a rumour cache with 10 entries or less performs very poorly even with very few Yentas. It can be seen, therefore, from the data in Fig 2, that the cache size needs to be over 30. Taking Fig 3 now, where the rumour cache is varied against the number of different interests, there is certainly a dependency with increasingly varied interests.

It appears that with high numbers of distinct interests a rumour cache of 50 is still too small, whereas with a small number of distinct interests there is no improvement once the rumour cache size is greater than 5!

3.5 Further Questions

Scaling issues for up to 1000 Yentas have been investigated. Although this is a reasonable number for a system to work with in a small-to-medium-sized company, it does not get anywhere close to the size of the Internet community, for which it was originally intended. It can be seen from the results that, with large numbers of different interests, as the number of Yentas is increased to 1000, not all Yentas (about 15%) have been updated after 500 iterations, and this would get worse as the number of Yentas is increased still further. It does appear though that it would scale acceptably to approximately 1500 without any changes, and would improve if the size of the rumour cache were increased. From this work, it cannot be predicted how the system would perform with tens or hundreds of thousands of Yentas and more experiments would need to be undertaken to determine its performance.

4. Related work

There are many experiments in distributed AI and multi-agent systems which could be considered relevant; here only other matchmaking systems and related approaches are considered.

A common technique in systems that support computation among a group of users is to centralise a server and have its users act like clients. Systems that match user interests to each other, and have such a centralised structure, include Webhound [7] and HOMR/Ringo [1].

Kuokka and Harada [14] describe a system that matches advertisements and requests from users and hence serves as a brokering service. Their system certainly is a matchmaker, but it assumes a centralised matchmaker and a highly structured representation of user interests.

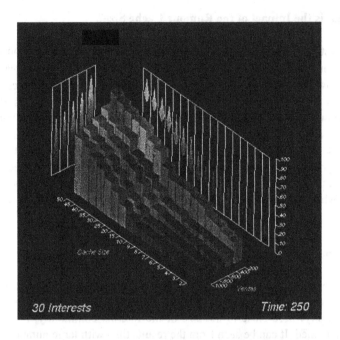

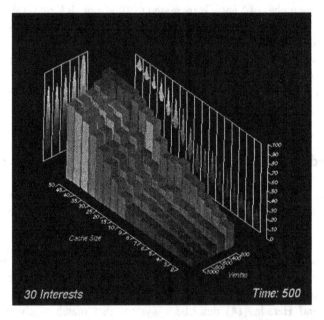

Fig. 2. Varying the rumour cache size and number of Yentas.

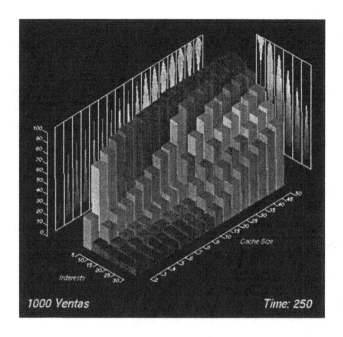

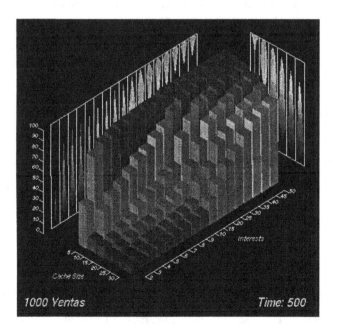

Fig. 3. Varying the number of interests and rumour cache size.

Others have taken a more distributed approach. For example, Kautz, Milewski and Selman [15] report work on a prototype system for expertise location in a large company. Their prototype assumes that users can identify who else might be a suitable contact, and uses agents to automate the referral-chaining process; they include simulated results showing how the length and accuracy of the resulting referral chains are affected by the number of simulated users and the accuracy and helpfulness of their recommendations. Yenta differs from this approach in using ubiquitous user data to infer interests, rather than explicitly asking about expertise.

5. Conclusions and Future Work

These results demonstrate that referral-based matchmaking can provide acceptable results without requiring any one agent to know about all other agents, and without requiring unreasonable messaging traffic or local computation.

Work is currently proceeding on several aspects of the final Yenta design:

* implementing the requisite privacy safeguards and user interface to permit a networked implementation with real user data;

* experimenting with different comparison metrics to enhance Yenta's ability to determine accurately a match in user interests;

* experimenting with the prototype with agents representing users from both BT and MIT Media Lab.

Acknowledgments

The authors would like to thank undergraduates Jon Litt, for figuring out the intricacies of a large system like SMART [16] and for his systems administration expertise, Bayard Wenzel for implementing the initial prototype of these ideas, and Simon Greatrix of BT Laboratories for creating the animations.

References

1. Lashkari Y, Metral M and Maes P: 'Collaborative Interface Agents,' Proceedings of the Twelfth National Conference on Artificial Intelligence, MIT Press, Cambridge, MA (1994).

2. Maes P: 'Agents that Reduce Work and Information Overload', Communications of the ACM, 37, No 7 (July 1994).

3. Kozierok R and Maes P: 'A Learning Interface Agent for Meeting Scheduling,' Proceedings of the 1993 International Workshop on Intelligent User Interfaces, ACM Press, New York (1993).

4. Foner L N: 'What's an Agent, Anyway? A Sociological Case Study,' Agents Memo 93-01, MIT Media Lab, Cambridge, MA, http://foner.www.media.mit.edu/people/foner/Julia/ (1993).

5. Mauldin M: 'ChatterBots, TinyMuds, and the Turing Test: Entering the Loebner Prize Competition,' Proceedings of the Twelfth National Conference on Artificial Intelligence, MIT Press, Cambridge, MA, http://fuzine.mc.cs.cmu.edu/mlm/aaai94.htm (1994).

6. Fisk D: 'Application of Social Filtering to Movie Recommendation', BT Technol J, 14, No 4, pp 124—132 (October 1996).

7. Shardanand U and Maes P: 'Social Information Filtering: Algorithms for Automating Word of Mouth', Proceedings of the CHI '95 Conference (1995).

8. Mockapetris P: 'Domain names — implementation and specification,' Internet RFC1034 (1987), {http://fuzine.mc.cs.cmu.edu/mlm/aaai94.html}

9. Horton M and Adams R: 'Standard for interchange of USENET messages,' Internet RFC1036, ftp://ds.internic.net/rfc/rfc1036.txt (1987).

10. Huberman B A (Ed): 'The Ecology of Computation', Elsevier Science Publishers B V (1988).

11. Foner L N: 'A Multi-Agent Referral System for Matchmaking', PAAM'96 Proceedings, pp 245—262 (April 1996).

12. Foner L N: 'Clustering and Information Sharing in an Ecology of Cooperating Agents, or How to Gossip without Spilling the Beans,' Proceedings of the Conference on Computers, Freedom, and Privacy, Student Paper Winner, Burlingame, CA (1995).

13. Foner L N: 'Clustering and Information Sharing in an Ecology of Cooperating Agents,' AAAI '95 Spring Symposium Workshop Notes on Information Gathering in Distributed, Heterogeneous Environments, Stanford, CA, http://www.isi.edu/sims/knoblock/sss95/foner.ps (1995).

14. Kuokka D and Harada L: 'Matchmaking for Information Agents,' Proceedings of the International Joint Conference on Artificial Intelligence (IJCAI) (1995).

15. Kautz H, Milewski A and Selman B: 'Agent Amplified Communication,' AAAI '95 Spring Symposium Workshop Notes on Information Gathering in Distributed, Heterogeneous Environments, Stanford, CA (1995).

16. Zumoff J: 'Users Manual for the SMART Information Retrieval System,' Cornell Technical Report 71—95 (1995).

An Application of Social Filtering to Movie Recommendation

D Fisk

Data Mining Group, BT Laboratories, Martlesham Heath,
Ipswich, Suffolk, IP5 7RE, UK.
E-mail: donald@info.bt.co.uk

The system described in this paper (MORSE — movie recommendation system) makes personalised film recommendations based on what is known about users' film preferences. These are provided to the system by users rating the films they have seen on a numeric scale. MORSE is based on the principle of social filtering. The accuracy of its recommendations improves as more people use the system and as more films are rated by individual users. MORSE is currently running on BT Laboratories' World Wide Web (WWW) server[1]. A full evaluation, described in this paper, was carried out after over 500 users had rated on average 70 films each. Also described are the motivation behind the development of MORSE, its algorithm, and how it compares and contrasts with related systems.

1. Introduction

We all have our own film preferences, and so take the risk, every time we watch a film, that we will not enjoy it. We can use a variety of methods to decide whether a film is worth watching, including the following:

- reading reviews;

- asking our friends (i.e. 'word of mouth');

- finding out who starred in it or who directed it;

- consulting the cinema or video charts;

- some combination of the above.

All of these approaches have disadvantages. In the first two, the viewer is relying on somebody else's opinion about the film, which will not always agree with their own.

---

[1]At URL http://www.labs.bt.com/innovate/multimed/morse/morse.htm

The third method does not work reliably, as films from the same director can vary considerably in quality, and film stars can be miscast or give lack-lustre performances. The fourth does not indicate popularity so much as the rate of change of people's expectations. It measures the rate at which tickets are bought or videos hired, with no feedback indicating whether the viewer actually liked the films that they watched.

Of course, one may ask whether it is possible at all to predict anyone's likes or dislikes in any area where preferences are to a high degree subjective. Is there not truth in the old adages, 'there's no accounting for taste', and 'one man's meat is another man's poison'?

The answer, which has been shown in the results presented below, is that, to a certain extent, it is possible to predict preferences [1]. This is true because people's tastes are not unique and films are not all dissimilar.

The breakdown of the rest of the paper is as follows — section 2 explains the social filtering approach, its possible applications and its commercial exploitation, and summarises related systems. Section 3 describes the MORSE system's architecture and algorithm, section 4 presents the results of its evaluation, and in section 5, some alternative algorithms are evaluated. Section 6 concludes the paper.

2. Background and Motivation

2.1 Social Filtering

Social filtering is based on the 'word-of-mouth' approach to recommendation in that it relies on the opinions of others. However, it makes use of considerably more data than other word-of-mouth approaches typically do. The general method can be summarised as:

- the user rates some films, CDs, etc;

- those ratings are compared with ratings given to the same films by other users;

- if you share similar tastes with others, it recommends to you those films that they liked, from among the films you have not rated.

As will be shown later, it is possible to improve the accuracy of the recommendations by taking into account ratings by people with dissimilar tastes too.

2.2 Possible Applications

Similar techniques could be used to provide recommendations in other areas with similar properties, such as television programmes, personalised newspapers, music, novels, beers or wines. In common with films, these have similarities between items of both the domain (people) and range (the thing which is recommended). Also, in these areas, people cannot be sure about whether they like something until they try it. However, within each of these areas, the correlation between items is sufficient for information about one item to help in predicting a person's liking for other items. If these conditions are not met, content-based filtering (where a user specifies their likes and dislikes and the system checks items against these) could be used instead [2, 3].

2.3 Potential Commercial Benefits

Although, for the foreseeable future, a significant part of BT's revenue will come from narrowband services such as voice and data, it is expected that in the near future BT will provide broadband services to customers' homes by exploiting asymmetric digital subscriber line (ADSL) technology [4]. A substantial part of this bandwidth will be used for entertainment services, probably in the form of films and other video material. BT is already carrying out customer trials of video on demand [5].

As other companies (e.g. video shops, cable TV companies, telecommunications companies) will be competing with BT in the supply of such services, it is important that BT differentiates its services from those of the competition. There are two obvious ways of service differentiation — price and range. The scope for price cutting may be limited because of the costs of both launching and supplying such a service, and the intense competition expected in future markets. The problem with increasing the range of films is that it becomes impractical to browse around even a small fraction of a database in order to find an interesting film, and even then the selected film might be disappointing.

However, there is a third way — taking some of the chance out of the customer's film selection process. This can be achieved by making customised recommendations (by a method similar to the one outlined below) while at the same time providing objective information about how the recommendations were made. This will increase customer satisfaction by decreasing the likelihood that customers watch films they do not enjoy.

2.4 Related Systems

Several systems have been developed which attempt to predict user preferences. Some of these are summarised in Table 1.

3. Description and Evaluation of MORSE

A large body of data was collected to evaluate the algorithm. In order to facilitate its use by as many people as possible and thereby improve its accuracy, MORSE had to satisfy the following two requirements:

- accessibility by as many people as possible;
- ease of use.

Table 1. Related user preference systems.

System	Domain	Comments
Movie Select [6]	Films	This is a CD ROM system claimed to incorporate artificial intelligence and fuzzy logic. It is accompanied by a comprehensive film database.
videos@ bellcore.com	Films	This is accessible by e-mail. It is unclear whether it uses social filtering [7], or is a neural network which makes use of film-specific information [8].
Movie Critic[a]	Films	This uses social filtering. Its algorithm is the subject of two patents.
Movie Recommen-dation Engine[b]	Films	No information on how this works is publicly available.
AgentMC[c]	Films	The developer "...hopes to get better performance [than Firefly, described below] by using multiple information sources and by adopting a well principled Bayesian approach"[9].
Ringo, HOMR [7]	Music	Developed at MIT. Ringo was accessible by e-mail, and was superseded by HOMR, and later Firefly.
Firefly[d]	Music, Films	This system was developed by the Autonomous Agents Group at MIT Media Labs, and is the successor to HOMR and Ringo. It uses social filtering.
The Similarities Engine[e]	Music	No information on how this works is publicly available.
GroupLens[f][10]	Usenet News	Developed at MIT Media Labs, this uses social filtering (Pearson-r algorithm).
NewT [11]	Usenet News	Also developed at MIT Media Labs, this uses genetic algorithms, with further non-genetic learning taking place between generations.
Yenta [12]	Match-making	Developed at MIT Labs, Yenta is a co-operating agents system which finds people with similar interests, clusters them and introduces them to each other.

a   http://www.moviecritic.com/
b   http://phoebe.dws.acs.cmu.edu/cgi-bin/movie
c   http://HTTP.CS.Berkeley.EDU/~murphyk/AgentMC AgentMC.html
d   http://www.agents-inc.com/
e   http://www.ari.net/se/
f   http://www.cs.umn.edu/Research/GroupLens

For this reason, it was decided to put MORSE on the World Wide Web, with data entered using forms. This had the additional advantages that the user interface (Netscape) would be familiar, so that instructions for users were unnecessary, and that it was straightforward to provide links into the Internet movie database, which contains comprehensive information about most films in the MORSE database.

A flow diagram for MORSE is given in Fig 1.

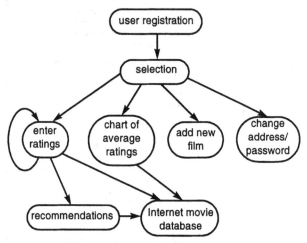

Fig. 1. Flow diagram of MORSE.

3.1 Description of MORSE's Main Modules

After registration (in which the user enters an e-mail address and password), the user selects from a menu which includes entering ratings and getting personalised recommendations, seeing a chart of films' average ratings, and some database management functions (see Fig 1). On choosing to enter ratings, the user is presented with a screen similar to Fig 2. The user can then rate films on an integer scale from 0 to 10, and repeat this on subsequent pages if desired.

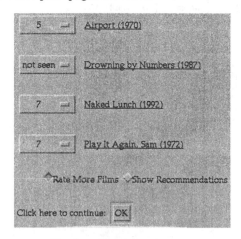

Fig. 2. Entering ratings.

After the user indicates to the system that the rating process is complete, recommendations are made by MORSE from among the films which remain unrated (see Fig 3). Both the predicted rating and the estimated error on it are taken into account when making recommendation. A film is:

- strongly recommended when its predicted rating, minus its estimated error, is at least 7,

- recommended when it is at least 6;

- weakly recommended when it is at least 5;

- not recommended if it falls below 5.

					Predictions for anonymous:
	score	± error	count	mean	film
weakly recommended	9.21	± 4.05	21	8.10	Heavenly Creatures (1995)
recommended	8.78	± 2.06	71	7.90	The Remains of the Day (1993)
recommended	8.71	± 1.97	51	7.75	Chinatown (1974)
recommended	8.71	± 2.30	45	7.87	Hoop Dreams (1994)
strongly recommended	8.71	± 1.60	38	8.00	Lawrence of Arabia (1962)
strongly recommended	8.70	± 1.63	24	7.54	Heat (1995)

Fig. 3. Recommendations.

The user can obtain more information about the films by clicking on the films' titles. The relevant pages are then downloaded from the Internet movie database.

3.2 The MORSE Algorithm

The principle of the MORSE algorithm is as follows. The rating a user i would give to a film k is estimated by normalising the ratings other users gave to the same film, and then plotting them against the correlation between the users' ratings and extrapolating (see Fig 4) the best-fitting straight line to correlation = 1.0. The normalisation process involves plotting the user i's ratings, for films whose ratings are closely correlated with those of film k, against those of each other user j, and using the best-fitting straight line to convert user j's rating for k into an equivalent rating for i (see Fig 4).

The steps taken by the program are.

- *Step 1* — calculate the correlation between k and each other film.

For each other user j, do:

- *Step 2* — plot the ratings given by i to the N films most closely correlated with k against the ratings given to the same films by j (see Fig 4).

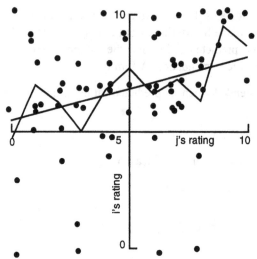

Plot of *i*'s rating against *j*'s rating for *n* films. The zigzag
line is the average value of *i*'s ratings for each value of
j's ratings, and is included to show how it closely follows
the best-fitting straight line.

Fig. 4. *i*'s rating plotted against *j*'s rating.

- *Step 3* — determine the best-fitting straight line through the points plotted in *Step 2* (see Fig 1). The best-fitting straight line is a function for converting the ratings given by *j* to *k* into equivalent ratings. Equivalent ratings are used because different users use the 0-10 scale differently.

- *Step 4* — determine the correlation between *i* and *j* for the *n* films most closely correlated with *k*.

- *Step 5* — plot the equivalent ratings for *k* (obtained in *Step 3*) against the correlation between *i* and *j* (obtained in *Step 4*) (see Fig 5).

end for:

- *Step 6* — find the best-fitting straight line through the points plotted in *Step 5*. Where this crosses the line *correlation* = 1.0 is the estimated rating (see Fig 5). *Correlation* = 1.0 is equivalent to a hypothetical user who exactly shares the tastes of user *i*.

- *Step 7* — calculate the error on the extrapolation.

- *Step 8* — base recommmendations on the value obtained by subtracting the error (*Step 7*) from the estimated rating (*Step 6*). If results exceed a threshold, the film is recommended.

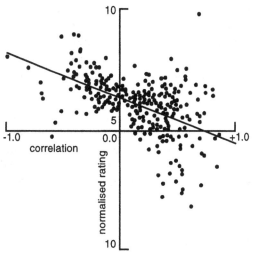

Plot of each user's rating (normalised) against their correlation with *i*. *i*'s rating is estimated by extrapolating the
best-fitting straight line to correlation = 1.0

Fig. 5.   Normalised ratings plotted against correlations.

4. Data Analysis and Results

The MORSE algorithm, and a number of alternatives, were evaluated by masking out
the known ratings one by one, estimating each rating by using the algorithm, and then
calculating the root mean square of the difference between each estimated rating and
the actual rating given by the user.

At the time the results were evaluated, there were a total of 729 registered users,
562 of whom had rated at least one film (users are not deleted if they do not enter
ratings), and there were 675 films to rate. In all, there were 38 982 ratings entered, an
average of 69 films per user. Unless stated otherwise, predictions were made for a total
of 37 877 ratings in all. (Some of the films had been seen by fewer than ten people, and
so their ratings were not predicted.)

4.1   Results

It was decided not only to measure the accuracy and certainty of MORSE's predictions,
but also to determine the effect on accuracy of the number of correlated films used in
the normalisation process, the number of users, and the number of films rated by
individual users.

- The root mean squared (RMS) error was calculated to be 1.805 (between 1.792
  and 1.818 with 95% confidence) for the MORSE algorithm — this is a significant
  improvement on the value 2.00 obtained when the average rating for the film was
  used as the prediction.

- 95.28% of recommendations (not predictions) were found to be satisfactory (here, a satisfactory recommendation is one where a film is recommended and the user enjoyed it) — more precisely, a recommendation is satisfactory if the film is strongly recommended and the user rated it 7 or above, or if it is recommended and the user rated it 6 or above, or it is weakly recommended and the user rated it 5 or above.

Because unsatisfactory recommendations would contribute to customer dissatisfaction, it is important to keep them to a minimum. Non-recommendations may have contained cases where a film would have been enjoyed by the user but was not recommended. This would not have contributed (significantly) to customer dissatisfaction, as the user would have wasted neither time nor money (the cost of video rental, for example) in not seeing the film.

- The correlation between the average predicted error for each user and the average RMS error was calculated to be + 0.43 (see Fig 6) — the correlation's positive value demonstrates that it is worth using the predicted error for determining the certainty of recommendations.

- The RMS error is a minimum when n, the number of correlated films used in the normalisation process, is equal to 11, though results are only significantly worse than this if n is outside the range 7 to 23.

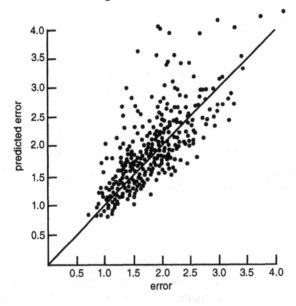

Fig. 6.   Accuracy of predicted errors.

The number of correlated films, n, used in the normalisation process (Fig 4) was varied, and the mean error was measured, in order to determine the value at which the error is a minimum. The results are shown in (Fig 7). If N is too low, the range of films used appears to be too small to be statistically significant, and, if n is too high, unrelated (and hence 'irrelevant') films are used in predicting the rating for a particular film.

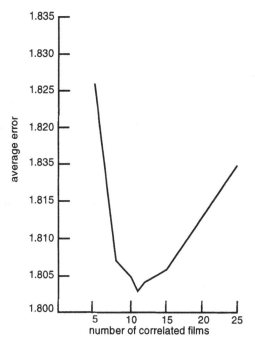

Fig. 7. Variation of RMS error with n.

- The RMS error on predictions was found to decrease slowly, from over 2.2 to 1.8, as the number of users increased (see Fig 8).

To explore the effect of increasing the number of users, fixed sets of films were rated (those which have been seen by fixed numbers of users (200, 100, 50 and 10) taken from the full data set). Then, the performance of MORSE was investigated as the number of users was varied (by deleting randomly selected users from the database). The results are plotted in Fig 8. They show a steady improvement as the number of users increases, and a slight improvement as the film range is progressively narrowed to the films rated by the most people. Intuitively, this was expected, since the quantity of information on which the predictions are based increases as the user base increases. In particular, the number of users with very similar (and also very dissimilar) tastes to any particular user increases, resulting in a more accurate extrapolation of the best-fitting straight line (as previously illustrated in Fig 5).

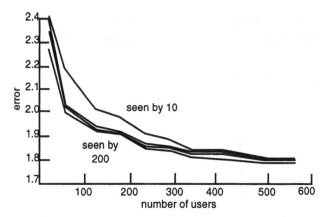

Fig. 8. Variation of RMS error with number of users.

- The RMS error for a user was found to decrease slowly, from over 2.2 to under 1.6, as the number of films seen by the user increased (see Fig 9).

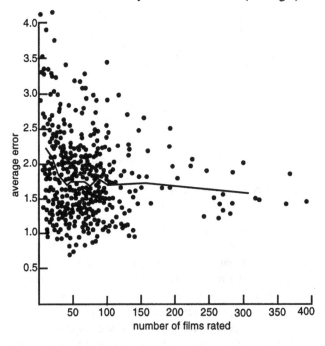

Fig. 9. Variation of RMS error with number of films rated.

The results show that, for users to get accurate recommendations (RMS error < 2.0), they should rate at least 30 films, and that predictions improve in accuracy as more films are rated. The reason for this might be that, when predicting the rating for a given film, the n films used to calculate the normalised ratings (Fig 4 above) are more closely correlated with it. Also, the correlations between users can be more accurately determined, resulting in more accurate extrapolation (as previously shown in Fig 4).

The line through the points on Fig 9 was obtained by grouping the points into sets of 50 with adjacent values of the x-co-ordinate (the number of films rated), and connecting the average values of the x-co-ordinate and the y-co-ordinate (the average error) in each set of points.

- The mean intrinsic error was found to be 1.535 (between 1.466 and 1.610 with 95% confidence).

There are several reasons for people varying the rating they give to a film. The first is that, as they grow older, their tastes change (for most people, one would expect a secular decrease in their rating of a Disney cartoon, for example). The second is a tendency to give more recently released or viewed films a higher rating than the same film would have if it was less recent. A perusal of the top 100 films in the Internet movie database[1] will confirm this. The third (the intrinsic error or variance) is essentially random and depends on how consistently or carefully the user rates a film. Even though a user may systematically rate films higher or lower on different occasions, the amount by which they do is still likely to be random.

The intrinsic error is an absolute limit on the accuracy of MORSE or any similar system — no system could generate more accurate results than the user who originally produced the ratings.

This third source of error was estimated by asking 14 users to rate the first 100 films in the database a second time, without them referring to the ratings they originally gave to the list of films. Although these users were not picked at random (it would have been difficult to pick volunteers at random), they were not selected by any other criterion than their availability. Altogether, 882 ratings were used.

4.2 Filtering out spurious data using Chauvenet's criterion

A slight modification of the algorithm, intended to remove possibly spurious data, was attempted. This involves the use of Chauvenet's criterion.

Chauvenet's criterion [13] assumes that data points follow a Gaussian distribution. The fewer points there are, and the greater the distance from the centre of the distribution, the less likely it will be that any points will be found beyond that distance. If the probability of finding a single point beyond a certain distance is less than a fixed value (usually taken to be 0.5), any points which do lie beyond it can be disregarded as they are likely to:

- be spurious,

- disproportionately influence any deductions which are based on the distribution, e.g. the intercept and slope of the best-fitting straight line.

---

[1]http://us.imbd.com/

The best-fitting straight line, and the error on this, is calculated. After points are removed using Chauvenet's criterion, the best-fitting straight line, and hence the predicted rating, is recalculated.

The result was a slight improvement, but not a significant one, on the basic MORSE algorithm.

The RMS error was 1.801 (between 1.788 and 1.814 with 95% confidence). If it is a real effect, it may have been because a few users were careless when entering ratings, or maliciously entered false ratings, or have such idiosyncratic tastes that their ratings cannot be used to predict other people's. When n was increased from 10 to 11, the use of Chauvenet's criterion gave the same result.

5. Alternative Algorithms

There are potentially an infinite number of alternative algorithms. These can be categorised into trivial algorithms and more complex ones.

5.1 Trivial Algorithms

Three trivial algorithms were tried because, while they are not useful for predicting users' ratings, they provide a baseline against which the performance of more complex algorithms can be measured.

- Using the average rating given by the user as the prediction, the RMS error on predictions was found to be 2.072 (between 2.057 and 2.087 with 95% confidence).

  This is equivalent to providing the user with no information, because users can calculate this by averaging their ratings.

- Using the average rating given to each film as the prediction, the RMS error was found to be 2.000 (between 1.986 and 2.014 with 95% confidence).

  This is an improvement on the previous figure of 2.072 and suggests that there is a certain amount of consensus as to which films are good, and which are bad.

- Using the nearest neighbour's rating for each film as the prediction, the RMS error was found to be 4.177 (between 4.147 and 4.207 with 95% confidence).

  Each rating is estimated to be the rating given by the user who has seen the film and who has the closest tastes to the user whose rating is being estimated. That this method is so inaccurate is surprising, especially since it is similar to what so many people do in practice, namely to ask one of their friends for recommendations.

5.2   The Pearson-r Algorithm

Using the Pearson-r algorithm, the RMS error was 1.940 (between 1.897 and 1.984 with 95% confidence).

Pearson-r is the algorithm used in GroupLens [8]. This algorithm ran considerably slower than the MORSE algorithm, probably because the data structures used were designed for the MORSE algorithm rather than the Pearson-r algorithm. Because of the slow processing speed, it was decided to run the algorithm on a randomly selected 10% sample of the data set (3826 ratings). The simultaneously calculated RMS error for the MORSE algorithm was 1.793 (between 1.754 and 1.834 with 95% confidence). It is 2.018 (between 1.974 and 2.064 with 95% confidence), if the average is used as the predicted rating. Thus, the MORSE algorithm makes more accurate predictions than the Pearson-r algorithm when using the same data.

5.3   Average of M Nearest Neighbours

The lowest RMS error obtained using the average of M nearest neighbours was 1.926 (between 1.912 and 1.940 with 95% confidence).

To predict user i's rating for film k, the films are sorted in order of their correlation with k, and the closest n selected. Then, the ratings given by the M users most closely correlated with i (using only the closest n films to calculate the correlation between i and other users), who have seen film k, are averaged. The average value is the predicted rating for user i and film k.

The prediction improves as n increases, and is best if all the films are used in the comparison (n = maximum). This is different from the results using the MORSE algorithm, where the best results were obtained with $n = 11$ (see Fig 7). The reason for this is unknown.

If $M = 1$ (i.e. only the nearest neighbour is used), the prediction is very poor. It should be noted that this is equivalent to asking the person, whose film tastes most closely match your own, what they thought of the film, and is a frequently adopted strategy. If all users are employed in the comparison, the predicted rating is the average rating (and the error on this is 2.000). Values of M close to 25 are, however, improvements on this. The error minimised at 1.926 (between 1.912 and 1.940 with 95% confidence), a significant improvement on using the average as the prediction, but not as good as MORSE (Fig 10).

The implication of this is that film recommendations made by one friend (e.g. the one with tastes most similar to your own) is not a good way of deciding which film to watch. It is better to ask all your friends (preferably at least 20 of them) before making a decision (better still, use MORSE). This may be because we are more similar to an average of all our friends than to any individual friend. The same principle would apply even if the 'friends' are anonymous, as is typically the case in systems which employ social filtering.

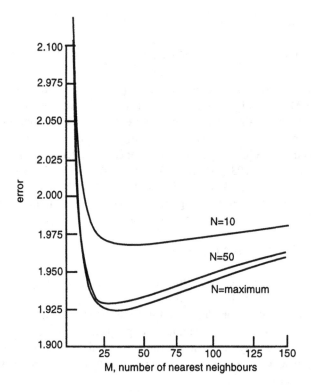

Fig. 10. Error plotted against number of nearest neighbours.

6. Conclusions

The research has confirmed that it is possible to provide personalised film recommendations using only the ratings given by users for those films. The recommendations obtained by applying the MORSE algorithm were more accurate than the other algorithms tried. This confirms that it is possible and worthwhile to predict people's subjective tastes. It should be possible to use similar techniques in other areas where personal tastes determine user preferences.

Acknowledgements

Thanks are due to Richard Titmuss for helping with some of the low-level C Unix hacking, to data mining colleagues for advice on statistical techniques, and to Hyacinth Nwana and Robin Smith for suggesting improvements to the paper.

References

1. Fisk D: 'Recommending Films Using Social Filtering', BT MSc Dissertation (1995).

2. Information Filtering Bibliography — http://ils.unc.edu/gants/filterbib.html

3. Information Filtering Resources — http://www.enee.umd.edu/medlab/filter/filter.html

4. Young G, Foster K T and Cook J W: 'Broadband delivery over copper', BT Technol J, 13, No 4, pp78—96 (October 1995).

5. Whyte W S: 'The many dimensions of multimedia communications', BT Technol J, 13, No 4, pp 9—20 (October 1995).

6. Medior Incorporated: 'Movie Select: The Intelligent Guide to Over 44,000 Videos', (CD ROM) Paramount Interactive (1995).

7. Shardanand U: 'Social Information Filtering for Music Recommendation', MIT Media Laboratory Learning and Common Sense Group Technical Report 94-04 (1994).

8. Karunanithi N and Alspector J: 'A Feature-Based Neural Network Movie Selection Approach', Proceedings of the International Workshop on Applications of Neural Networks to Telecommunications, Stockholm (1995).

9. Murphy K P: 'CS289 Final Project Proposal: A Bayesian Movie Critic', http://HTTP.CS.Berkeley.EDU/~murphyk/AgentMC/proposal .ps

10. Resnick P, Iacovou N, Suchak M, Bergstrom P and Riedl J: 'GroupLens: An Open Architecture for Collaborative Filtering of Netnews', Proceedings of the ACM Conference on Computer Supported Cooperative Work, Chapel Hill, NC, pp 175—186 (1994).

11. Maes P: 'Evolving Agents for Personalized Information Filtering', Proceedings of the Ninth Conference on AI for Application, CAIA '93 (1993).

12. Foner L: 'A Multi-Agent Referral System for Matchmaking', Proceedings of the First International Conference on the Practical Application of Intelligent Agents and Multi-Agent Technology (PAAM '96), London (April 1996).

13. Barford N C: 'Experimental Measurements: Precision, Error and Truth', p102, Addison Wesley (1967).

14. Fisk D: 'Programme Transmission and Reception System', EP Application No. 95305539.9 (BT Case Reference A25026) (1996).

Agents of Change in Business Process Management

P D O'Brien and M E Wiegand

Intelligent Systems Research, Advanced Applications & Technolody Department,
BT Laboratories, Martlesham Heath, Ipswich, Suffolk, IP5 7RE, UK.
E-mail: paul/mew@info.bt.co.uk

Successful enterprises are built on change. Increasingly, businesses
operate in a rapidly evolving environment where the response to
changing markets may of necessity be measured in hours and days
instead of months and years. Responsiveness and adaptability will be
the hallmarks of business success. BT is strategically placed as both a
major potential facilitator of this change, as well as benefiting from its
technology. This paper describes how agent-based process management systems can provide powerful tools for managing the enterprise of
the future. It explores recent work combining distributed computing
technology with autonomous software agent techniques for business
process management, and argues that these represent a viable supplement and even an alternative to existing workflow management
systems. This is supported by the results of a number of projects,
including ADEPT[1], BeaT[2] and a number of other related schemes,
which are exploring how leading edge technology can improve the way
business processes are managed. This paper provides a vision of how
agent-based process management systems can support the needs of the
'virtual' enterprise of the future and the integration of the information
systems of small to medium-sized enterprises (SME).

1. Introduction

Workflow systems provide powerful automatic mechanisms for managing the
execution of business processes. The workflow approach helps to separate the business
logic represented by a business process from the underlying information systems which
support that process. This separation allows business processes to be designed without

---

[1]ADEPT is a three-year collaborative project involving BT, ICI Engineering Technology, Loughborough
University and Queen Mary and Westfield College. The project is part of the DTI/EPSRC Intelligent
Systems Integration Programme (ISIP). This work also draws from a number of other BT projects looking
at the development of intelligent business process management systems.

[2]BeaT has investigated the engineering aspects of applying agent-based process management systems to
actual BT business processes and the information systems that underpin them.

requiring major changes to be made to the underlying computing infrastructure. Workflow automates the enactment of business processes, improving the speed and efficiency of an organisation. However, workflow management systems have certain limitations which need to be addressed if business process management systems are to be applied more successfully and to more business processes.

1.1 Existing Workflow Systems

Workflow management systems at present are ideal for managing business processes which are fully dimensioned and where all logical paths have been carefully considered in detail and fully described.

However, not all business processes are like this. In commercial environments decisions are not always clear cut but involve the balancing of various vested interests and policies, and resource levels can change. Such business processes highlight a number of shortcomings in existing workflow management systems [1]. They lack:

- reactivity — workflow management systems require an *a priori* representation of a business process and all potential deviations from that process;

- semantics — many workflow management systems lack an appreciation of the content of a business process and do not make decisions based on the nature of the information generated by a business process;

- extensibility — many systems are not extensible on-line;

- resource management — workflow management systems do not control the resourcing of a business process and so rely on a business process being dimensioned beforehand;

- heterogeneity — workflow management systems tend to take a centralised view with a single workflow management engine that does not operate across multiple-server platforms or multiple-client operating systems.

1.2 Agent-based process management systems

Agent-based process management systems (APMSs) combine the latest distributed computing technology with agent-based techniques [2, 3] providing an intelligent extension and alternative to workflow management systems. They provide :

- intelligent decision making — APMSs can represent management strategy and policy from a range of perspectives;

- anticipation — APMSs plan tasks and schedule available resources in anticipation of their use in a business process;

- explicit resource management — APMSs represent the levels, limitations and value of resources and manage them in support of business activities;

- reactivity — APMSs react to changing circumstances and have the capacity to generate alternative execution paths in response to unique exceptions;

- heterogeneity — APMSs can be distributed over multiple platforms across LANs and WANs using the latest distributed computing technology which is fully open across machines and operating systems.

APMSs offer an alternative technology to existing workflow systems. Most importantly, they also offer an alternative vision of how organisations can be structured and managed. APMSs take a 'service-oriented' view of business process management, where the resourcing and co-ordination of activities to support an end-to-end business process involves negotiation and collaboration between customer and provider agents.

Figure 1 contrasts workflow management systems, which have a centralised workflow engine, with APMSs which consist of autonomous systems that represent the respective concerns of various business units involved in a business process. The service-oriented approach of APMSs can reflect the inherent distributed nature of large organisations and make the management of an organisation transparent to its logical or physical structuring. Similarly, this approach allows an organisation to adapt and evolve with minimal disruption so that new services or tasks can be defined incrementally, without the need to redesign an entire distributed system. This empowers local semi-autonomous groups to define how they will perform and manage tasks and processes; see Armson and Paton [4] for detailed discussions on the empowerment of personnel in large organisations.

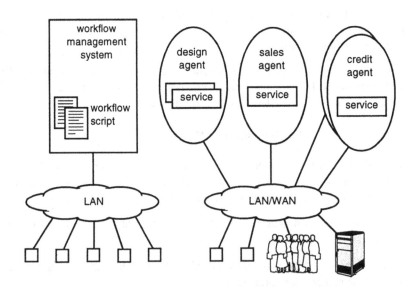

Fig. 1. Workflow management systems compared with APMS.

An important feature of APMSs is that dimensioning of business processes is brought on-line and integrated with process enactment resulting in improved redeployment of resources and increased flexibility during exception handling. Therefore, unlike workflow management systems APMSs have two objectives — firstly, the timely execution of business functions and, secondly, the efficient use of resources.

2. APMS — A Service-oriented Approach

A business process is made up of a number of process activities or tasks which are combined to express the functioning of the process. Dependencies exist between tasks, so they have to be executed in a controlled and ordered way. The execution of a task consumes resources which typically are grouped into business units that have semi-autonomous control over the way in which the resources are deployed.

Autonomous software agents communicate with each other over a communications network and negotiate over how they can collaborate to support an overall business process. Each agent offers services to other agents and can take the role of provider (server) or customer (client) for a service.

This client/server view of a business process has parallels with the ActionWorkflow methodology [5], although in an APMS this is reflected in the system architecture, with agents performing the roles of provider and consumer of services. There are also parallels with some aspects of the organisation of large enterprises, where service-level agreements may exist between groups and departments.

A service is a packaging of tasks and other (sub-) services that allows an agent to offer or to receive from another agent, some functional operation. A service can be reused as a component of another service. A task represents a primitive functional component of a business process.

Figure 2 depicts an example of five agents managing a business process. Each agent provides service(s) in support of a typical customer-sales business process.

Agent C, representing the sales department, would negotiate for services from other agents to support their sales function. This could involve negotiating for manufacturing capacity with agent E, and delivery services from agent B. These agents in turn might require other services, for example the agent E might negotiate for services from stores through agent A. As agreements are reached between the agents (as both client and server agents), contracts are established.

Each agent has to ensure that it has sufficient capacity to provide a service before it commits itself to delivering that service. This requires the agent allocating sufficient resources to support those tasks under its direct control, as well as ensuring it has access to sufficient component services offered by other agents.

An agent may need to guarantee the existence and availability of a particular service with some fundamental level of assurance and reliability. There can be three basic levels:

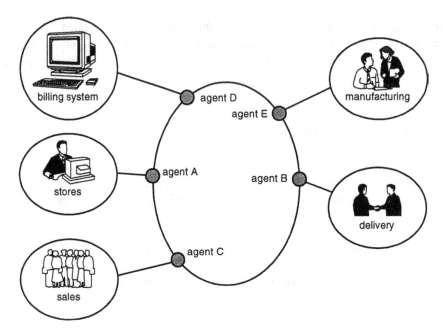

Fig. 2. Agents and the virtual enterprise.

- one-off — this allows a single execution of the service, the time of activation being agreed during negotiation;

- regular (or scheduled) — this allows multiple execution of the service, at agreed and pre-scheduled times;

- on-demand — this allows execution of the service at any time to a specified volume, within an agreed time window.

When a customer requests a service from the sales team, an instance of this business process is enacted. The agents manage the execution of the business process ensuring that each task and service is performed in a timely and efficient way within the constraints of the agreed contracts. Agents interact to co-ordinate enactment, facilitate the exchange of information and handle exceptions; this might require rescheduling and/or renegotiation.

3. The APMS Reference Model

The APMS reference model comprises three main components — the agent, the business task, and the APMS business monitoring and engineering (BME) system together with the interfaces between them. Agents exchange information during negotiation and service enactment via interface 1. Agents manage business process tasks, information and resources via interface 2. The development and in-service administration and maintenance of agents is performed by the BME system which accesses agents via interface 3. During enactment, information can be exchanged between business tasks via interface 4. These interfaces are depicted in Fig 3.

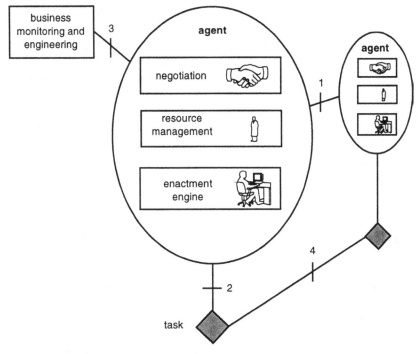

Fig. 3. APMS reference model.

An APMS agent comprises three core modules:

- negotiation module;

- resource management module;

- enactment module.

3.1 Negotiation Module

Negotiation is the process whereby two agents seek a mutual agreement and commitment on the delivery of a service. Quality, time and cost are three typical parameters which would form the basis for negotiation. As is the case with all negotiations, agreement cannot always be reached.

A contract is the result of an agreement between client and server agents during the negotiation process. The contract contains a list of agreed values for parameters, establishing the terms and conditions for the delivery of the service. For example, the agreed time(s) at which the service will be available and/or activated, the maximum duration of the activation, the minimum quality of the service, etc, will be defined.

In order for agents to be able to communicate effectively about these different parameters a common negotiation information model and language are required. The language consists of agreed primitives and a protocol to allow agents to suggest modification, and give consent, to the value of parameters in a contract. The negotiation language protocol defines the valid ordering on sending and receipt of primitives during negotiation between agents.

In a realistic business process an agent will be required to negotiate for multiple contracts simultaneously. Therefore the negotiation management module of an agent must be multi-threaded so that it can support multiple negotiations for different services concurrently.

During negotiation, an agent correlates and balances multiple criteria both within the negotiation for a single service, and across all the negotiations with which the agent is involved. The criteria can be modelled as (partial) ordinal value spaces that represent parameters such as quality, time, cost, etc.

3.2   Resource Management Module

An important aspect of an APMS is its ability to perform direct management of resources — the systems, databases, equipment and people that make up an organisation. Resource management is one of the key advantages of the APMS approach.

When a set of resources is under some form of semi-autonomous common ownership, there is usually a requirement to exercise some control over the commitment of those resources, in order to maximise speed, efficiency, etc, and to minimise cost, waste, etc. Delegating a single agent some form of executive responsibility for the set of resources is a way of achieving this. Resource management functionality (in particular scheduling) is either implemented in, or available to, the agent.

One way in which resources may be managed in an APMS is within an 'agency'. An agency represents a grouping of resources under the ownership of a single agent. An agency is the unit for which an agent performs resource management. The agency itself may be physically distributed, but it is logically centralised and managed by a controlling agent. An agency reflects the grouping of tasks for which there is some reason to attempt to optimise the use of resources in the execution of those tasks. The collection of tasks and (sub-)agents in an agency does not necessarily reflect a functional grouping (though in most organisations this effect may be expected).

During provisioning, an agent can commit to a contract without performing detailed resource allocation. The negotiation management module of an agent can commit that agent (as server) to provide a service. In this way, an agent decouples negotiation from detailed resource management in order to support real-time performance during the negotiation process.

3.3   Enactment Module

Enactment involves the activation of tasks and agreed (sub-) services in order to meet the obligations established in a contract. Server agents activate tasks and services when triggered by client agents. This can involve the execution of software or the sending of a work schedule by facsimile to an operative. An agent executes multiple services and tasks simultaneously. The agent must be multi-threaded to allow the agent to activate concurrent operations and handle multiple negotiations.

When tasks and services fail, agents can perform corrective actions and try to resolve the failure. The enactment module receives exceptions from the tasks within its agency and from other agents (as servers). Exceptions can be resolved by either:

- re-resourcing the task/service by the resource management module;

- renegotiating the terms of the contract (as the defaulting server agent);

- relocating the service with another agent (as the aggrieved client agent);

- ignoring the exception and accepting a penalty (if appropriate).

3.4   Business Monitoring and Engineering

The APMS BME system supports developers of organisations to engineer and monitor agent-based business process management systems.

Within APMS, agents offer services to each other based upon process activities (tasks). These services are combined in order to realise business processes. The techniques for defining services that may be useful in such a scenario correspond to business-process definition tools, though it is important to note that these services are not expressing what the complete process is. The service definition phase must be linked to a methodology that ensures that the defined services are useful to the enterprise (and will therefore be used) and that they will together realise an end-to-end business process. These conditions are termed 'necessary' and 'sufficient' service definitions.

The APMS languages and interfaces allow developers to implement and maintain the distributed business processes that have been conceived for the organisation. The design of an agent-oriented business process management system involves the principled transformation of some description of that business process into a number of communicating and co-operating software agents and the services they provide. The structure of an integrated system should reflect the structure of the existing organisation(s) rather than impose structure on them.

Each agent manages business functions that are under its direct control. The realisation of an end-to-end business process could involve contributions from many different agents. The monitoring and administration of a business process based on the APMS approach demands the ability to collate information from all the agents involved, filter this information, and present it in a way that allows a business process owner/manager to understand the contribution from all agents in the enterprise, and to see where problems might occur. The BME has to strike a balance between the autonomy of agents and the overall business requirement.

4. Realising Agent-based Process Management Systems

The following two sections describe aspects of the development of APMS. Section 4.1 describes the ADEPT approach providing an example of an implementation of an APMS, its functionality and how it has been developed. Section 4.2 describes the BeaT study of how APMSs can be integrated into actual systems which support an end-to-end business process.

4.1 ADEPT — An APMS Prototype

Project ADEPT [6] has developed a prototype APMS which demonstrates multiple autonomous agents managing nearly one hundred business tasks which make up a typical BT business process. The ADEPT infrastructure consists of a community of agents that can negotiate concurrently with one another in order to reach agreement on how resources are to be assigned to support a business process. The ADEPT agents are used for resourcing business processes, co-ordinating process tasks, and exception handling when business processes break down. Further details of the ADEPT demonstrator system are available elsewhere [7, 8].

The ADEPT Architecture

The ADEPT agent consists of three core modules — the interface management module (IMM), situation assessment module (SAM) and service execution module (SEM), each respectively mapping into the reference model outlined in the previous section. The IMM manages the negotiation for services with other agents during the service provisioning stage. The SAM ensures that commitments made by the IMM can be discharged using available resources. The SAM maintains a schedule of how and when available resources are to be used. The SEM manages the execution of tasks and services as the business process is enacted.

Resource management is achieved by encapsulating resources into tasks and managing the assignment of tasks to support a business process. In the ADEPT system, resources are managed implicitly via the assignment to task interfaces.

The ADEPT Demonstrator

The ADEPT demonstrator prototype (see Fig 4) is a full integration over the Common Object Request Broker Architecture (CORBA)-compliant platform, DAIS, from ICL. CORBA supports the distribution of computing objects across different machine and operating-system architectures. The ADEPT demonstrator consists of the following main components:

- a community of nine agents using the ADEPT agent architecture;

- a BT task simulator that emulates the relevant behaviour of nearly one hundred distinct business tasks;

- an Agent Visualiser, providing a limited part of the monitoring requirements for the APMS BME.

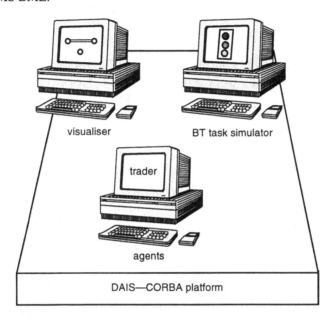

Fig. 4. The ADEPT prototype.

The ADEPT agents are multi-threaded, supporting the concurrent execution of several business processes. The CLIPS rule-based language (freeware developed by NASA) has been used in the implementation of the agents. Each agent contains a separate CLIPS environment and is registered with the DAIS trader.

The BT task simulator emulates the relevant behaviour of distinct business tasks providing a simulation environment for the agents which is used for both testing and demonstration. Tasks may have varying execution times and different probabilities of success or failure. Quintus Prolog and Quintus Objects have been used to implement the task simulator. Each task object is registered separately on the DAIS trader.

Agent visualisation tools provide the means of displaying agent communication and interaction. The visualiser does not register itself as a server with the trader, rather it contacts agents as a client and passes them its own object reference to allow them to send information back for display. The visualiser can be seen to contain functionality that would be included in an APMS BME.

4.2 BeaT — Engineering APMSs in BT

Project BeaT has studied the linking of APMSs to new business tasks within a large organisation like BT and has considered the engineering aspects of an APMS.

In a real application, the tasks that APMSs manage will be based on systems that have some direct access to, or effect upon, the real resources in an organisation. These resources may be information systems, databases, applications, even people. There are three main approaches to interfacing APMSs with business tasks [9].

- Direct access to databases — if there is direct access to databases, a wide variety of products are available that can provide object-oriented access to this data. If the data is in an object-oriented database, then object adapters may be available in a CORBA Object Request Broker (ORB) that permit the database objects to integrate seamlessly with the implementation objects.

- Application program interface (API) — more usually perhaps, the databases would be protected by an application layer that is designed to help keep them in a consistent state. If an application program interface is provided, it should be possible for the task object 'wrapper' to communicate with the application layer and gain direct access to the application functions.

- Screen-scraping — there are a number of reasons why no API may be available. The task may be one that is performed manually; in this case the task object needs a way of messaging the person or people involved. The task may be based upon a system that was never designed to operate in an open, distributed computing environment (so-called 'legacy' systems). In this case, one option may be to access and manipulate directly from the screen buffer that was intended originally for a human user — this is sometimes referred to as screen-scraping. Performance issues and the maintenance of the connection are major considerations with this approach. The back-end system may not have been designed to cope with the loading imposed by multiple automated task clients, and this may even cause the system to fail in its original objective.

A major issue for organisations is that significant parts of a business process are 'locked up' within large-scale operational support systems (OSS). This can impede improvements to business processes, making the company slow to react to change. The application of workflow management systems to middleware has led the way in separating business logic from the underlying information systems. This approach provides a suitable foundation for the introduction of APMSs into an enterprise (see Fig 5).

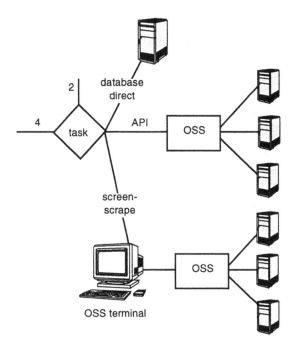

Fig. 5. Different ways to access information systems.

4.3 Distributed Computing Platforms for APMSs

APMSs rely upon a robust computing platform for accessing distributed functionality throughout an organisation. The technology that allows agent software to access distributed resources in an organisation is developing rapidly:

- CORBA — a number of workflow management systems as well as project ADEPT have used products based upon the CORBA standard, which allows the distribution of software across heterogeneous computing platforms — in APMSs, this technology can be used to support agent interaction, as well as access to distributed tasks and resources in an organisation;

- NextSTEP — adopts the CORBA approach, but incorporates it into a complete development environment for system designers, and an associated user-interface presentation environment;

- Internet — including Java, which represents a further advance in technology which is expected to make access to distributed resources easier.

5. Conclusions

Agent-based process management systems have a number of key advantages over existing workflow systems:

- they reflect the inherent distribution of large organisations;

- they make the management of an organisation transparent to the logical or physical structuring of its components;

- they allow organisations to adapt and evolve with minimal disruption, new services or tasks being defined incrementally, without the need to redesign an entire distributed system;

- they support the decentralisation of control in an organisation, thus empowering local (in a logical or physical sense) autonomous groups to define how they will perform tasks and processes.

6. Future Work

Research and development of APMSs is continuing within the Intelligent Systems Research group at BT Laboratories. Project IBS (Intelligent Business Systems) is integrating leading-edge agent and scheduling technology in the development of an APMS. Work is continuing also on the application of this technology to the enhancement of existing workflow management systems within BT.

Acknowledgements

The authors would like to acknowledge the support of the ADEPT consortium, and their colleagues Nader Azarmi, Robin Smith and Hyacinth Nwana.

References

1. Trammel K: 'Workflow without fear', Byte (April 1996).

2. Smith R: 'Software Agent Technology', Proceedings of the 1st International Conference on the Practical Applications of Intelligent Agents and Multi-Agent Technology, London, UK, pp 557—551 (1996).

3. Nwana H S: 'Software Agents : An Overview' Knowledge Engineering Review, 11, No 3 (1996).

4. Armson R and Paton R: 'Organizations : Cases, Issues, Concepts', (2nd edition), Paul Chapman Publishing Ltd (1994).

5. Medina-Mora R, Winograd T, Flores R and Flores F: 'The ActionWorkflow Management Technology', The Information Society, 9, pp 391—404 (1992).

6. Alty J L, Griffiths D, Jennings N, Mamdani E, Struthers A and Wiegand M E: 'ADEPT-Advanced Decision Environment for Process Tasks : Overview and Architecture', Proceedings of the BCS Expert Systems 94 Conference, Cambridge, UK, pp 359—371 (1994).

7. Jennings N, Faratin P, Johnson M J, O'Brien P D, and Wiegand M E: 'Using Intelligent Agents to Manage Business Processes', Proceedings of the 1st International Conference on the Practical Applications of Intelligent Agents and Multi-Agent Technology, London, UK, pp 345—360 (1996).

8. Wiegand M E and O'Brien P D: 'ADEPT: An Application Viewpoint', Proceedings of Intelligent Systems Integration Programme Symposium, Ambleside, UK (1996).

9. Wiegand M E: 'Building Practical Agent-based Systems', (Tutorial Notes) given at The 1st International Conference on the Practical Applications of Intelligent Agents and Multi-Agent Technology, London, UK, pp 345—360 (1996).

Agents, Mobility and Multimedia Information

R Titmuss, I B Crabtree and C S Winter

Intelligent Systems Research, Advanced Applications & Technology Department,
BT Laboratories, Martlesham Heath, Ipswich, Suffolk, IP5 7RE, UK.
E-mail: titmussrj/baz/wintercs@info.bt.co.uk

This paper describes the design philosophy and implementation of a system which manages the location, retrieval and processing of multimedia information for mobile customers. The system uses intelligent agents in all aspects of management and allocation of service components to perform the most appropriate translation and movement of information through the network.

The agents use an open market model to provide the services. The strategy of the management agents is to stimulate demand to use their services, which is offset by quality-of-service factors, leading to balanced utilisation of the network. Agents also act as proxies for the user to take into account personal preferences.

1. Introduction

Multimedia services present a telecommunications provider with many interesting options when compared to traditional voice telephony. The latter is based around a single, standard offering over which universal and common services are provided. It is questionable whether such an approach is either desirable or obtainable with multimedia. A plethora of sources and displays are available, varying from phones and video cameras that plug into telephone networks, to top-end workstations capable of displaying pseudo-3D virtual reality graphics. When users want to send multimedia documents they will have to give a great deal of thought to what equipment the receiver has available to display the document, and to the ability of the network to deliver it at a reasonable transmission rate. This complexity will inhibit the use of such services. Simply, users want to send documents and leave the 'network' to make intelligent choices about where and how to process, translate and display them.

These problems are particularly acute for the mobile user. Mobile equipment rarely has the display or processing power of 'fixed' items due to the need for low-power consumption and robust build quality. Thus the mobile user will only have access to lower processing power terminal facilities. Additionally, the mobile customer is normally attached to the network via a wireless tail which normally has less bandwidth than the fixed network. In the future the situation will almost certainly become more complex with users able to access information over an enormous number of different networks each of which will have different advantages and limitations.

The provision of intelligent management systems that select the optimum format of reception and the best network for the purpose and cost will be essential to give customers the necessary flexibility, and network operators a competitive edge. The network should be capable of taking information and delivering it to the user in the most appropriate form, depending on the equipment in the vicinity and the user's personal preferences. It is this problem that has been addressed using intelligent agents to provide the flexibility for a solution that is:

- robust — in that the network solution should be resilient to or be able to route round component failures or provide alternative solutions;

- scalable — so that the solution will work for local networks, but also be appropriate for large corporate networks or at a national or international level;

- flexible — so that new components that become available can be introduced into the system and used where appropriate with the minimum of intervention or manual re-configuring of the system.

The rest of this paper goes on to describe the rationale behind the agent approach used in the Multimedia Information Interchange (MII) system, then outlines the architecture and different types of agents that are involved in this system. At this point the approach is compared with alternative methods of achieving the same goal. The final section gives examples of the kind of services that can be achieved from the office-based prototype that has been in operation for the last few months.

2. Design Philosophy and Architecture

For the purposes of this paper, an intelligent agent is an autonomous computer program that continuously learns about its environment, adjusts its behaviour appropriately and negotiates with other agents to buy and sell resources needed for the overall system to undertake some task. Autonomy, learning and negotiation are the basic attributes of this agent definition [1].

A number of key ideas about what agents are and how agent systems should function drove the design of the agent model and architecture. As can be seen from the list below, the three major criteria in designing an agent-based network and service management system [2] are scalability, flexibility and robustness:

- each agent manages one resource, thus allowing for flexibility and robustness — a resource is viewed as either a component part of a service, such as a basic translation service, up to a whole network, which may be managed by an agent or hierarchy of agents;

- it should be possible to remove any agent from the system so that it still operates effectively but possibly in a reduced capacity;

- there should be a minimum messaging overhead — it is essential that, when there are some ten million users, the inter-agent messages do not swamp the system;

- agents should form hierarchies (scalability).

Fundamentally, there are three different problems the agents will need to tackle in this multi-network environment — the location of information, the allocation of network resources and the tracking of people and equipment. All have different characteristics, although only the latter two are actually implemented here, the proposed agent model can be extended to cover all three.

To best describe the architecture of the system it is first necessary to revisit briefly the service that the system is performing. Basically it has to deliver a multimedia document to a mobile user in the most acceptable form making best use of the resources it has available. This problem is depicted in Fig 1. If the receiver of the information is at a compatible workstation the multimedia document can be transmitted directly. If they only have access to a PDA (personal digital assistant), it will be unlikely to have the display capabilities and so the document must be decomposed, and perhaps only the text transmitted. The most extreme case is also shown where the only access to the person is via a phone. In this case a précis of the document must be made and that précis translated to speech to be delivered over the phone.

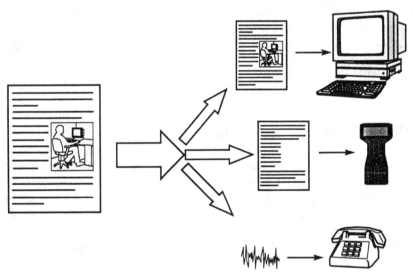

Fig. 1. The ubiquitous service problem.

To be able to perform this task effectively the system needs to know:

- the preferences of the recipient;

- the capabilities of the equipment near the recipient;

- the translation facilities that are available in the network.

One of the requirements was to ensure that the customer knew the cost of delivery of the message before it was sent, as some of the translation services may not be free. The delivery of a message is therefore split into two phases — a high-level pass to determine the possible delivery formats and cost, and whether it is possible to deliver it at all, given the cost and time constraints that may be imposed by the user. Then, once agreed, a second pass to actually implement the service in terms of routeing the message through the appropriate translation services to allow the message to be delivered in the correct form.

2.1   The First Phase

Figure 2 shows the agent communication involved in the management agent negotiation. The icons represent different types of agents, the lines between these icons represents the communication between the agents (the thicker the line the greater the communication). In Fig 2, negotiation between a geography database, network agent and two customer agents is shown. During this negotiation the agents calculate the document formats and cost of delivery by using statistical knowledge of the network resources. This is analogous with the management structure of a company where a customer would request a service from the manager of a group. This manager knows approximately what resources are available to him, how long the job will take and how much it will cost. Using this information the manager provides a quote for the work.

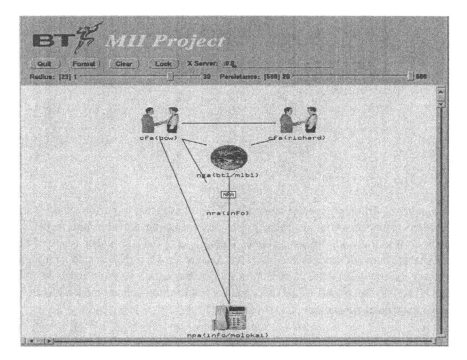

Fig. 2.   Management agent negotiation.

2.2 The Second Phase

Each translation service is controlled by resource agents which combine dynamically to provide any type of translation service that is necessary. The resource agents are involved in the second stage of the negotiation. This can be seen in Fig 3, where the resource agents (for the link, service and terminal resources) can be seen in a negotiation to determine exactly which resources are needed in the service and in what order they should occur. Returning to the analogy of the management structure, this phase of the negotiation is the same as the employees of the manager working out how they will do the work required. Each multiple translation service requested is built on the fly in this way.

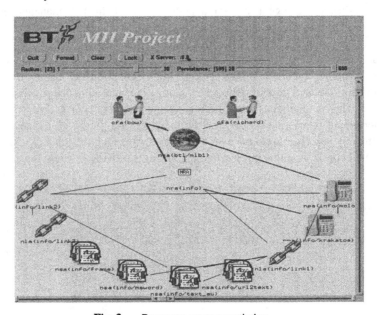

Fig. 3.   Resource agent negotiation.

2.3 The Agents Involved

A number of different types of agent have been constructed to perform these various resource management tasks. There are agents managing the user interfaces to the network which are known as customer facing agents (CFAs). Other types of agent manage the network services at a high level and are known as NRAs, and a third group manage the low-level network resources such as translation services and links (NSAs and NLAs). To keep track of the users and current location of equipment a hierarchical geographic database is used.

Customer-facing Agents

All customers subscribing to the network have a personalised CFA. This agent provides a single point of contact and is responsible for learning the customer's profile allowing the best to be obtained from the network.

This agent negotiates with the geography and the network agents to determine how the service can be provided. As the network agents may return with more than one possibility, an offer is sent to the customer describing the service which best matches the request. If the customer accepts the offer then the customer-facing agent buys the service in from the network, otherwise the customer-facing agent may provide another offer if more choices exist.

Network Agents

The network agents manage how the network resources are used to provide services. These agents are structured in a hierarchy so that the agents at the leaves of the hierarchy manage a network resource, e.g. a network link or an information translation service. These agents are collected into agencies based on the local network topology; each agency is co-ordinated by a manager agent, and in turn collections of manager agents can be an agency and controlled by a higher level manager agent — Fig 4 shows this organisation.

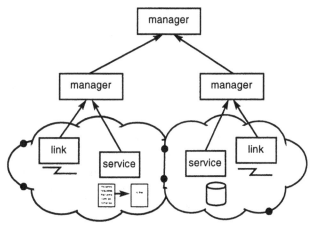

Fig. 4.   Network resource agents.

The service requests that come from customer-facing agents are processed starting at the top of the hierarchy and filtering downwards. The manager agents compare the requirements of the service with their network model. If the agents' network could be used in the service then the agent will enter a bid. This bid is used to construct the service offer for the first phase of the service as discussed earlier. If the agents' bid is accepted then the manager must negotiate with the agents in its agency to provide the resources required to fulfil its bid (the second phase). If the managers fail to provide the service or the service provisioning fails, this is indicated up the hierarchy and this failure is used by the learning mechanisms to alter the network model in the managers to reduce the chance that unsuccessful services will be contracted in the future.

The peer-to-peer bidding process of the resource manager agents used to link together the necessary service components performs a distributed search through the resources taking account of the availability, cost and abilities of the different resources. A representation of this search can be seen in Fig 5. The icons represent different media formats and agents. In this example, the service needs to translate a Microsoft Word document (on the left) to speech output (on the right). Terminal agents (represented by the telephone icons on both sides) move the information into and out of the network. A service agent can be seen converting the Word document into text. This search graph is only partially complete. A number of 'gaps' can be seen where the search has yet to be completed. It can be seen that a gap exists between the text document and the speech file. As the negotiation between the agents continues from this point, an agent managing a text-to-speech resource will be consulted and will be able to fill this gap.

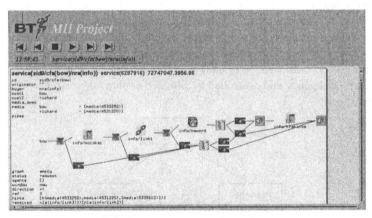

Fig. 5.   Resource search graphs.

One of the primary goals of the system is to be robust. To achieve this, resources can be added and removed from the network without affecting the system as a whole. When a resource is added to the network the agent controlling the resource informs its manager about its resource abilities. The manager uses this information to update its model describing the abilities of its whole agency. If the changes are significant then the agent will inform its manager. It is possible for agents to build an abstract view of the effectiveness of the part of the network they are managing using statistical state information and by monitoring significant deviations from the expected state. This means that the agents do not need a detailed model of the underlying network; rather they can learn abstract views of the performance and abilities of the network. The intelligence and flexibility of the resulting system can be used to provide a universal mechanism to cope with updating, network failure and service management.

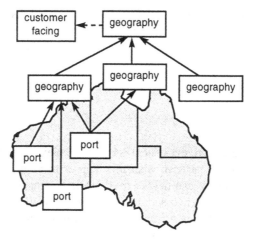

Fig. 6.   Geographical databases.

2.4   Geography Databases

The geographic database needs to provide a flexible, fast search that enables the network to track people and equipment and their relationship. A number of distributed database models exist that have been exploited or analysed. The Home Location Register-Visiting Location Register is used in current mobile networks and the REMUS architecture [3] is more closely linked with the system used here. The design philosophy used was to build a distributed database using the same tools as used in the network domain and so keep the system design simple. As will be seen, this gives a particularly robust and flexible database.

To provide the best use of the terminal equipment available to the customer, the network needs to know the geographical relationship between the customer and the terminals (see Fig 6). The geography databases are responsible for maintaining and using information about these relationships.

The geographical databases are organised in a hierarchy which reduces the amount of communication required to track customer and equipment movement. At the bottom of the hierarchy every geographical database is responsible for a small region, e.g. a floor within a building. The other databases represent the union of the areas managed by the agents reporting upwards. At the lowest level the information is very detailed, for example which terminal each customer is using and the exact capabilities of the terminal.

When a customer logs on to a new terminal a message moves up the hierarchy. This message only needs to propagate upwards until it reaches a geographical database which already knows about that customer. This database then adds a new pointer to the sub-hierarchy indicating the customer has logged on in a new place. Log-off operations are handled in a similar way. This system reduces the communications overhead when customers are moving around different areas of the network because most of the communication occurs locally to the customer. When a service is requested via the customer-facing agent the requirements from the customer include the media type of the information being transmitted and constraints on the delivery media (if any). The geographical databases use the location and terminal information to recommend terminals near the customer for this service.

3. Discussion

From what has been described, the system is quite complex with interactions between different types of agents to perform what may appear to be quite a simple delivery service. After all, the WWW can deliver multimedia documents to the desktop in a fairly straightforward way and, in theory, mime-compliant mail readers can also offer a document, delivered in the most appropriate form depending on the terminal capabilities. Various Web browsers use helper applications to do this which are fired up depending on the mime-type of the document to display the document, while mail readers can interpret multipart mime documents (multipart/alternative) to display the appropriate form. So, why is such a complex system needed?

3.1   Why Not The WWW Model?

There are a number of reasons why the WWW model was not thought suitable. The first thing to note is that the document source, be it Postscript, plain text, html, etc, is made available 'as is' on the Web server. The provider of the information cannot reasonably be expected to make it available in a number of different formats to please a wide audience (although some benevolent people have made documents available both as (say) Microsoft Word format and html). If a user wants to look at one of these documents, they must have the appropriate helper application available on their machine. In the most common cases this will not be a problem, but it is unlikely that everyone will have every helper application available to be able to read the documents. The majority of the Unix community for example will be unable to read any Microsoft Word document that may be made available.

With the MII approach, this is not a problem. If the appropriate helper application is not available, the document is translated, on-the-fly, to a format that is most suitable for the end user. With the translation facilities being network-based, there is no computational overhead at the destination end, and the service provider can make available the latest versions of the translation software, ensuring a highly effective service.

Bandwidth may be an issue; some Web sites are notoriously slow, or the delay might be on the receiving end. The user may only have available a low-bandwidth link, such as a modem to connect to the network. In these cases, the user has no option but to wait for the whole download to see if the document is worthwhile. With MII this could be taken into account by the user's customer- facing agent which would place a limit on the amount of data to be sent at any one time, and any documents to be delivered would be routed through some summarisation service [4] to ensure maximum content for minimum bandwidth.

3.2   Why Not the Intelligent Mail-Reader Approach?

Mime-compliant mail readers are able to take mail of the form multipart/alternative and deliver the document in the most appropriate form for the terminal capabilities available. The argument against this is simply that the document needs to be made available in all the different formats that are possible. For example a document written in Microsoft Word would ideally need to be made available in the following formats:

- as is;

- rich text format (in case you do not have the same version of Microsoft Word);

- plain text format;

- summarised plain text.

This approach is not thought to be practical, as it would place much more effort on the part of the document provider to try to second-guess the formatting capabilities of the reader of the document. Additionally, this method also probably doubles or triples the amount of data needed to be sent across the network, which again may be an issue if one of the links is of low bandwidth.

3.3   Related Work

The IBM Intelligent Communications Service [5] claims to provide services which are very similar to those in MII. Routeing and translation allows the customers of this service to communicate over a variety of networks and terminals. Differences between the systems exist on how the service to be delivered is determined. With the IBM system, a set of customer-specified rules [6] determine the routeing and translation required by the Intelligent Communications Service, whereas in MII the translations and networks to be used are determined dynamically based on the availability of translation services in the network and terminals near to the customer. The current status of IBM's Intelligent Communications Service is unknown.

3.4   Do We Need Agents At All?

The problem tackled here was to provide a very flexible method of delivering information, making appropriate choices of delivery format. The advantages that agents bring in this application are the following:

- a very robust approach to the management of the delivery service, covering failure of elements and allowing dynamic re-routeing;

- flexible configuration management — new translation services are added locally, and the management agents pass on the availability of these new services as necessary;

- a personalised approach from the user's viewpoint allowing information to be delivered in the most appropriate form, learned over a period of time.

4. Example Services

A demonstrator system has been operational in an office environment for a number of months, allowing a range of the services and facilities, that the agent system provides, to be demonstrated. The prototype runs over a LAN, and integrates a number of Sun workstations, including a portable. A number of media-translation services have been provided to the system such as text-to-speech [7], Microsoft Word-to-text, FrameMaker-to-text, etc.

4.1 Document Translation

The first example service depicts one customer sending a Microsoft Word document to another customer who can only be contacted using a mobile phone. Service requests from the customer consist of a number of attributes which describe the service required (Fig 7). The request contains a contact address for the person to whom the document should be sent, the document type, when the document needs to be received, the cost of the document and who should be billed. The template which the customer is required to fill in is shown in Fig 7. In this example, a Microsoft Word document is being sent to Richard which needs to be received as soon as possible. The icons at the bottom of the form indicate that a Microsoft Word document is being sent by the customer and the format in which the document is received is unknown.

Once the service request has been received by the agents, a high-level negotiation occurs between the customer-facing agents and the network agents, making use of the geographical database. The agents realise collectively that it is possible for the document to be translated into a text document then into a speech file and read out over the mobile phone. This results in a service offer being sent to the customer as shown in Fig 8. The icons on this form show that the document will be converted into speech for delivery to the customer at the other end of the phone. The customer then has a choice to accept or reject the offer made to the network. If the offer is accepted then the network agents enter the second stage of negotiation that sets up the necessary resources for the service. The information is then received by the network, processed as necessary and then delivered to the receiving customer.

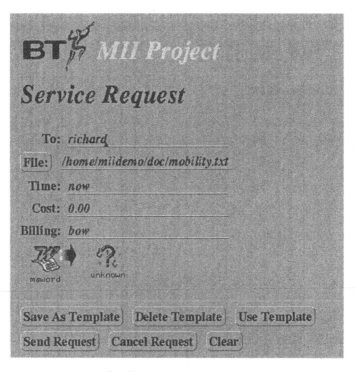

Fig. 7. Customer request.

4.2 Document Redirection

The redirection of services to a more appropriate terminal near the customer has also been demonstrated. For example, a VRML (virtual reality modelling language) document can be sent to a customer who is using a workstation with an unsuitable graphics card. The agents exploit the geographical knowledge about the relationship of the terminals to determine that a high specification workstation is nearby. Both customers are then informed where the document is to arrive. Where possible the network will strive to achieve the highest accuracy of transfer at the specified cost, rather than downgrading the message type simply because the recipient is not currently on a suitable machine. This decision is made by the manager agents during the first pass of the negotiation.

In Fig 9, the graph constructed during the first phase of this service is shown. On the left it can be seen that a VRML document is being sent into the network. On the right all the possible target document types for the service are shown. It can be seen in the figure that some of these types are repeated; this is because the receiving customer is near two terminals, one a high-power workstation which can cope with many different format types, the other a simple PDA with text and limited graphics abilities.

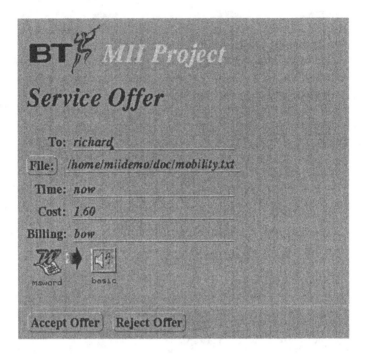

Fig. 8. Network offer.

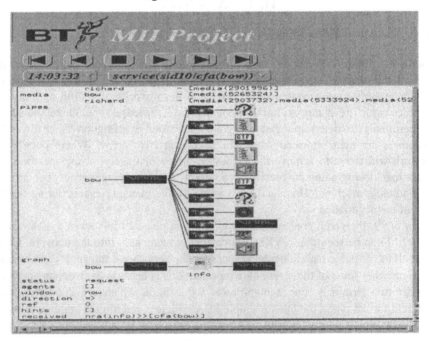

Fig. 9. Negotiation during a redirection service.

This exploitation of the communication and computing environment around a user allows the system to create a virtual communications shell wherever the customer moves. The network carries out this function continuously without input from the user — a key feature of the ubiquitous communications system vision of the future.

5. Conclusions

It has been shown that communities of intelligent agents can be used for effective management of a flexible document delivery service. The ability of agents that manage services being able to bid to supply services provides a simple but powerful mechanism to give flexibility in the use of service components and enables performance management to be handled in a dynamic manner.

Acknowledgement

The authors would like to acknowledge Bharat Purohit for his work on the user interface.

References

1.   Nwana H S: 'Software Agents: An Overview', Knowledge Engineering Review, 11, No 3, pp 205—244 (1996).

2.   Busuioc M: 'Distributed Co-operative Agents for Service Management in Communications Networks', in 11th IEE Teletraffics Symposium, Cambridge (England) (1994).

3.   Novoa I and Wileby M: 'Knowledge and Location', Proc of IJCAI 95 workshop on AI and Telecommunications (1995).

4.   Netsumm, http://www.labs.bt.com/innovate/informat/netsumm/index.htm

5.   Reinhardt A: 'The Network with Smarts', Byte (October 1994).

6.   Roschenstein J and Zlotkin G: 'Rules of Encounter', The MIT Press (1994).

7.   Laureate, http://www.labs.bt.com/innovate/speech/laureate/index.htm

A Real-Life Experiment in Creating an Agent Marketplace

A Chavez, D Dreilinger, R Guttman and P Maes

MIT Media Laboratory, 20 Ames Street, Cambridge, MA 02139, USA
E-mail: anthony@microsoft.com   daniel/guttman/pattie@media.mit.edu

Software agents help people with time-consuming activities. One relatively unexplored area of application is that of agents that buy and sell on behalf of users. We recently conducted a real-life experiment in creating an agent marketplace, using a slighly modified version of the Kasbah system. Approximately 200 participants intensively interacted with the system over a one-day (six-hour) period. This paper describes the set-up of the experiment, the architecture of the electronic market and the behaviours of the agents. We discuss the rationale behind the design decisions and analyze the results obtained. We conclude with a discussion of current experiments involving thousands of users interacting with the agent marketplace over a long period of time, and speculate on the long-range impact of this technology upon society and the economy.

1. Introduction

Software agents help people with time consuming activities [1]. In the past, a range of roles for agents have been explored, such as filtering information, automating repetitive tasks and making referrals and introductions [2, 3]. One relatively unexplored area of applications is that of agents that buy and sell on behalf of their users. It currently requires a large effort from a user to do price comparison shopping, to search for all parties interesting in selling/buying what the user wants to buy/sell, or to negotiate with an interested party for a price that the user feels comfortable with. The activity of buying and selling among end-consumers is especially time consuming and inefficient. The few means that we resort to are classified ads, yard sales and flea markets. We believe that these activities could benefit from the introduction of software agents.

The wide pervasiveness and growing popularity of networks such as the Internet and online services have made it possible to facilitate transactions in an automated way. Existing efforts in the area of electronic commerce are still fairly simple, in the sense that they don't radically change the way transactions happen or don't create any new markets. Current efforts include the ability to pay at online stores with a credit

This paper will also appear in PAAM'97 (http://www.demon.co.uk/ar/paam97/index.html).

card or with electronic cash and online listings of goods for sale which are more easily searchable. Some more interesting experiments which change the way transactions normally occur (and hence raise many issues) include Bargain Finder and Fido. Both of these systems present the concept of an agent which can shop for the best price for an item on behalf of a user. The Telescript white paper also provides some inspiring scenarios for how transactions can be implemented by agents; however, to our knowledge, these scenarios have not yet been implemented.

The Artificial Intelligence (AI) literature includes a substantial body of work on negotiating agents [4], but little of this work has been used in real applications. Since 1994 the Software Agents group of the MIT Media Laboratory has embarked on a research program to create electronic agent marketplaces. Chavez and Maes describe the architecture of Kasbah, an electronic marketplace where agents buy and sell to one another on behalf of their users [5]. The current paper reports on an actual experiment that was performed in October 1996 which involves a large group of people using a slightly revised Kasbah system.

More specifically, about two hundred people intensively interacted with the system in a one-day, six hour experiment. The paper reports on the setup for the experiment, the architecture, and the methods used for the electronic market and the agents. We also discuss the rationale behind the design decisions and, most importantly, describe the results obtained. The paper concludes with a discussion of a current experiment which involves up to 10,000 users interacting with the electronic marketplace over a long period of time and, finally, we speculate about the impact of a widespread usage of this technology upon society and the economy.

2. The Experimental Set-up

On October 30th 1996, the Media Laboratory organized a symposium on 'Digital Life' for approximately 200 attendees from industry. Many of these people were not technically inclined. None had been introduced to the Kasbah concept beforehand. The attendees were given a total of three objects as well as some money (50 'bits', as we called our denomination of money)[1]. We invited the attendees to create 'selling' agents to sell some of the objects they owned but did not want and to create 'buying' agents to buy some of the objects they wanted to own. When a user created an agent, the user would determine its characteristics such as: is it a buying or a selling agent, what does the agent buy or sell (chosen from a limited list of goods), what is the initial asking price (or offer), what is the final lowest asking price (or final highest offer) and what is the 'strategy the agent will use to lower (or increase) its price over time. Figure 1 shows some users interacting with the Agent Marketplace.

---

[1] We decided to use 'fake' money, because we did not want to upset our test users in case some things did not work as planned. However, we could have used real money or digital cash/credit, which would not have fundamentally changed the experiment.

Fig. 1   Participants interacting with the Agent Marketplace.

People were able to create agents all day long. At the end of the day, they could exchange their money for wine (70 bits for one bottle). Hence, wine could be said to correspond to the 'gold standard' of the economy created; people would decide how many bits objects were worth to them based on the fact that a bottle of wine was worth 70 bits.

Participants in the agent marketplace experiment were immersed in an environment involving interactive kiosks, a transaction center, and several large scale displays. Users created and interacted with their agents via 20 keyboardless kiosks which consisted of a computer workstation, monitor, mouse, and bar-code reader. Users initiated a personalized session by scanning their name tag badgewith the bar-code reader. Once automatically logged in, users were provided with a list of their actrive agents (see Fig 2), a list of completed transactions, and options for creating new agents and changing old ones. The interface was entirely mouse driven — users navigated a simple point-and-click interface to create, modify, and monitor their agents. No keyboard input was required. The interface was designed to facilitate short interactions, so that the 200 people could use the 20 kiosks during the 30 to 60 minute breaks. A typical user session involved the creation of three or four agents and laster about five minutes.

In addition to the kiosks, several other devices and displays were used to disseminate information. Each participant received a personal pager which would notify them whenever one of their agents had made a deal. For example, if Andy had created an agent named James Bond to sell a lunch pail, and this agent then made a deal with one of Pattie's agents, Andy was paged with the message: "Andy, I sold your Media Lab lunch pail to Pattie Maes for $53. — James Bond". Pattie was paged with a similar message from her agent. At one point, about halfway through the day, buying and selling agents sent suggestions to users' pagers when it seemed unlikely that they would make a deal by the end of the day with the price parameters given by the user. For example, if a user created an agent to buy a box of chocolates and the maximum price the agent would offer was 20 percent lower than the average selling price of chocolates throughout the day, that agent would page the user with a message like: "Tip: you may want to raise my maximum offer if you want to buy those chocolates — James Bond."

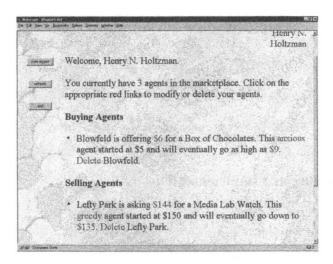

Fig. 2   Part of the welcome screen shown to user upon login.

A 10 foot high projection display and two large monitors provided visualizations of marketplace statistics, including histograms of buying and selling prices for each of the nine items, as well as a time series projection illustrating the trend in actual transaction prices for each item. Figure 3 shows a screenshot taken from the time series display. A scrolling LED 'ticker-tape' displayed up-to-the-minute market information about each of the items being traded, such as the highest bid, lowest asking price, and last transaction amount.

Upon being notified of a transaction (either via the pager or the user interface) users were told to report to the transaction center to exchange the good for the price agreed upon. We anticipated situations where one party would arrive several minutes after the other party (or fail to show up altogether), and wanted to avoid making the participants wait around since they had very busy schedules. Thus, when two users arrived asynchronously, the transaction center, which had a supply of extra money and surplus items, completed the one-sided deals. If the two users arrived at the same time, they carried out the transaction privately between themselves. The transaction center was also used to provide general information and assistance, to make change, and to sell the wine at the end of the day.

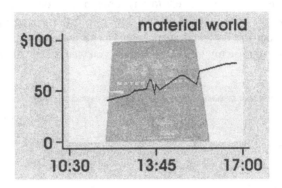

Fig. 3.   Screenshot taken from the time series display.

3.   Architecture and Implementation

3.1   Overall Architecture

The architecture of the agent marketplace system can be divided into three primary components.

- Front-end: a Web interface handles all the user interaction. It consists of a set of Perl CGI scripts located on a Web server.

- Back-end: the marketplace engine is where the agents actually 'live' and interact with one another. The back-end is implemented as a Java program.

- Auxiliary components: there are several auxiliary components, that do things such as:
  — generate the visual display files;
  — send out notification pages to users;
  — send marketplace data to ticker tape displays;
  — implement the login process.

The architecture was designed to be fairly well modularized, so that changes to one component would cause at most minimal changes to be made to the others. The interfaces between components was designed to be as general and flexible as possible. This design decision proved to be a wise one, as the front-end design was constantly in a state of flux, yet most of these modifications were made without requiring constant changes to the back-end. Figure 4 shows the overall architecture of the Agent Marketplace system.

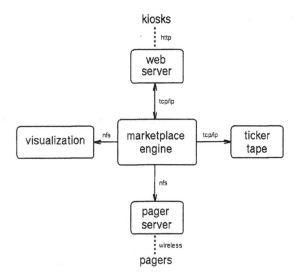

Fig. 4   Architecture of the Agent Marketplace system.

As for the physical topology of the system: the front-end CGI Perl scripts resided on two Web servers. The back-end marketplace engine was located on a single high-performance workstation. The other auxiliary components were scattered across several other servers. The user kiosks consisted of 20 Intel computers running a specially modified version of Microsoft Internet Explorer. The kiosks were set up so that user interaction was done entirely via the mouse and special barcode scanners (to read people's name badges and log them on). The front-end and back-end communicated with one another via TCP/IP sockets. The user kiosks communicated with the two front-end servers via HTTP.

3.2   The back-end engine

The back-end engine is the actual 'guts' of the agent marketplace. It implements a request-response service: a client sends it a request, the back-end services that request, and then sends back to the client a response. From a high-level functional viewpoint, these are the marketplace services that the back-end provides:

- add a new user (a person) to the marketplace;

- create a new selling or buying agent for a given user;

- list all the agents and their corresponding properties for a given user;

- delete a specified agent for a given user;

- modify parameters of a specified agent for a given user;

- get current market data.

The front-end sends requests for the above services to the back-end via a simple protocol that we devised. In addition to handling requests from the front-end, the back-end is where the agents actually do their negotiating and deal-making. Conceptually, one should think of the back-end as the place where agents are 'running around' talking to one another, 'haggling' and trying to find the best possible deal on behalf of their users, all in parallel.[1]

3.3 Selling and Buying Agents

Software agents are long-lived programs that perform some task on behalf of a user [1]. In our case, the agents try to buy or sell some good for the best possible price on behalf of the user which created them. To do this, the agents negotiate with other users' agents in the marketplace, trying to find the best deal subject to a set of user-specified constraints. When two agents 'make a deal' with one another, they notify their respective users so that the transaction can be physically consummated.

The best way to understand how our selling and buying agents work is to look at the parameters that a user must specify when creating a new agent. The design of the agents is derived from that of Kasbah [5]. However, the functionality was simplified somewhat after some early user tests indicated that people may feel uncomfortable delegating a buying/selling task to an agent whose behavior is complex and difficult to predict. In fact, the tests which we performed lead us to believe that the level of intelligence or sophistication of a buying/selling agent may be limited more by user acceptance constraints than by limitations of AI technology. This was particularly the case when agents have the authority to complete transactions as in our experiment.

Selling and buying agents are architecturally symmetrical. The description below lists the parameters for a selling agent (parentheticals correspond to a buying agent). The relatively simple set of agent parameters include:

- good to sell (buy) — in order to keep the user interface for the experiment simple, we decided to only have 9 goods which users could buy or sell; these included several books, a mug, a camera, a box of chocolates, and so on;

- desired price to sell (buy) for — this is the price for which the user ideally would like to sell (buy) the good, i.e. the initial price which the agent will ask (offer);

- lowest acceptable price (highest offer) — this it the lowest price (highest offer) for which the user would ultimately be willing to sell (buy) the good;

- date to sell (buy) by — this parameter was hard-coded to 5:00pm for the experiment reported upon in this paper (i.e., users were not allowed to set it);

---

[1] In reality, the agents are not really running in parallel, but it is a useful abstraction. After all, the actual implementation of the back-end is sure to change in the future — for instance, becoming more distributed.

agent strategy — this allows the user to specify the negotiating 'behavior' of their agent; here were three options to choose from:
— 'anxious': the agent is in a big hurry to sell (buy) the good;
— 'cool-headed': the agent is well-balanced; it's not in a big hurry to sell (buy), but it doesn't want to wait forever either;
— 'frugal': the agent is a cheapskate; it really wants to sell (buy) for the highest (lowest) price possible.

By specifying these parameters, the user defines and constrains the behavior of his or her agent. The behavior of a selling agent is as follows (with buying agents behaving similarly). The agent will try to sell the specified good. It will initially start by asking the desired price. If it is able to find someone willing to pay that price or more, then it makes a deal (at the highest price). Otherwise, the agent lowers its asking price and continues to negotiate. By the end of the day (the hard-coded date to sell by), if the agent has not yet made a deal, it will have lowered its asking price to the lowest acceptable price.

The way in which a selling agent lowers its price throughout the day is dependent upon its strategy. An 'anxious' agent, in a big hurry to sell, will lower its price very quickly towards the lowest acceptable price. A 'frugal' agent, on the other hand, will lower its price slowly, waiting until the very end of the day before lowering its price substantially. A 'cool-headed' agent will strike a balance between these extreme strategies. The section on agent behavior explains how these strategies were implemented.

From observations made during the experiment, it appeared that users of the system had little difficulty in understanding what their agents were doing. They seemed to perceive the agent behavior in the way described above. Some users even created three agents with different strategies to sell the same good, so as to test whether the agents displayed the right behavior.

3.4   Agent Communication

In order for agents to negotiate in the marketplace, they need to be able to communicate with one another. Agent communication is based upon a request-response protocol and is strictly agent-to-agent. There is no broadcasting of messages and an agent cannot eavesdrop on a conversation between two other agents. The flow of a single 'conversation' between agent x and y is as follows:

• agent x sends request message to agent y;

• agent y processes request message;

• agent y sends a response message back to agent x.

In the implementation used for the agent marketplace experiment, there were just two types of request messages an agent could send:

- What are you currently asking?": the agent responds with its current asking price (i.e., the price at which it is willing to buy/sell);

- "I offer X. Will you accept?": the agent responds with either "yes" or "no" — note that this request message is considered binding; that is, the agent making the offer (sending the message) is implying that if the response is "yes", it is bound to that deal. Likewise, the agent responding "yes" has bound itself as well.

Clearly, the current conversation space is rather simple. For more sophisticated agents interactions, a richer language will be needed. The current work section expands on this.

3.5   Agent Behavior

Now that we have described the user's perceived behavior of their selling or buying agent, let us turn to the actual implemented behavior of the agent. It should be obvious that the actual behavior of the agent needs to correspond closely to the user's perception of how it will behave; if not, then the user is sure to be disappointed or possibly upset. This is a general challenge facing agent research, namely to make sure that the agent lives up to the user's expectations.

Given this, here is a selling agent's actual implemented behavior (again, the strategy for a buying agent would be the intuitive opposite). An agent has an internal variable called 'current ask price'. This is always set to the price which the agent is currently willing to sell the good for. As time passes, the agent will adjust this price — selling agents will lower it, buying agents will raise it. The price will never be set lower than the lowest acceptable price that the user had specified. When the agent is first created, 'current ask price' is set to the desired price. How the agent adjusts its 'current ask price' over time is described below.

Agents must be able to adjust their asking prices over time in order to be able to make deals. Currently, these price adjustments are deterministic, i.e. they follow some function of time. In the future, we plan on building agents which can adjust their price according to real-time marketplace factors (e.g. the number of other agents selling the same good, the number of interested buyers, etc). The three agent strategies described above map directly to price adjustment curves, as shown in Fig 5. These price adjustment curves show the agent's 'current asking price' as a function of time. As you can see, the 'current asking price' always starts at the user-specified desired price. By the date to sell by (a hard-coded date in this particular experiment), the current asking price is always at the user-specified lowest acceptable price.

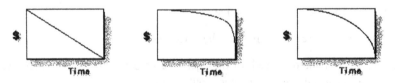

Fig. 5.   Price adjustment curves for selling agents.

Between highest and lowest price is where the curves for different strategies differ. For the 'anxious' strategy, the curve decays linearly. For the 'frugal' strategy, the curve decays much more slowly following an inverse-cubic shape. Intuitively, this makes sense — a 'frugal' selling agent will naturally lower its asking price more slowly than one that is 'anxious' to sell. Naturally, the 'cool-headed' strategy's curve lies between that of the 'frugal' and 'anxious' strategies following an inverse-quadratic shape. At any point in time, the agent can compute its current asking price using these curves. This calculation is done whenever the agent needs to access the 'current asking price' variable in order to make a decision (e.g. whether or not it should accept an offer).

When an agent (buying or selling) makes a deal, it sends out a notification message to its owner (the user who created it) telling him or her with whom it made a deal (that is, the owner of the agent it made a deal with) and what the deal price is. For the agent marketplace experiment, the notification messages were delivered via pagers. Once an agent makes a deal, it ceases to negotiate with other agents and asks the marketplace to remove it from the list of 'active' agents. This ensures that other agents will not be able to send it messages. For all intents and purposes, the agent has terminated.

Agents have two behavior modes: passive and pro-active. The passive behavior is what the agent will do when other agents make initiatives towards it. The pro-active behavior is what steps the agent will take towards making the best possible deal. We believe it is important for agents to have both passive and pro-active behaviors, especially in long-term marketplaces that include a multitude of agents whose internal behaviors and strategies are not publicly known. If an agent has only a passive strategy, and makes no active attempts to find deals, there is the danger that all other agents in the marketplace will also only have a passive strategy. In this case, no deals will ever be made, because all agents are waiting for others to make contact, which no one ever does.

In the experiment performed, an agent's passive strategy includes the following. If the agent is made an offer for a good which is greater than or equal to the 'current ask price', it will accept it. Otherwise, it will reject it. The agent's passive behaviors are only triggered when it is made an offer by another agent. An agent's pro-active behavior includes finding the agent X who is willing to pay the most for the good it is selling. Ask agent X what it is currently willing to pay. If X's offer is greater than the agent's 'current ask price', then make an offer to X at that price. Otherwise, make an offer at the 'current ask price'. The point of the agent first asking X its own asking price is that X might be willing to pay more than the agent is currently asking. After all, the agent's job is to find the best possible deal; if there's a customer in the marketplace who will pay more than the asking price, then the agent should grab that deal if it wants to be considered competent by its owner. The agent's pro-active behavior is triggered by the marketplace. Basically, the marketplace acts as a scheduler which cycles through the agents and tells each to 'do its thing'. Note that in running its pro-active behavior, the agent will send a message to another agent, thus triggering that agent's passive behavior.

3.6   The Marketplace

The marketplace houses all agents and user information. It keeps track of:

- all the 'active' agents: the agents which have not yet made deals;

- all the agents for each user: the marketplace tracks all of their agents, including the 'terminated' ones which have already made a deal;

- marketplace data: statistics on deals that have been made, current asking prices for each type of good, etc.

The marketplace also provides a useful 'finding' service to the agents which inhabit it. By providing this service, the marketplace frees the agents from having to do this additional work. This 'finding' service works as follows. An agent can ask the marketplace to find an agent, either buying or selling, who has the current best asking price for a particular good. For selling agents, this would be the agent with the current lowest asking price. For buying agents, this would be the agent with the current highest asking price. Recall from above that the agent negotiation strategy is to always make offers to the agent with the current best asking price (for a specified good).

The marketplace is also responsible for 'running' the agents. By this we mean triggering the agent's 'pro-active' behaviors described above. The back-end is implemented as a Java program; the marketplace and the agents are Java objects within that program. The behaviors of the agents (as well as the marketplace) are embedded as methods in these objects. For each agent, there is a 'run-pro-active-behavior' method which, when called, will take the appropriate actions. For various reasons, we chose not to have each agent run within an individual thread (mainly due to synchronization difficulties), thus, every agent needs to have its 'run-pro-active-behavior' method called frequently, in order to achieve the illusion of all agents running 'in parallel'. The marketplace takes care of this. It continuously cycles through all the active agents in the marketplace and calls their 'run-pro-active-behavior' method. When it makes this call, the marketplace passes execution control of the thread to the agent. The agent can then send requests to the marketplace, to other agents, or whatever else its 'run-pro-active-behavior' method implements.

It is important to note that the 'run-pro-active-behavior' method should terminate within a reasonable amount of time (no infinite loops!!) for fairness. Since we built the agents for the agent marketplace experiment, this was easy to ensure, but in a more open market system, where third-parties can submit their own agents, it will be necessary to take more explicit steps to ensure fairness (e.g. going to a thread model). As the marketplace cycles through all of the active agents and 'runs' them, some of them will make deals and remove themselves from the set of active agents. Others will expire (run past the user-specified date to sell by) and be removed by their owner. The order in which the marketplace 'runs' the active agents is constrained by the following rule: once an agent is 'run', it will not be 'run' again until all other active agents have also been 'run'. This rule ensures that no agent will have more opportunities to make a deal than any other agent.

In addition to running the agents, the marketplace also services the requests coming from the Web server scripts. The list of requests handled was given above. It was a design criteria that requests to the marketplace be processed as quickly as possible, so that the end-user standing at the kiosks experience minimal delay. To achieve this goal, the marketplace interleaves running the agents with polling the socket from the web server to see if a request has arrived. If that is the case, then the marketplace processes it immediately. A high-level pseudo-code description of how the marketplace runs is given below:

```
While (true) do
        poll the socket
        if (request pending) then
                process the request
                    and return result
        else
                run another agent
        end % if
end % while
```

This control flow gives priority to processing Web server requests. If there is queue of five pending requests, all of these will be processed before an agent will be run.

4. Results, Analysis and Observations

The quantitative and qualitative results from our agent marketplace experiment were largely as expected with a few surprises. We first look at and analyze quantitative data and then discuss some qualitative observations.

4.1 Quantitative Analysis

Between 11:00am and 5:00pm, the 171 participants created 625 agents of which 510 made deals as shown in Fig 6. This graph also shows how many agents were created and how many made deals where made for each good. For example, many agents were created for cameras (145) and much fewer were created for lunch pails (14). Two factors that we observed which determined how many agents were created for each good was (1) the overall quantity of the good (which varied widely) and (2) the participants' interest in trading it.

Figures 6 and 7 show the total number of agents, the number of active agents (those agents that have not yet made deals), and the cumulative number of completed deals made over the course of the day. The kiosks were accessed heavily during program intermissions and more moderately during lunch. This coincides with the number of agents spikes at the start of the experiment and at particular times — roughly between 11am and 12pm, 1pm and 2pm, and again at 3pm. The noticeable agents spike just before the 5:00pm market close was due to the transaction center infusing agents into the marketplace to distribute the remaining goods.

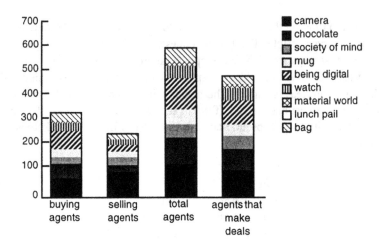

Fig. 6. Number of agents and agents that made deals.

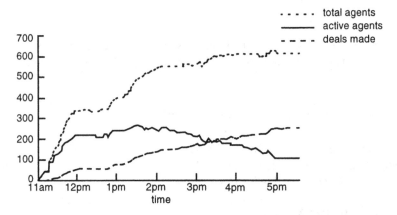

Fig. 7. Number of agents and deals over time.

We can see that after about 1:30pm, the number of active agents left in the marketplace began to decrease due to active agents making deals. This corresponds with the substantial rise in deals made around that 1:30pm time frame. The flatline of agents and deals at 5:00pm is due to kiosks being switched off and the convergence of each agent's negotiation price to its termination price at its 5:00pm hard-coded deadline.

One intriguing aspect of the agent marketplace experiment was the participants' ability to choose for each agent one of three negotiation strategies: frugal (or greedy for a selling agent), anxious, or cool-headed as discussed in the last section. Among other factors (e.g. initial price), the chosen strategy helps determine the likelihood that the agent will make a deal and at what price. Figure 8 shows a histogram taken after the market closed at 5:00pm of how many agents there were of each strategy broken down by good.

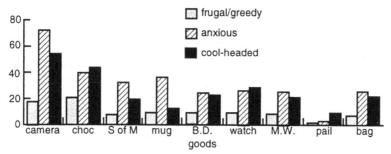

Fig. 8.   Number of agents (of each strategy for each good).

It is interesting to see that by the end of the day most agents were given an anxious strategy and very few agents were given a frugal or greedy strategy. It should be noted that the user interface did not default to any choice and that anxious was the last listed of the three strategies. Either the participants were more eager to trade goods initially and as the marketplace drew to a close or the names given to this general strategy were somehow a deterrent. A few informal surveys indicate the former.

A more interesting question than how many agents of a given strategy were created is how did each strategy perform in general? One would expect to see a higher percentage of deals being made by anxious agents than frugal (or greedy) agents since they more quickly change their price over time and thus would more quickly find an agent willing to trade. This is true for mugs as shown in Fig 9. For mugs, 90% of all anxious buying agents made deals whereas only 65% of all frugal buying agents made deals. However, the other goods show non-intuitive results. In most cases, frugal agents made the highest percentage of deals.

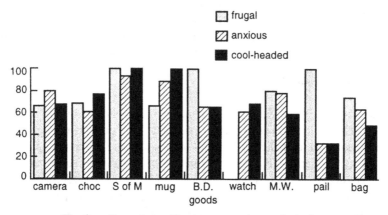

Fig. 9.   Percentage of buying agents that made deals.

A possible explanation for this is that participants were able to (and did) modify their agents prices throughout the day in order to make deals more quickly. This behavior of manually negotiating for an agent would change the nature of any negotiation strategy. An alternate explanation is that we should instead be looking at each agent's lifespan (i.e. how much time it took each agent to make a deal). Unfortunately, this data was not adequately captured to perform such an analysis.

Another expectation based on strategy is that purchases made by anxious agents should be higher priced on average than deals made by frugal agents since they more quickly increase their price over time. (The inverse would be expected for sales.) As shown in Fig 10, this expectation holds for virtually all goods. If we look at mugs again, we see that the average price paid by an anxious agent is about $45 whereas the average price paid by an frugal agent is about $25.

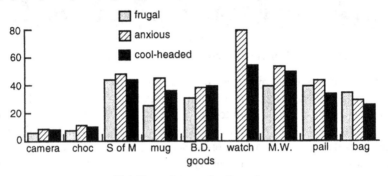

Fig. 10.   Average buying price.

Two other incidents happened which can be identified in Fig 11. At some point in the middle of the day, one of the participants spread a rumor saying that at the end of the day, every person present would receive a free Media Lab watch. As a result the price of watches plummeted because people hurried to change the prices of their watch-buying agents. When it was pointed out later that this news was false, the price of watches picked up again. Another phenomenon that took place is that the prices of items generally rose towards the end of the day. This is the case because at the end of the day, people could only buy wine if they had more than 50 bits. Anyone owning less than 50 bits was happy to spend all their money on whatever good they good buy, because the money became useless at the end of the experiment.

4.2   Qualitative Analysis

Throughout the day, we had several students stationed around the kiosks to assist participants. The feedback observed and reported to these students was quite positive. Most participants had no difficulty logging into the system (by scanning their badge), creating agents, or checking the status of their agents. Except for some people having trouble operating their pagers and overcrowding at the transaction center, the participants found the experiment to be highly compelling to the point where some skipped sessions to be at the kiosks following their agents' every move.

Although the focus of the experiment was in the digital trading realm, we also anticipated the occurence of black-market trading. This is because we see the electronic agent marketplaces as complementing rather than competing with existing means of transactions. In general, we see agent marketplaces as helping reduce transaction costs associated with certain types of transactions (e.g. classified ads) where financial, time, and trust issues can impede negotiations and commerce. Many black-market trades were observed throughout the day.

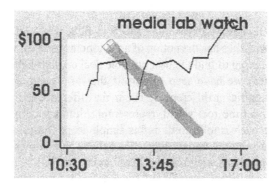

Fig. 11.   Price of watches over the day.

Another anticipated behavior we observed was participants buying more than they had money to spend. Interviewing several participants revealed several reasons for this behavior. A few people misunderstood the negotiation tactics of their agents. Others were not able to sell goods fast enough to cover purchase costs. Some just assumed credit was available or they didn't expect any negative consequences for their actions (after all the money was 'play money'). While some of these reasons are user interface issues, the underlying issue involves the inherent discrepancy between how much money the owner has and how much money the owner's agents 'think' they can offer. This problem has a number of potential solutions.

One solution could be to let agents know how much money an owner has to spend and ensure that collectively they don't make bids greater than that amount. This would require greater inter-agent communication and collaboration than currently exists in the system. While not a foolproof solution (because the user could spend some money in real-life as well), it could be useful to help place price caps on total agent spending. Another solution may allow agents to directly access an owner's financial account(s) (e.g. credit cards or digital cash). In this scenario, no mapping of funds between the analog and digital worlds would be necessary since agents would be transacting with actual currency. Obviously, issues of trust, security, and price caps are still relevant here.

A more interesting solution to the problem of buying more than one has money to spend could involve a collaborative way for an owner's agents to negotiate. For example, a user may specify conditions on when an agent or group of agents should buy or sell a good. Perhaps an owner is interested in buying one of three goods and doesn't care much which good is purchased as long as one of the three goods is bought and the price paid is good. In this scenario, an owner could create three agents in a mutually-exclusive relationship where once one of the agents makes a deal, the other two stop negotiating (until instructed otherwise). This addition to the system was considered but left out of the actual system deployed in the experiment because we assumed it would take too much time to teach the participants about instructing agents.

5. Related Work

There are many Web sites where people can go to find, buy, and sell goods [6—9] However, none of these sites has the notion of an autonomous agent which will actually do the work of *negotiating* to find the best possible deal on your behalf.

The closest system we have seen to ours is that of Tsvetovatyy and Gini [10], although there are significant differences. The main difference is that they attempt to more completely model the real world, representing things such as banks, accounts, money, etc. Our approach is to keep things as simple as possible, and focus primarily on the negotiation aspects of transactions. We believe this allows our system to be integrated into the already existing real world of buying and selling more easily.

Autonomous or intelligent agents have been actively researched for many years. The overarching goal of this work is to help people deal with 'information and work overload' [1].

The notion of autonomous agents is not a new one. It appears extensively throughout computer science literature, in several different contexts. In the field of Distributed AI, agents are entities which collaborate to solve a specific problem [11]. In Decentralized AI, the focus is more on the interactions of agents with different motivations. The underlying notion, though, is still that the agent interaction should further some organizational goals [11].

Agents are often seen as a general technique for solving problems, be they very specific (planning the path of a robot) or broader (managing resources). This notion of agents is somewhat different from the one we take, which is more task-oriented. Also, our agents not only don't share common goals, they have diametrically opposing aims. This contrasts to a system such as Firefly [12], where agents serve individual users (to make music recommendations), yet cooperate and exchange information in a mutually beneficial fashion.

There has also been a lot of work done on market-based systems [13]. The typical approach is to model an optimization problem, such as resource allocation, as a marketplace consisting of multiple agents, each trying to maximize their own 'utility'. Notice how this differs from the traditional AI approach mentioned above where the agents are cooperating. Here the agents are not cooperating but acting selfishly. This can be a powerful and effective technique when dealing with difficult optimization problems. A good example of a market-based system is the Challenger system for allocating processing resources within a network of workstations [14].

Our agent marketplace is in a sense very similar to a market-based system, in that we are trying to efficiently and optimally match buyers and sellers. Unlike most market-based systems, though, which exist strictly in a virtual world, our system is intended to be used by real people. Because of this human factor, a lot of issues have to be considered that do not in more 'artificial' systems.

Finally, a multiple agent system implies agent communication. This is also an area which has been extensively researched. KQML is perhaps the most notable attempt to design a general purpose agent language [15]. We chose not to use KQML, since our agents are all locally built and thus can be made to communicate via a predefined set of methods.

More advanced agents might require a richer semantics of communication to enable more complex and subtle negotiations. The field of speech acts has investigated such theoretical issues in depth [16].

6. Current Work

We received a lot of useful feedback from our first agent marketplace experiment. Our current efforts include using this feedback (along with our own analysis) to create an agent marketplace for the MIT-wide community. We will initially allow MIT members and sponsors to trade books, music, and Magic Cards™. We intend to have this system up and running by early 1997. This experiment will run for several months.

Unlike the first experiment, we will not have a transaction center for one party to complete their half of a transaction if the other party doesn't show up to complete the deal. Having parties renege on deals made by their agents can lead to many unhappy people. To provide a means for recourse for this likely scenario, we are implementing a limited 'Better Business Bureau' feedback mechanism where users can 'report' untrustworthy people. The logistics of this facility is judiciously being worked out now; however, one use of this information is to disallow one's agents from negotiating with anyone's agents who are under a user-specified trust level.

Depending on the feedback we receive from this new MIT-wide agent marketplace experiment, we will add more types of goods with a means for users to create their own good templates. These will be used for defining goods that the system has not yet seen. We are also exploring protocols and semantics for defining more extensible agent marketplace communications and are researching several alternative protocols [15]. The chosen protocol will be used to support the distribution of agents so they can either execute on the marketplace server or on a user's local machine. This marketplace protocol will be 'open' to allow third-party agents (with their own unique strategies) to participate in the agent marketplace. For example, we envision developers creating sophisticated commerce agents that require a non-trivial amount of resources to complete its market analysis. Such agents could potentially be run more efficiently on a user's local machine and communicate/negotiate with other agents via the open marketplace protocol. Other technologies we're looking at include electronic cash/ credit and all-digital transactions involving online information.

At the same time that we are building an architecture to support distributed and third-party agents, we are also exploring how agents can negotiate better in the marketplace on their users' behalf. To do this, we are beginning to merge microeconomics theories with AI techniques such as collaborative filtering and machine learning. Ultimately, agents can be created that make better deals than their owners without the owner needing to intervene. We anticipate that our agent marketplace combined with sophisticated agent strategies will offer a more compelling consumer experience over today's online auctions and marketplaces.

7. What We Learned

We created an electronic marketplace where agents buy and sell goods and negotiate with interested parties on behalf of their users. In general, we see such agent marketplaces as helping reduce transaction costs associated with certain types of transactions (end-consumer to end-consumer transactions) where currently financial, time, and trust issues can impede negotiations and commerce. User testing of such agents has revealed that the level of intelligence or sophistication which a buying/ selling agent could ultimately demonstrate is limited more by user-agent 'trust' issues than by limitations of AI technology. In particular, in order for these agents to be widely accepted, it is crucial that the agent's behavior can easily be understood and controlled by the user.

The experiment raises a lot of issues about the implications of this type of marketplace for our society and economy. While the experiment was limited to a very small set of goods, one could envision setting up similar marketplaces for all consumer goods as well as for services. It is still an open issue what the effects of such wide deployment would be. One could argue that this type of market will approach the concept of an ideal market more so than our current markets resulting in a more efficient and effective economy. Another potential effect may be that more types of goods will be bought and sold because it is easier in this kind of system to find a buyer/ seller for a good, even if it's a good that very few parties might be interested in. For example, we hope that the wider deployment of this technology will encourage people to buy and sell more second-hand goods, thereby supporting the reuse of objects in our society. Finally it is an open issue what happens to current brokers in this future scenario, since an important role of brokers, namely to bring buyers and sellers together, is automated by this agent system.

References

1.   Maes P: 'Intelligent software', Scientific American, 273, No 3, pp 84—86 (September 1995).

2.   Proceedings of the First International Conference on the Practical Application of Intelligent Agents and Multi-Agent Technology, London, UK (April 1996).

3.   Bradshaw J: 'Software agents', MIT Press, Cambridge, MA (March 1997).

4.   Rosenschein J S and Zlotkin G: 'Rules of encounter', MIT Press, Cambridge, MA (1994).

5. Chavez A and Maes P: 'Kasbah: an agent markeplace for buying and selling goods', Proceedings of the First International Conference on the Practical Application of Intelligent Agents and Multi-Agent Technology, pp 75—90, London, UK (April 1996).

6. Bargain Finder: http://bf.cstar.ac.com/bf/

7. FIDO: http://www.shopfido.com/

8. Infomaster: http://www.infomaster.stanford.edu/

9. Telescript 96: http://www.genmagic.com/Telescript/

10. Tsvetovatyy M and Gini M: 'Toward a virtual marketplace: architectures and strategies', Proceedings of the First International Conference on the Practical Application of Intelligent Agents and Multi-Agent Technology, pp 597—613, London, UK (April 1996).

11. Demazeau J and Muller J: 'Decentralized artificial intelligence', Elsevier Science Publishers, North Holland (1990).

12. Shardanand U and Maes P: 'Social information filtering: algorithms for automating word of mouth', Proceedings of CHI 95 Conference, Denver, CO (1995).

13. Clearwater S: 'Market-based control: a paradigm for distributed resource allocation', World Scientific Publishing, Singapore (1996).

14. Chavez A, Moukas A and Maes P: 'Challenger: a multi-agent system for distributed resource allocation', to appear in Proceedings of the First International Conference on Autonomous Agents, Marina del Ray, California (February 1997).

15. Larou Y and Finin T: 'A semantics approach for KQML — a general-purpose communication language for software agents', Proceedings of CIKM 94, New York (1994).

16. Winograd T and Flores F: 'Understanding computers and cognition: a new foundation for design', Addison Wesley, Reading, MA (1986).

Section 3

Soft Computing — Concepts and Applications

The Roles of Fuzzy Logic and Soft Computing in the Conception, Design and Deployment of Intelligent Systems

L A Zadeh

Computer Science Division, University of California, Berkeley, USA.
E-mail: zadeh@cs.berkeley.edu

The essence of soft computing is that, unlike the traditional, hard computing, it is aimed at an accommodation with the pervasive imprecision of the real world. Thus, the guiding principle of soft computing is: '...exploit the tolerance for imprecision, uncertainty and partial truth to achieve tractability, robustness, low solution cost and better rapport with reality'. In the final analysis, the role model for soft computing is the human mind.

Soft computing is not a single methodology. Rather, it is a partnership. The principal partners at this juncture are fuzzy logic, neuro-computing and probabilistic reasoning, with the latter subsuming genetic algorithms, chaotic systems, belief networks and parts of learning theory.

In coming years, the ubiquity of intelligent systems is certain to have a profound impact on the ways in which man-made intelligent systems are conceived, designed, manufactured, employed and interacted with. It is within this perspective that the basic issues relating to soft computing and intelligent systems are addressed in this paper.

1. Introduction

To see the evolution of fuzzy logic in a proper perspective, it is important to note that we are in the throes of what is popularly called the information revolution. The artefacts of this revolution are visible to all. The Internet, World Wide Web, cellular phones, facsimile machines and home computers with powerful information processing capabilities have all become a part of everyday reality. The centrality of information in almost everything that we do is a fact that few would care to challenge.

Much less visible, but potentially of equal or even greater importance, is what might be called the intelligent systems revolution. The artefacts of this revolution are man-made systems which exhibit an ability to reason, learn from experience and make rational decisions without human intervention. I coined the term MIQ (machine intelligence quotient) to describe a measure of intelligence of man-made systems. In this perspective, an intelligent system is a system which has a high MIQ.

I will have more to say about MIQ at a later point. A question that I should like to raise now is the following. We have been talking about artificial intelligence for over four decades. Why did it take AI so long to yield visible results?

Let me cite an example that bears on this question. When I was an instructor at Columbia University I wrote a paper entitled 'Thinking Machines — A New Field in Electrical Engineering' which was published in a student magazine [1]. In the opening paragraph of that article, I quoted a number of headlines which appeared in the popular press of the time. One of the headlines read: 'An Electric Brain Capable of Translating Foreign Languages is Being Built'. The point is that my article was published in January 1950, about six years before the term 'artificial intelligence' was coined. What is obvious today is that a translation machine could not have been built in 1950 or earlier. The requisite technologies and methodologies were not in place.

We are much more humble today than we were at that time. The difficulty of building systems that could mimic human reasoning and cognitive ability turned out to be much greater that we thought at that time. Even today, with a vast array of powerful tools at our disposal, we are still incapable of building machines that can do what many children can do with ease, e.g. understand a fairy tale, peel an orange, or eat food with a knife and a fork.

At this point, let me return to the concept of MIQ. A basic difference between IQ and MIQ is that IQ is more or less constant whereas MIQ changes with time and is machine-specific. Furthermore, the dimensions of MIQ and IQ are not the same. For example, speech recognition might be an important dimension of MIQ but in the case of IQ, it is taken for granted.

At this juncture, we do not have as yet an agreed set of tests to measure the MIQ of a man-made system, e.g. a camcorder; but I believe that such tests will be devised at some point in the future and that eventually the concept of MIQ will play an important role in defining and measuring machine intelligence.

In realistic terms, we are just beginning to enter the age of intelligent systems. Why did it take so long for this to happen?

In my perception, there are several reasons. Until recently the principal tools in AI's armamentarium were centred on symbol manipulation and predicate logic, while the use of numerical techniques was looked upon with disfavour. What is more obvious today than it was in the past is that symbol manipulation and predicate logic have serious limitations in dealing with real-world problems in the realms of computer vision, speech recognition, handwriting recognition, image understanding, multimedia database search, motion planning, common-sense reasoning and in the management of uncertainty.

2. Soft Computing and Fuzzy Logic

During the past several years, our ability to conceive, design and build machines with high MIQ has been greatly enhanced by the advent of what is now referred to as soft computing. Soft computing (SC) is not a single methodology. Rather, it is a consortium of computing methodologies which collectively provide a foundation for the conception, design and deployment of intelligent systems. At this juncture, the principal members of SC are fuzzy logic (FL), neuro-computing (NC), genetic computing (GC), and probabilistic reasoning (PR), with the last subsuming evidential reasoning, belief networks, chaotic systems, and parts of machine learning theory. In contrast to the traditional hard computing, soft computing is tolerant of imprecision, uncertainty and partial truth. The guiding principle of soft computing is: '...exploit the tolerance for imprecision, uncertainty and partial truth to achieve tractability, robustness, low solution cost and better rapport with reality'.

What is important about soft computing is that its constituent methodologies are for the most part synergistic and complementary rather than competitive. Thus, in many cases, higher MIQ can be achieved by employing FL, NC, GC and PR in combination rather than singly. Furthermore, there are many problems which cannot be solved if the only tool is fuzzy logic, neuro-computing, genetic computing or probabilistic reasoning. This challenges the position of those who claim that their favourite tool, be it FL, NC, GC or PR, is capable of solving all problems. The proponents of such views will certainly shrink in number once a better understanding of soft computing becomes widespread.

Within SC, each of the constituent methodologies has a set of capabilities to offer. In the case of fuzzy logic, it is a body of concepts and techniques for dealing with imprecision, information granularity, approximate reasoning and, most importantly, computing with words. In the case of neuro-computing, it is the capability for learning, adaptation and identification. In the case of genetic computing, it is the capability to employ systematised random search and achieve optimal performance. And in the case of probabilistic reasoning, it is a body of concepts and techniques for uncertainty management and evidential reasoning.

Systems in which FL, NC, GC and PR are used in some combination are called hybrid systems. Among the most visible systems of this type are the so-called neuro-fuzzy systems. We are beginning to see fuzzy-genetic systems, neuro-genetic systems and neuro-fuzzy-genetic systems. In my view, eventually, most high-MIQ systems will be hybrid systems. In the future, the ubiquity of hybrid systems will have a profound impact on the ways in which intelligent systems are designed, built and interacted with.

What is the place of fuzzy logic in soft computing? First, I should like to clarify a common misconception about what fuzzy logic is and what it has to offer.

A source of confusion is that the label fuzzy logic is used in two different senses. In a narrow sense, fuzzy logic is a logical system which is an extension of multi-valued logic. However, even in its narrow sense the agenda of fuzzy logic is very different both in spirit and in substance from the agendas of multi-valued logical systems.

In its wide sense — which is the sense in predominant use today — fuzzy logic is coextensive with the theory of fuzzy sets, that is, classes with unsharp boundaries [2]. In this perspective, fuzzy logic in its narrow sense is a branch of fuzzy logic in its wide sense.

What is important about FL is that any theory, T, can be fuzzified — and hence generalised — by replacing the concept of a crisp set in T with that of a fuzzy set. In this way, one is led to a fuzzy T, e.g. fuzzy arithmetic, fuzzy topology, fuzzy probability theory, fuzzy control and fuzzy decision analysis. What is gained from fuzzification is greater generality and better rapport with reality. However, fuzzy numbers are more difficult to compute with than crisp numbers. Furthermore, the meanings of most fuzzy concepts are context- and/or application-dependent. This is the price that has to be paid for a better rapport with reality.

3. Information Granularity

There is a point of fundamental importance which lies at the base of ways in which humans deal with fuzzy concepts. The point in question has to do with information granularity and its role in human reasoning, communication and concept formation. In what follows, I will attempt to explain why information granularity plays an essential role in dealing with fuzzy concepts and, in particular, in reasoning and computing with words rather than numbers.

The concept of information granularity motivated most of my early work on fuzzy sets and fuzzy logic. Basically, the point that I stressed is that most human concepts are fuzzy because they are the result of clumping of points or objects which are drawn together by similarity. The fuzziness of such clumps, then, is a direct consequence of the fuzziness of the concept of similarity. Simple examples of clumps are the concepts of 'middle-aged', 'downtown', 'partially cloudy', 'obtuse', etc. To underscore its role, a clump will be referred to as a granule.

In a natural language, words play the role of labels of granules. In this role, words serve to achieve data compression. The achievement of data compression through the use of words is a key facet of human reasoning and concept formation.

In fuzzy logic, information granularity underlies the concepts of linguistic variable and fuzzy if-then rules [3, 4]. These concepts were formally introduced in my 1973 paper 'Outline of a New Approach to the Analysis of Complete Systems and Decision Processes' [5]. Today, almost all applications of fuzzy logic employ these concepts. It is of historical interest to note that my introduction of these concepts was met with scepticism and hostility by many eminent members of the scientific establishment.

The importance of fuzzy rules stems from the fact that such rules are close to human intuition. In fuzzy logic, fuzzy rules play a central role in what is called Fuzzy Dependency and Command Language (FDCL). In an informal way, it is this language that is used in most of the applications of fuzzy logic.

In comparing fuzzy logic with other methodologies, a point that is frequently unrecognised is that, typically, the point of departure in a fuzzy logic solution is a human solution. Thus, a fuzzy logic solution is usually a human solution expressed in FDCL. An easily understood example of this point is the car parking problem in which the objective is to place the car near the curb and almost parallel to it. A fuzzy logic solution of the parking problem would be a collection of fuzzy if-then rules which describe how a human parks a car. The parking problem is hard to solve in the context of classical control. In this context, the point of departure is not a human solution but a description of the final state, the initial state, the constraints and the equations of motion.

A further example which illustrates the essentiality of information granularity is the following. Consider a situation in which a person A is talking over the phone to a person B whom A does not know. After a short time, say 10-20 seconds, A can form a rough estimate of the age of B expressed as:

the probability that B is very young is very low
the probability that B is young is low
the probability that B is middle-aged is high
the probability that B is old is low
the probability that B is very old is very low

These estimates may be interpreted as a granular representation of the probability distribution, P, of B's age. In a symbolic form, P may be represented as a fuzzy graph:

P = very low\very young + low\young + high\middle-aged
+ low\old + verylow\very old

In this expression, '+' is the disjunction operator and a term such as 'low\old' means that low is the linguistic probability that B is old .

The important point is that humans can form such estimates using linguistic, i.e. granulated, values of age and probabilities. However, humans could not come up with numerical estimates of the form 'the probability that B is 25 is 0.012.'

It should be observed that in many cases a human would estimate the age of B as middle-aged omitting the associated probability. The omission of probabilities may be justified if there exists what might be called a p-dominant value in a probability distribution, i.e. a value whose probability dominates the probabilities of other values. The omission of probabilities plays a key role in approximate reasoning [6].

A question which arises is: 'Could the use of a methodology within soft computing provide an estimate of the age of B without human intervention?' In my view, the answer is in the negative. More specifically, neuro-computing and genetic computing techniques would fail because of the complexity of input/output pairs, while fuzzy logic would fail — even though a human solution exists —because humans would not be able to articulate the rules by which the age estimate is arrived at.

In sum, information granularity lies at the centre of human reasoning, communication and concept formation. Within fuzzy logic, it plays a pivotal role in what might be called computing with words, or CW for short. CW may be viewed as one of the most important contributions of fuzzy logic. What is computing with words? As its name suggests, in computing with words the objects of computing are words rather than numbers, with words playing the role of labels of granules. Very simple examples of CW are:

Dana is young and Tandy is a few years older than Dana, $\therefore$ Tandy is (young + few) years old

Most students are young and most young students are single, $\therefore$ most^2 students are single

In these examples, young, few and most are fuzzy numbers; + is the operation of addition in fuzzy arithmetic and most[2] is the square of most in fuzzy arithmetic.

In Western cultures, there is a deep-seated tradition of according more respect to numbers than to words; but, as is true of any tradition, a time comes when the rationale for a tradition ceases to be beyond question. In my view, the time has come for questioning the validity of the tradition of according more respect to numbers than to words.

What we need at this juncture is a system which allows the data to be expressed as propositions in a natural language. This is what CW attempts to provide. The point of departure in CW is a collection of propositions expressed in a natural language. This collection is referred to as the initial data set (IDS). The desired answers or conclusions are likewise expressed as a collection of propositions expressed in a natural language. This collection is referred to as the terminal data set (TDS). The problem is to arrive at TDS starting with IDS. A very simple example is one where the initial data set is the proposition, 'most Swedes are tall', and the terminal data set is the answer to the query, 'What is the average height of Swedes?' The answer is expected to be of the form, 'the average height of Swedes is A, where A is a linguistic value of height'. In this example, the aim of CW is to compute A from the information provided by the initial data set.

In CW, words play the role of fuzzy constraints and a proposition is interpreted as a fuzzy constraint on a variable. For example, the proposition 'Mary is young' is interpreted as a fuzzy constraint on Mary's age. In symbols:

Mary is young → Age(Mary) is young

In this expression, '→' represents the operation of explicitation; 'Age (Mary)' is the constrained variable, and 'young' is a fuzzy relation which constrains 'Age(Mary)'.

More generally, if p is a proposition in a natural language, the result of explicitation of p is what is called the canonical form of p. Basically, the canonical form of a proposition, p, makes explicit the implicit fuzzy constraint in p, and thus serves to define the meaning of p as a constraint on a variable. In a more general setting, the canonical form of p is represented as:

X isr R

where X is the linguistic constrained variable, e.g. Age(Mary), R is the constraining fuzzy relation, e.g. young, and isr is a variable in which r is a discrete variable whose values define the role of R in relation to X. In particular, if $r = d$, isd is abbreviated to 'is' and the constraint 'X is R' is said to disjuncture. In this case, R defines the possibility distribution of X. What is the reason for treating r as a variable? The richness of natural languages necessitates the use of a wide variety of constraints to represent the meaning of a proposition expressed in natural language. In CW, the principal types of constraints that are employed — in addition to the disjuncture type — are: conjunctive, probabilistic, usuality, random set, rough set, fuzzy graph and functional types. Each of these types corresponds to a particular value of r.

In CW, the first step in computing the terminal data set is that of explicitation, i.e. the representation of propositions in IDS in their canonical forms. The second step involves constraint propagation, which is carried out through the use of the rules of inference in fuzzy logic. In effect, the rules of inference in fuzzy logic may be interpreted as the rules of constraint propagation.

The third and final step in the computation of the terminal data set involves a retranslation of induced constraints into propositions expressed in a natural language. In fuzzy logic, this requires the use of what is referred to as linguistic approximation.

What is important to recognise is that the steps sketched above may require an extensive use of computing with numbers. However, as a stage of CW, computing with numbers takes place behind a curtain, hidden from the view of a user.

So what is it that CW has to offer? The ability to infer from initial data sets in which information is conveyed by propositions expressed in a natural language, opens the door to the formulation and solution of many problems in which the available information is not precise enough to justify the use of conventional techniques. To illustrate, suppose that the problem is that of maximising a function which is described in words through the fuzzy if-then rules:

if X is small then Y is small

if X is medium than Y is large

if X is large then Y is small

in which small, medium and large are defined through their membership functions. Another problem in this vein is the following. Assume that a box contains ten balls of various sizes of which several are large and a few are small. What is the probability that a ball drawn at random is neither small nor large?

In these examples, the propositions in the initial data set are quite simple. The real challenge is to develop CW to a point where it could cope with propositions of much greater complexity which express real-world knowledge.

At this juncture, computing with words is a branch of fuzzy logic. In my perception, in coming years computing with words is likely to evolve into an important methodology in its own right, providing a way of coping with the pervasive imprecision and uncertainty of the real world [6]. In this perspective, the role model for computing with words, fuzzy logic and soft computing is the human mind.

4. Conclusions

The conception, design and deployment of intelligent systems presents a great challenge to those of us who are engaged in the development and applications of fuzzy logic and soft computing. Hopefully, our efforts will contribute to the creation of a society in which intelligent systems will serve to enhance human welfare and intellectual freedom.

References

1. Zadeh L A: 'Thinking Machines — A New Field in Electrical Engineering', Columbia Eng, No 3 (1950).

2. Zadeh L A: 'Toward a theory of Fuzzy systems', in: 'Aspects of Network and System Theory', Rinehart and Winston, NY (1971).

3. Zadeh L A: 'The concept of linguistic variable and its application to approximate reasoning', Inf Sci, $\underline{8}$ (1975).

4. Zadeh L A: 'The Calculus of Fuzzy if-then Rules', AI Expert, $\underline{7}$, No 3 (1992).

5. Zadeh L A: 'Outline of a New Approach to the Analysis of Complete Systems and Decision Processes', IEEE Trans Syst Man Cybernet, $\underline{SME-3}$, No 1 (Jan 1973).

6. Zadeh L A and Yager R R: 'Uncertainty in Knowledge Bases', Springer-Verlag, Berlin (1991).

An Introduction to Soft Computing — A Tool for Building Intelligent Systems

B Azvine, N Azarmi and K C Tsui

Intelligent Systems Research, Advanced Applications & Technology Department,
BT Laboratories, Martlesham Heath, Ipswich, Suffolk, IP5 7RE, UK.
E-mail: ben.azvine@bt-sys.bt.co.uk
azarmin@info.bt.co.uk
tsuikc@info.bt.co.uk

"The essence of soft computing is that unlike the traditional, hard computing, soft computing is aimed at an accommodation with the pervasive imprecision of the real world. Thus, the guiding principle of soft computing is: '...exploit the tolerance for imprecision, uncertainty and partial truth to achieve tractability, robustness, low solution cost and better rapport with reality'. In the final analysis, the role model for soft computing is the human mind." [1]

In this paper terms associated with soft computing are defined and its main components are introduced. It is argued, using a number of practical applications, that the hybrid approach of soft computing can provide a methodology for increasing machine intelligence.

1. Introduction

One of the primary issues in artificial intelligence (AI) has been the choice between two fundamentally different (and often viewed as competing) approaches to building intelligent systems — traditional symbolic AI and numeric (sub-symbolic) artificial neural networks (ANNs). This has been an issue engaging the AI community for three decades, and there have been attempts to bridge the gap between these two paradigms in order to take advantage of the relative merits of each [1].

In an attempt to model the human mind/brain it has been necessary to oversimplify the structure (resulting in ANNs) and the function (resulting in precisely defined symbolic- AI programmes) of the brain. Symbolic AI attempts to pre-program intelligence into a deterministic algorithm. On the other hand, most ANNs are equipped with relatively weak forms of learning (i.e. tuning a fixed set of parameters or weights). It has been argued [2] that despite the seemingly different approaches that symbolic AI and ANNs take to building intelligent systems, they both share common origins, and are both based on the hypothesis that cognition can be modelled by computation. Tasks performed by ANNs can be performed by symbolic AI and vice versa as both paradigms rely on different but essentially equivalent models of computation [2]. Decades of collective experience by theoreticians and practitioners in several areas of computer science have shown that it is efficiency, robustness and elegance that determine the best approach. Hybrid systems resulting from the integration of concepts and technologies drawn from both traditional AI systems and ANNs clearly demonstrate the potential benefits for the design of truly robust, flexible and adaptive intelligent systems in a wide application domain. This paper concentrates on one of many promising approaches for developing hybrid intelligent systems known as soft computing (SC). SC is not a single methodology, rather it is a partnership. The principal partners at this juncture are fuzzy logic (FL), neuro-computing (NC), and probabilistic reasoning (PR) which subsumes genetic algorithms (GA), chaotic systems, belief networks and parts of learning theory.

The term soft computing was coined by Zadeh, the inventor of fuzzy set theory, to be an extension to fuzzy logic by merging it mainly with neural networks and evolutionary computing. A concise definition for SC is: 'A term that describes a collection of techniques capable of dealing with imprecise, uncertain or vague information'. Zadeh advocates that SC has the means to extend what conventional AI has achieved in the past 40 years, and that a prerequisite to building an intelligent machine is a model of human cognitive capability [3]. The philosophical argument for SC is stated elegantly in Mamdani [4].

It is obvious that humans deal with uncertain and imprecise information everyday and are remarkably consistent in processing such information. This is the primary aim of SC — to exploit the tolerance of imprecision, uncertainty and partial truth associated with almost every aspect of real-world problems.

The aim of this paper is to describe SC in terms of the techniques associated with it, and how they are being combined to produce hybrid systems. There are three sections describing three techniques accepted as the main (but by no means the only) constituents of SC — fuzzy logic, neural networks and genetic algorithms. The final section describes hybrid techniques and their applications in the industry.

2. Intelligent Systems from a Soft Computing Perspective

There are many features that can be attributed to an intelligent system. Among them one can mention robustness, adaptivity, autonomy and the ability to communicate, including man/machine communication in multiple modalities. Dealing with real-world uncertainty or robustness is one of the most important characteristics of an intelligent system (Fig 1).

Uncertainty arises from many sources among which are nonlinear behaviour, time-varying behaviour (e.g. degradation over time) and interaction with uncertain environments. All of these features are present in human behaviour and therefore are important in the context of machines that interact with, co-operate with or replace humans in certain tasks. Humans do not seem to be as affected by uncertainty in sensory data as present-day computing machines. One explanation is that humans do

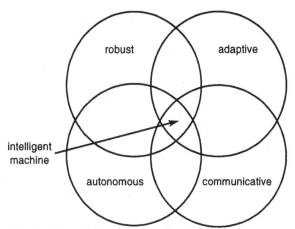

Fig. 1. Essential features of an intelligent machine.

not rely directly on raw data for decision making but on abstract, uncertain rules, e.g. in the rule 'if it is cold, put on an extra jumper', the actual temperature is not important, neither is the season nor the time of day. A definite advantage of using abstract rules is that a large amount of irrelevant information can be filtered out and the decision-making process is simplified. This is particularly important in the context of machines that rely on search techniques. It can be argued that in many real applications the relevant information belongs to a class that is not well defined, and its membership changes from time to time. To use the above example 'cold' means one thing today and its meaning may change next week, or next month. A fixed rule may be able to deal with this particular task, but it lacks the degree of adaptability required to work in changing environments. Humans seem to have the ability to change with their environment. Adaptive behaviour can be captured in a machine by using symbolic meta-level rules. For example, a rule can be defined that adjusts other rules according to a mean temperature based on the season, such that 'if it is winter then the mean temperature is 10°C', and 'in summer the mean temperature is 30°C', and define cold relative to these. This provides a fixed meta-level rule and an adaptive base-level rule. This is a partial solution, but what if there is an exceptional circumstance such as a particularly cold winter. This highlights one of the shortcomings of such an approach, namely that fixed symbolic meta-level rules can be restrictive in some circumstances.

The question that arises is how are these rules derived? Humans develop general rules from specific observations and then generalise from specific instances to new situations. For example, it can be seen that touching a specific hot object will result in pain and personal injury, so a general rule is developed — 'if an object is hot, do not touch it'. In this case it is assumed that we have some sensory information received by one or several of our five senses as to the temperature of an object. On the other hand, generally, humans do not develop rules for recognising friends' faces. Picking a familiar face in a crowd is performed instantaneously. Humans recognise vast numbers of patterns and exhibit many skills without having to develop rules for them or even know the rules that would result in such behaviours. Studies of the human brain have shown that the pre-attentive processing of stimuli is carried out in as few as 70 to 100 ms. We look, see, pay attention and then recognise without using rules. Then we address the higher cognitive functions such as reasoning, decision making, planning and control using rules. An intelligent machine therefore should be able to combine signal-level (sub-symbolic) intelligence with symbolic, more abstract level intelligence (rules). In this sense intelligence can become a property of a hybrid dynamical system.

SC enables the pre-processing of sensory information, reasoning using symbolic rules, and learning directly from observations. Adaptive systems must be able to develop rules for themselves and update the rules in view of new sensory data, i.e. learn from their experience. Learning (adaptability) is the second important feature of an intelligent system (Fig 1). Learning can be viewed as change in system behaviour based on experience. From a dynamical system's point of view, learning is the rate of change of an analytic function describing the system's behaviour [5]. As the analytic function is a mapping from the input to the output space, it can therefore be a collection of rules or a mathematical function. Clustering techniques are one aspect of learning addressed by SC.

Application of SC to real-world problems has been aimed at increasing machine intelligence quotient (MIQ). MIQ is measured by the level of control that a system can have over its own operation (autonomy) (Fig 1). For example a robot that can navigate its way around obstacles has a certain MIQ, another that can navigate and cope with unforeseen moving obstacles has a higher MIQ. Another measure for MIQ is the degree to which the machine assists humans in a particular task, e.g. a washing machine that chooses its own program has a certain degree of MIQ, another one that can program itself and use cheap electricity has a higher MIQ.

3. Fuzzy Logic in Brief

There are two reasons for using fuzzy logic in real applications. Firstly, in certain circumstances the definition of the problem is vague and uncertain. The information available does not lend itself readily to precise mathematical reasoning as in rule-based systems. A second class of applications are well defined but a precise solution is not necessary; the tolerance for imprecision can be exploited to simplify the solution. Most of the applications of fuzzy logic today fall into the second category.

Fuzzy logic can be viewed as a superset of Boolean logic in the sense that it can handle the concept of partial truth [6]. This concept has been used to develop more general extensions such as fuzzy calculus and fuzzy differential equations. Fuzzy logic is based on the principle of fuzzy subsets. In classical set theory, based on Boolean logic, membership of a subset U can be defined as a mapping from the elements of a set S to the elements of another set L with two members: 0 and 1. So an element is mapped to 0 if it is not a member of S and to 1 if it is. In fuzzy sets, a similar mapping exists to a set F with the difference that F contains all values between 0 and 1. This gives rise to the concept of degree of truth. A mapping to 0.3 is less true than a mapping to 0.6. The degree of membership of a set is defined by a membership function μ. Boundaries of fuzzy subsets are not sharp but fuzzy and overlapping. This implies that a particular entity A could be a member of two subsets with different degrees of membership — $\mu_1(A)$ and $\mu_2(A)$.

There are two important concepts that are central to the application of fuzzy logic:

- a linguistic variable;

- fuzzy if-then rules.

A linguistic variable is a variable that takes linguistic values such as height, age, speed, quality, etc. Such variables can take linguistic values like tall, young, fast, good, etc. A linguistic value is a label for a fuzzy set. Within fuzzy sets, degree of membership is characterised by membership functions, e.g. a membership function 'tall' determines the degree of tallness of someone of a certain height as shown in Fig 2. For example, it depicts a person who is 180 cm as tall with a degree of membership 0.45, while someone who is 185 cm tall is 'tall' with a degree of membership 0.6.

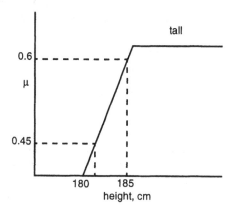

Fig. 2   Membership function 'tall' in a fuzzy set height.

A linguistic variable can be defined as a micro-language with context-free grammar and attributed-grammar semantics [3]. The context-free grammar defines the legal linguistic values for the variable and the grammar semantics defines the membership functions for any value within the linguistic variable, using the membership functions of primary terms. For a linguistic variable height, the legal values could be tall, short, very tall, not very tall, almost tall. The grammar semantics in this case define the membership functions for all values in terms of two primary membership functions — tall and short. For example:

$$\mu_{\text{not very tall}}(A) = 1 - (\mu_{\text{tall}}(A))^2$$

This introduces the idea of linguistic hedges or modifiers such as very, more or less and almost. Such terms are used extensively in natural language in a purely subjective way and therefore do not have a universal definition within different applications.

However, once they have been defined, consistency can be ensured within a particular application. Some common definitions are:

$$\mu_{very}(A) = \mu(A)^2$$

$$\mu_{more\ or\ less}(A) = \mu_{tall}(A)^{\frac{1}{2}}$$

The reason fuzzy logic includes such terms is that linguistic terms are essential to the way humans perceive, reason and communicate. By using words, people compress data to achieve economy of communication. Fuzzy logic aims to exploit this important feature of natural language combined with the consistency of a logical approach.

Another way of looking at the degree of membership of a value in a fuzzy set is a possibility distribution, e.g. $\mu(A) = 0.45$ is equivalent to the statement: 'the possibility that A is tall is 0.45'. It should be noted that this is quite different to the statement: 'the probability of A being tall is 0.45', since probability represents randomness and depends on the frequency of observations, while the possibility depends on uncertainty and vagueness and remains the same irrespective of the number of observations. As long as the definition of tall is fixed by the membership function, A would always be tall to the same degree.

Fuzzy rules in their most simple form can be expressed as if X is A then Y is B, where A and B are fuzzy values. This can be represented by the cartesian product of A and B i.e. $A \times B$, so that the membership function of the above rule can be written as:

$$\mu_{A \times B}(X,Y) = \mu_A(X) \wedge \mu_B(Y)$$

where $\wedge$ is the conjunction operator usually defined as $min(A \times B)$. For example, a fuzzy rule can express a simple rule of thumb. If X is tall then X is a good basketball player'.This rule can be visualised in terms of two membership functions defining 'tall' and 'good_basketball_player' as shown in Fig 3. Any player of any height has a certain degree of being a good basketball player between 0 and 1.

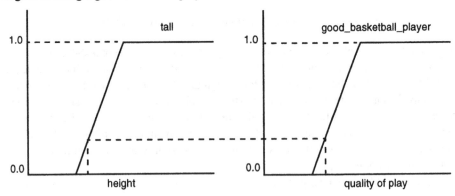

Fig. 3. Visualisation of a fuzzy rule.

A collection of fuzzy rules can be represented as a fuzzy graph. Fuzzy rules can be written as if X is A_i then Y is B_i, $i = 1...n$. For example, consider the following simple rules:

- if X is small then Y is large;

- if X is medium then Y is small;

- if X is large then Y is large.

This system can be represented by a fuzzy graph, $f*$ as shown in Fig 4. A fuzzy graph represents a coarse characterisation of functional dependency between X and Y. In this context, interpolation of rules becomes an important issue, i.e. what value of Y results if the input X is not a perfect match with any of the antecedent variables defined. This is carried out by considering each fuzzy rule and its degree of truth. Then defuzzification of the outputs is performed using one of many available techniques. The most widely used is the centre of gravity method. Interpolation is one of the most important features of fuzzy systems which can be exploited in situations where complex functional relationships are to be represented by a small number of fuzzy rules. This has been demonstrated in a number of complex industrial problems where the number of fuzzy rules have been typically between 10 and 20 [7].

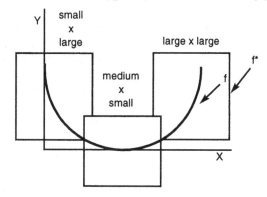

Fig. 4. Visualisation of a fuzzy graph.

One of the central issues in fuzzy logic is how to induce rules from observations. This is the problem of obtaining deep structure from surface structure [8]. It is relatively easy to write down a set of fuzzy rules to describe a particular behaviour. However, to calibrate these rules, i.e. to choose the type and characterisation of the membership functions, is not a trivial problem. A number of techniques have been used to solve this problem, such as dynamic and gradient programming (developed for multi-stage optimisation), genetic algorithms, reinforcement learning, and trial and error [8].

4. Artificial Neural Networks

The structure of the brain has been the subject of intense research in the past several decades. Many of the pioneers of AI drew upon biological inspiration for their work. Analogies were established between artificial processing elements and real neurons, between network connection and axions, and between connection strengths and synapses. A key aspect of the brain that ANNs try to imitate is its parallelism. ANNs achieve this by using densely interconnected simple processing units to store and process information. Each aspect of the neuron is represented mathematically by real numbers. The basic processing unit, or artificial neuron, is characterised by a set of input connections, a set of output connections, an activation level, an output level, and a bias value (Fig 5).

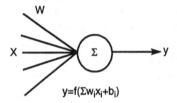

Fig. 5.   A simple artificial neuron.

The output level of a neuron is determined according to a function of the activation level, which is a weighted sum of the signal from the input connections. ANNs have many characteristics such as nonlinear mapping, self-organisation and learning. Learning in ANNs is viewed as the problem of finding a set of connection weights so that given a set of inputs the desired outputs are generated. ANNs effectively perform a parallel version of curve fitting and their capabilities should be assessed as adaptive function approximators [5]. When viewed in this manner they are powerful tools that can be used in an intelligent system to give it the learning capability. Many learning algorithms have been proposed, mostly network-architecture-specific. Supervised-learning algorithms rely on a teacher module to provide a set of training data which contains the input and the associated expected output. The learning algorithm then minimises the difference between the network output and the expected output. A possible application is a function- learning task. Unsupervised-learning algorithms take only the input patterns as training data and try to organise the neurons which best classify the data [9]. With reinforce-ment-learning algorithms, instead of providing a desired output for each input as in supervised learning, only a scalar reinforcement signal is used, which may be available only occasionally. Typical application of reinforcement learning algorithms is in automatic control applications like the pole balancing problem [9].

A most common ANN architecture, called the feedforward net, arranges neurons into layers, namely input, hidden and output layers. Connections are restricted to the area between neurons in different layers. Many learning algorithms have been developed to train such neural networks. Most applications that employ feedforward net use the backpropagation algorithm for learning. In a multi-layer network, the input is coded into an internal representation, and it is this internal representation that generates the outputs. Given a large enough set of hidden units, it is possible to perform any mapping from the input set to the output set.

Another common type of ANN that allows connections between any two neurons is called the recurrent net. This allows complex interaction between the neurons. An example is the Hopfield net which has been used as an associative memory. There are connections between any two neurons in a Hopfield net, and some neurons are designated as input while others, not necessarily different, as output. Upon completion of training, a Hopfield net is capable of retrieving the stored information when a part of the string used during training is presented to the network. Relaxing the restriction of having only inter-layer feedforward connections leads to the development of a network architecture called the Elman net. For each neuron in the hidden layer, there are backward connections to some neurons in the input layer. These extra connections allow the network to include temporal information during its course of deriving a solution [10].

It is clear that the most important contribution that ANNs make to a smart system is that they make it adaptive. ANNs can automatically adjust their weights using the learning algorithm to optimise the system behaviour. This capability allows ANNs to continually track solutions in changing environments. However, it is not true to say that ANNs would be able to compete with conventional techniques at performing well-defined, precise, numerical calculations such as matrix inversion. They have produced the best results in problems that not only involve ambiguity but are also difficult to model, such as pattern recognition. It is this key characteristic of ANNs that is exploited within the framework of SC.

5. Genetic Algorithms

Genetic algorithms (GAs) are search techniques which derive their inspiration from biological natural selection and genetics. The starting point is a population of individuals, each representing a possible solution to a problem. Each individual is allocated a fitness measure according to the quality of the solution it produces. The fittest individuals survive to the next generation while the individuals that produce unsatisfactory solutions are eliminated. This represents survival of the fittest. The transition from one generation to the next is by means of reproduction among the survived individuals only. The reproduction results in new individuals as offspring who share some features taken from each parent.

A basic GA processes a finite population of binary strings. There are three basic operations — selection, crossover and mutation. Selection chooses two individuals to produce offspring. The primary objective of selection is to produce a partial ranking of the population so that fitter individuals will have a higher chance to reproduce. Crossover takes the two selected individuals and divides randomly their binary representation into two sections, called heads and tails. The two tails are then swapped to produce new individuals. For example 11111 and 00000 can produce two new strings 11000 and 00111, or 11110 and 00001. Mutation is applied to each offspring after crossover. It is an occasional alteration of a bit (gene) position. The quality of the offspring is evaluated in the same way as the parents.

The GA's application domain is wide. It can be applied to any optimisation problem and has produced impressive results in a number of applications [11]. General Electric developed a CAD system that combined expert systems with genetic algorithms. This system was used on a 100-variable portion of a gas-turbine design and produced a 92% increase in efficiency over human designers.

Variations to the basic form of the GA described above include real number and integer representation, different selection schemes that give various reproduction advantage to fitter individuals, and crossover operators that divide a string into more than two sections. Common to various forms of GA is their robustness in reaching an optimal solution in the presence of minimal, if any, prior knowledge of the problem at hand. It is also best used in situations which involve a large number of parameters. As a result, the search conducted by a GA is very computationally intensive. Recent research has produced an analytical theory of GAs based on stochastic differential equations which may further establish GAs as an efficient tool for optimisation and simulation of distributed systems.

6. Soft Computing and Hybrid Systems

In the past decade a number of hybrid techniques have been developed that take advantage of the relative merits of fuzzy systems, ANNs and GAs [12]. In the previous sections, these merits were discussed and can be summarised as shown in Table 1.

There are five categories in Table 1 used for the comparison — learning and optimisation refer to sub-symbolic learning and optimisation. (The techniques have been assessed on the basis of whether learning and optimisation are implicit features or have to be built in.) Knowledge extraction refers to symbolic knowledge extraction as defined in conventional AI systems. Real-time operation is linked with implementation issues, i.e. whether each method lends itself readily to hardware implementation or not. Knowledge representation is either symbolic or numeric. The entries for fuzzy systems, ANNs, GAs and conventional systems are as shown. It should be noted that Table 1 also assumes a simplistic binary set of entries — yes and no. In reality, they could themselves be fuzzy.

Two observations can be made from Table 1. Firstly, there is a good case for combining fuzzy, ANNs and GAs for building intelligent systems because each method can complement the other. Secondly, such a combination can enhance the capabilities of conventional AI systems. Some proponents of SC [13] use this as a strong argument for developing new ways of producing hybrid systems to address the shortcomings of conventional AI.

It has been argued [3] that the success of SC (as indicated by an explosion of applications in the present decade) is due to its emphasis on computational intelligence (CI) which is for the most part numeric rather than symbolic. CI is defined by Bezdek

[14] as the first step of achieving biological, or human-level, intelligence (BI), and it is purely based on numerical computation using sensory signals. AI lies somewhere between CI and BI and can be achieved by extending CI with symbolic representation and manipulation of non-numeric data (see Table 2). Fuzzy models are particularly suitable for a smooth transition between CI and AI because they can accommodate both numeric and symbolic information in a common framework.

Table 1. Relative merits of Fuzzy, ANN, GA and conventional AI systems.

	Sub-symbolic learning	Symbolic knowledge extraction	Real-time operation	Knowledge repre-sentation	Optim-isation
Fuzzy system	no	yes	yes	symbolic/ numeric	no
ANN	yes	no	yes	numeric	no
GA	yes	no	no	numeric	yes
Conven-tional AI systems	no	yes	no	symbolic/ number	no

Table 2. The ABC of intelligence [14].

Complexity →		
Biological Human knowledge + sensory inputs	BNN	BI
Artificial Symbolic + numeric + sensor data	ANN	AI
Computational Numeric	CNN	CI

(vertical axis label: Complexity)

Bezdek presents the case for combining symbolic and sub-symbolic techniques by introducing a distinction between computational neural networks (CNNs) and artificial neural networks (ANNs). He argues [14] that ANNs result from the combination of CNNs, which are based purely on numerical processing of sensory data, and some knowledge usually in the form of non-numeric rules.

The most widely researched hybrid system in the area of SC is neuro-fuzzy systems. Here the learning capabilities of ANNs are exploited within the framework of fuzzy logic. In some systems, ANNs can be used to generate and tune the membership functions in a fuzzy system (Fig 6). A number of models have been suggested for such hybrid systems, e.g. fuzzy ART [15], Fuzzy LVQ [16] and radial basis functions [17]. The process of obtaining and tuning the fuzzy rules is one that is particularly suitable for ANNs, resulting in substantial reductions in cost and development time. Here, gradient descend methods have been used to define the shape and position of membership functions. This hybrid method has been used to design triangular, Gaussian, sigmoidal and bell-shaped membership functions [18].

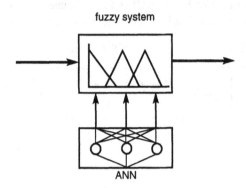

Fig. 6. ANN for tuning membership functions.

A number of applications have been reported in which fuzzy systems and ANNs are employed in series [19]. In such situations, either the sensor output is not suitable for direct input to the fuzzy system in which case an ANN pre-processes the input to the fuzzy system (Fig 7(a)), or the output of the fuzzy system is not suitable for direct interface with the external devices and an ANN is used as a post-processor to perform a mapping or conversion not easily achievable by other analytical techniques (see Fig 7(b)). For example, Toshiba's microwave-oven-cum-toaster estimates the temperature and the number of pieces of bread using an ANN and decides the optimum toasting time by using fuzzy reasoning, i.e. its model resembles closely Fig 7(a).

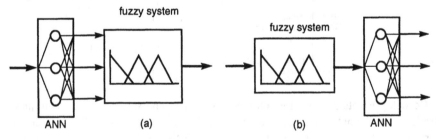

Fig. 7. Serial hybrid ANN-fuzzy systems.

In some applications ANN and fuzzy systems are used in parallel. One possible configuration uses a fuzzy system as the main system and an ANN to fine-tune the output to suit users' personal preferences. The ANN learns from the fine adjustments made by the user and corrects the output of the fuzzy system (Fig 8).

Another class of systems, known as neural fuzzy systems, have been used for knowledge acquisition and learning. In such systems, experts' knowledge in symbolic form is used to initialise a structured ANN. The ANN is then trained using the input/

output from an actual system. Symbolic knowledge is then acquired from the trained ANN in fuzzy logic representation (Fig 9).

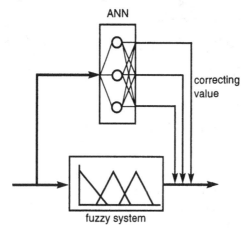

Fig. 8. Parallel hybrid ANN/fuzzy systems.

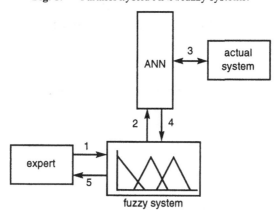

Fig. 9. Neural/fuzzy systems.

A significant number of researchers have concentrated their efforts on implementing fuzzy systems on a neural network representation. These include fuzzy weights, fuzzy neurons and fuzzy neural networks in which the neural network layers perform the fuzzification and defuzzification on crisp input/output data. The structure of fuzzy neural networks is shown in Fig 10. There are three groups of layers each performing one of the three functions of a fuzzy system.

The initial layers process crisp input data by assigning groups of nodes to the labels of linguistic variables and implementing membership functions in these nodes. The output of these layers goes to layers that function as fuzzy rules operating on fuzzy input. The final layer aggregates the results of applying the rules and defuzzifies the results [19]. GARIC [20] is an example of such a scheme which uses a five-layer neural network. It has been used in the space shuttle orbital operations control by NASA.

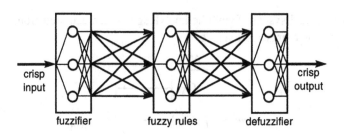

Fig. 10. Fuzzy/neural networks.

Development tools are becoming available for integrating fuzzy and neural networks which should pave the way for the exploitation of the available architectures in information systems applications. Two such tools are NEFCON-I [21] and O'INCA [19] by Intelligent Machines Inc.

Fuzzy-GA systems combine the optimisation capabilities of GAs with fuzzy logic (Fig 11). Such systems can develop the best possible set of rules for use by a fuzzy inference engine. They can also be used to optimise the choice of the membership functions.

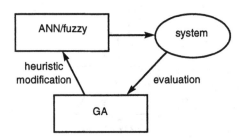

Fig. 11. GA for optimisation of ANN/fuzzy hybrid systems.

The applications of hybrid genetic and fuzzy systems are in adaptive process control, pattern recognition, robot trajectory generation and face recognition. GAs can be used to improve the performance of neural networks by changing their parameters, topologies or both. Applications include structure organisation of fuzzy neural networks, evolving ANNs and self-organising maps.

There are many other possible combinations of FL, ANN and GA. However, this paper has only presented the most widely published ways of combining these techniques within the context of SC. The references provide a more comprehensive list for further reading.

7. Some Applications of Soft Computing Techniques

Although SC is a relatively new field of research it has already been established as one of the fastest growing areas of AI technology in terms of consumer and industrial applications. Japanese companies lead the way both in research and development, although many European and American companies are allocating large resources to this technology and the products have already appeared in the market. The majority of the applications are in the areas of expert systems, control, pattern recognition, clustering and image processing. However, active research is being carried out in many other areas such as decision support systems, user interfaces, speech recognition, face recognition and natural language systems. This section gives a brief description of a small number of recent applications of this technology. The emphasis here will be on applications resulting from the fusion of SC techniques rather than applications of individual techniques.

7.1   A Smart Washing Machine

Hitachi has produced a washing machine that uses the parallel structure of Fig 8 [22]. The smart controller inside the washing machine determines the washing programme automatically by measuring the amount and type of clothes placed inside the machine. A fuzzy rule-based system then uses this information to control the water flow and the programme parameters such as washing time, rinsing time and spinning time. A neural network monitors the operation of the machine during a wash and uses the quality of the water inside the drum to fine-tune the output parameters of the fuzzy system. In this way, it acts as an adaptive correcting mechanism for the fixed fuzzy rules.

7.2   A User-seeking Electric Fan

The electric fan of Sanyo is designed to face the user as the user moves inside a room [23]. To solve this problem accurately a very sophisticated and expensive system is required, which is not suitable for a relatively cheap consumer product. The main problem is computing the distance of the user from the fan. Sanyo have designed a fuzzy system to estimate the distance given readings from an infra-red sensor. A neural network is then trained to use this information to compute the required turning angle of the fan. This technique has not only produced a financially viable solution but it has 2.5 times better accuracy compared to statistical regression methods.

7.3   A Photocopier with a 'Brain'

The Matsushita Electric photocopier machine controls its operation with a set of fuzzy rules [24]. All photocopier machines operate with a set of fixed parameters which can be adjusted manually by an engineer or the user. However, the quality of the copies can deteriorate with time or can be dependent upon the type of the original document. A fuzzy rule-based system can use the information about the state of the machine, the quality and type of the original document to make decisions regarding operating parameters of the photocopier. Some of the fuzzy input parameters used by the rules are temperature, humidity, toner density, image density and image background. The output of the system controls the parameters such as exposure lamp, drum voltage and toner density among others. Interestingly, the parameters of the fuzzy system were designed automatically by neural networks, i.e. the position and width of the fuzzy membership functions were tuned by a gradient method. It is important to note that the neural network was used during the development stage and not during the operation. The same approach has been used by Matsushita to design vacuum cleaners, rice cookers and washing machines.

7.4 A Rolling Mill with Fuzzy Recognition

Hitachi have manufactured and run a rolling mill system since 1991 [25] whose aim is to produce constant thickness metal rolls. The surface of the plate which is being driven through 20 rolls is scanned. The scanned pattern is matched against standard template patterns by a neural network. The standard templates are used as the antecedent of the fuzzy rules, for example:

IF pattern is *template_1* THEN action is *output_1*
IF pattern is *template_2* THEN action is *output_2*
IF pattern is *template_3* THEN action is *output_3*

The level of matching identified by the neural network is the strength of each fuzzy rule. The aggregated final output of the fuzzy system determines the output to the rolls. This approach is called neural network-driven fuzzy reasoning.

7.5 Other Interesting Consumer Products

Mitsubishi Electric Corp introduced fuzzy inference into their videoconferencing system in 1991 [26]. The aim was to improve the data compression coding method based on the extent of change in successive frames. The fuzzy rules improved the motion tracking ability of their product by 30—50%. A smart TV produced by Mitsubishi [26] continuously adjusts the controls on the TV set to produce optimum picture quality according to the brightness of the room and the viewer's distance from the set. Canon has used fuzzy logic in their camera to improve the auto-focus functions [26]. Sanyo have done similar work on their camcorders [26]. Siemens have done extensive work on the application of fuzzy reasoning to various aspects of ATM networks such as call admission control and usage parameter control [27].

There are many more of such applications as documented in many journals and books [24]. The wealth of sources of applications show that the soft computing technology is reliable, cost effective and applicable to real-world problems. These are the factors that make soft computing an attractive technology from an industrial point of view. However, there are many active research areas within the soft computing framework that are and will be producing new directions for exploiting this technology in other challenging areas of applications.

7.6 Human/Computer Interaction — A New and Challenging Area of Application

This area of research can benefit from soft computing in many different ways because of the inherent uncertainty and vagueness in natural language, image recognition, hand-writing recognition, speech recognition and gesture understanding. The uncertainty is either due to poor sensor technology and data, or lack of processing algorithms and background information. There are already products available that use component technologies of soft computing to perform many of the above mentioned tasks e.g. neural networks have been used extensively for image and speech recognition, fuzzy logic has been used in areas such as face recognition [28], hand-writing recognition and speech recognition. However, as discussed in section 2, the merger of these technique would improve the overall characteristics of the resulting system and therefore it is anticipated that this will be an active area of research in the next few years. In the next section we will briefly mention future trends in soft computing research.

8. Future Research Directions

The majority (70%) of the publications in this area are concerned with the fusion of fuzzy systems and neural networks (FS-NN). About 25% of the publications are in the area of combining neural networks and GAs (NN-GA), and the remainder are in the area of merging fuzzy systems and GAs (GA-FS). The most promising areas in FS-NN are in the automatic design of fuzzy systems using neural networks and in neural networks whose structure is based on fuzzy rules (generally similar to that shown in Fig 10) which has produced results significantly superior compared to conventional neural networks. Within NN-GA, GAs have been used for optimisation of synaptic weights in ANNs and have produced better results when combined with back-propagation (BP) compared to BP on its own. In the GA-FS area the performance of static GA has been improved by incorporating a set of fuzzy rules to dynamically change the parameters of the GA in order to improve its overall performance. On the other hand GAs have been used to optimise the selection of best fuzzy rules as well as optimising the rules themselves. In general, improvements are being made in the areas of soft computing where individual components seem to have deficiencies. In summary the future research directions are as follows:

- a better understanding of the trade-offs between training time and size of neural networks is necessary;

- neural network implementations of fuzzy systems must be able to learn on-line in order to respond to changes in their environment;

- we must be able to extract the knowledge learnt by neural networks;

- GAs must be able to handle qualitative fitness functions as well as quantitative ones;

- generic soft computing platforms are essential for further research in these areas.

These are just some of the challenges faced by the soft computing research community.

9. Conclusions

This paper has given a definition for soft computing and described its relevance to intelligent systems. The principal aim of soft computing is to achieve robustness, low solution cost and high machine IQ, through the exploitation of tolerance for imprecision and uncertainty. The individual components of soft computing each exhibit certain characteristics beneficial to the aim of increasing MIQ. Fuzzy logic provides a model for approximate reasoning, as well as a representation for smooth transition from a symbolic paradigm to a numeric one. Neural networks operate on numeric data and provide low-level, fast-processing units that can adapt and learn. GAs are used for optimisation to evolve better performance. A number of successful applications, particularly in the area of consumer products, have shown that synergism of these techniques can provide a route to building intelligent systems [29].

Acknowledgement

The authors wish to acknowledge the advice and encouragement provided by Professor Lotfi Zadeh in the preparation of this paper.

References

1. Zadeh L A: 'The roles of fuzzy logic and soft computing in the conception, design and deployment of intelligent systems', BT Technol J, 14, No 4, pp 32—36 (October 1996).

2. Uhr L and Honavar V: 'Introduction', in: 'Artificial Intelligence and Neural Networks — Steps Toward Principled Integration', Academic Press (1994).

3.   Zadeh L A: 'Fuzzy Logic, Neural Networks and Soft Computing', Comm of ACM, 37, No 3, pp 77—84 (March 1994).

4.   Mamdani E H: 'Towards Soft Computing', Proc BCS Expert Systems Conference, Cambridge (December 1995).

5.   Kosko B: 'Neural Networks and Fuzzy Systems — A Dynamical Systems Approach to Machine Intelligence', Prentice Hall (1992).

6.   Horstkotte E: http://www.quadralay.com/www/ Fuzzy/Fuzzy.html

7.   Munakata T and Jani Y: 'Fuzzy Systems: An Overview', Comm of ACM, 37, No 3, pp 69—76 (March 1994).

8.   Zadeh L A: 'Soft Computing and Fuzzy Logic', IEEE Software, 11, No 6, pp 48—58 (1994).

9.   Barto A, Sutton R and Anderson C: 'Neuro-like Adaptive Elements that can Solve Difficult Control Problems', IEEE Tran on Systems, Man and Cybernetics, No 13 (1983).

10. Dayhoff J: 'Neural Network Architectures', Van Nostrand Reinhold (1990).

11. Goldberg D E: 'Genetic and Evolutionary Algorithms Come of Age', Comm of ACM, 37, No 3, pp 113—119 (March 1994).

12. Fukura T: 'Fuzzy-neuro-GA Based Intelligent Robotics', in: 'Computational Intelligence Imitating Life', IEEE Press, pp 352—363 (1994).

13. Fox J: 'Towards a reconciliation of fuzzy logic and standard logic', Int J of Man Machine Studies, 15, pp 213—220 (1981).

14. Bezdek J C: 'What is Computational Intelligence', in: 'Computational Intelligence Imitating Life', IEEE Press, pp 1—12 (1994).

15. Carpenter G, Grossberg S, Markuzon N, Reynold H J and Rosen D B: 'Fuzzy ARTMAP: A Neural Network Architecture for Incremental Supervised Learning of Analogue Multi-dimensional Maps', IEEE Tran on Neural Networks, 3, No 5, pp 698—713 (1992).

16. Tsao E C K, Bezdek J C and Pal N R: 'Image Segmentation Using Fuzzy Clustering Networks', in North American Fuzzy Information Processing, pp 98—107 (1992).

17. Wang L X: 'Training Fuzzy Logic Systems Using Nearest Neighbourhood Clustering', Manuscript (1992).

18. Asakawa K and Takagi H: 'Neural Networks in Japan', Comm of ACM (March 1994).

19. Medsker A R: 'Hybrid Intelligent Systems', Kluwer Academic Publishers (1995).

20. Berenji H R: 'Fuzzy Systems That Can Learn', in: 'Computational Intelligence Imitating Life', IEEE Press, pp 23—30 (1994).

21. NEFCON: http://sol.ibr.cs.tu-bs.de/ibr/projects/ nefcon/

22. Hitachi News Release: 'Neuro and fuzzy logic automatic washing machine and fuzzy logic dryer', No. 91-024 (February 1991).

23. Sanyo News Release: 'Electric fan series in 1991', (March 1991).

24. Takagi H: 'Co-operative system of neural networks and fuzzy logic and its application to consumer products', in: 'Industrial Applications of Fuzzy Control and Intelligent Systems', IEEE Press (1994).

25. Nakajima M, Okada T, Hattori S and Morroka Y: 'Application of pattern recognition and control techniques to shape control of the rolling mill', Hitachi Review, 75, No 2 (1993).

26. Takagi H: 'Survey of fuzzy logic applications in image processing equipment', in: 'Industrial Applications of Fuzzy Control and Intelligent Systems', IEEE Press (1995).

27. Hellendoorn H, Metternich W, Nissel M, Seising R and Thomas C: 'Traffic management for broadband networks with fuzzy logic — call admission control and usage parameter control', Proceedings of EUFIT'96 (September 1996).

28. Baldwin J and Martin T: 'Basic concepts of fuzzy logic data browser with applications', in Nwana H and Azarmi N (Eds): 'Software Agents and Soft Computing: Towards Enhancing Machine Intelligence', Springer Verlag, Berlin (December 1996).

29. Zadeh L A: 'Foreword', in Medsker L R: 'Hybrid Intelligent Systems', Kluwer Academic Publishers (1995).

Basic Concepts of a Fuzzy Logic Data Browser with Applications

J F Baldwin and T P Martin

Advanced Computer Research Centre and Engineering Mathematics Department,
University of Bristol, Bristol, BS8 1TL, UK.
E-mail: {jim.baldwin/trevor.martin}@bristol.ac.uk

A fuzzy data broswer for classification and prediction is described and its use demonstrated with several examples. The browser is written in the AI language Fril and provides a friendly user interface for the user to test the performance, see the effect of changes in the rules, visualise the performance and try various different forms of modelling. The rules with their associated fuzzy sets are automatically determined from a learning set of examples given in the form of a database. The fundamental theory of this approach to the automatic extraction of rules from data and the method of inference using these rules to generalise is described in simple terms. The method has wide application to data mining, fuzzy AI modelling, pattern recognition and computing with words.

1. Introduction

Human knowledge is obtained by induction — we generalise from known cases to new cases which are similar. We use induction to make decisions and to classify, to draw conclusions, to form useful rules of thumb, to make models and to hypothesise. We can generalise by replacing values for a known case by fuzzy sets. The fuzzy sets allow nearby values to those for the known case to be accepted with membership values which decrease the further the values are from the original values. This is a form of case-based reasoning and nearest neighbour interpolation but can be expressed in a logic-style format that provides a knowledge representation which can be combined with other knowledge to provide further inferences.

Why should we be so interested to discover ways for computers to make inductions? Data is everywhere — we can easily collect large databases and store them for future use. Large volume data from various fields such as medicine, science and engineering, finance and economics, marketing, social welfare, education, advertising, law, the arts, etc, is there for the collecting. We store it away in large databases in the hope that it will be useful. To be useful we must be able to discover relationships between the various attributes of the database, find rules to predict values of one attribute when the others are known for cases which are not explicitly present in the database. A database will not necessarily have all its entries correct, there may be errors. Some entries will not be known exactly. We may not be sure of the exact context for which the database is relevant.

How can we extract knowledge from these databases where we understand knowledge to be useful relationships and useful rules. We may wish to report this knowledge in the form of a natural language summary.

We require a data browser in the form of a human/computer partnership where the human is the actual interested party and the computer has the appropriate software for making inductions and performing AI tasks. In this paper we describe such a data browser and show some applications which illustrate its use.

Imagine a group of sensors which are to be used to recognise certain objects. The response of each sensor might be different for each of the objects or at least the sensors taken as a group will give the required discrimination to provide the correct recognition. These responses can be modelled with fuzzy rules or more general linguistic descriptions involving fuzzy sets. The model can then be used for recognition purposes. We will call this the classification problem.

The behaviour of a dynamic system can also be modelled with fuzzy rules and at any instance the predicted output value can be determined using these rules. The inference using the values for the inputs and the model will result in a fuzzy value for the predicted output. This can be defuzzified to give a point value. This we will call the prediction problem. Of course, any function can be approximated as a set of fuzzy rules and the function value for any set of arguments corresponds to a defuzzified prediction.

In both classes of problem we will assume that we are presented with a data base of examples of the form $(x1, ...xn, y)$ where xi are feature values and y is the prediction or the classification. For the classification problem we will have at least one fuzzy rule for each classification . A rule could take the form:

classification is Ci   IFF

feature 1 belongs to **fi1** $\wedge$ feature 2 belongs to **fi2** $\wedge$ ... $\wedge$ feature n belongs to **fin**.

The vectors for each classification would be clustered and one rule for each cluster used for classification purposes.

For the prediction problem let the output variable y belong to the universe Y. A fuzzy partition of Y, namely **(g1, ..., gm)** is used and a rule for each fuzzy set **gi** of the form:

value of y is **gi** IFF

feature 1 belongs to **fi1** $\wedge$ feature 2 belongs to **fi2** $\wedge$ ... $\wedge$ feature n belongs to **fin**.

is used.

The fuzzy sets **gi** are such that

$$\mu \, \mathbf{g1}(y) + ... + \mu\mathbf{gm}(y) = 1$$

which is required for a fuzzy partition.

We can have other types of fuzzy rules but these will be discussed later. The important issue to discuss here concerns how we determine these fuzzy sets {**fi**} used in the body of the rules automatically from the data base. The methods used in this paper will be somewhat different to the usual fuzzy logic approach. This is why we have used equivalence rules above. The approach which we use is that used by the Fril fuzzy AI programming language [1, 2] and is based on the fuzzy set interpretation using mass assignment theory [3—6] We will not discuss the full details of this theory in this paper but present a simple version of the essentials of the theory which is relevant for the automatic method of finding the fuzzy sets in the rules from the data base of examples. The mass assignment theory is also useful to justify the inference rules used by the Fril system.

For the moment let us assume that we can automatically generate the fuzzy sets from the database and provide the required inference to give us a classification or prediction. The database is then being used to form rules from which we can provide a classification or prediction for a new case not present in the database. We are using the rules formed from the database to induce values for cases which are not in the database. The vector $(y, x1, ..xn)$ can be thought of as corresponding to attribute values of the database and y is the value of the attribute we are attempting to predict in terms of the other attribute values $x1, ..., xn$. The classification or prediction will correspond to the unknown value of one of the attributes when the other attributes are known. The known values of the attributes need not be known exactly but can be fuzzy sets defined on the appropriate attribute universe. This will include the case when some of the xi values are completely unknown.

It may be that the attributes of the database are not particularly good features to use in the rules. A better feature may consist of some algebraic combination of certain attribute values. Choosing a good set of features is a most difficult problem. We can use genetic programming for this purpose to generate good features [7].

For the above case we are providing a prediction or classification for y in terms of $x1...xn$ where xi takes values in Xi for all i. We could form a fuzzy set **f** on the cross product space $X1 \times X2 \times ... \times Xn$ corresponding to a particular classification or **gi** prediction. A rule for this cluster would say that:

y is Ci, (or gi) IF $(x1, ..., xn)$ belongs to **f**

We prefer not to work in this cross product space since we have a high dimensionality problem in general. Imagine that we are trying to classify faces into male and female categories. We would need about 18 features for this classification and **f** would be a fuzzy set on an 18-dimensional space. Therefore we prefer the rules of the form given earlier in which fuzzy sets on single spaces are used. This decomposition from a multiple space to single spaces can give rise to decomposition errors. In the method that we will describe below we do not decompose the fuzzy set because this will lead to large decomposition errors. Instead we form the marginal frequency distributions for feature values on each of the individual feature spaces. These marginal distributions are converted into fuzzy sets for the body of the rule. This method of decomposition leads to much smaller decomposition errors. We can illustrate this with a simple example. Consider that points inside the circle of Fig 1 are legal and points outside are illegal.

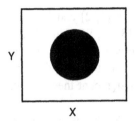

Fig. 1.

The fuzzy set on X × Y for legal points is uniform with membership 1 over the circle and has membership 0 outside the circle. If we decompose this fuzzy set on to the separate axes X and Y we will get the fuzzy sets **f1** and **f2** shown in Fig 2 and this will correspond to saying that all points in the enclosed rectangle are legal. The problem here is that f1 has membership 1 for a given x if there is at least one legal point with this x value. But if we know that a given point is legal it has a much higher probability of having an x value near the centre of the circle than at the ends of the edges of the circle. We should take this into account if we want to minimise the decomposition error. Fig 3 shows the marginal probability densities p1 and p2. These can be used, as we explain below, to find corresponding fuzzy sets which will have a similar shape to these distributions. When we use these fuzzy sets, say **fp1** and **fp2**, formed from the probability distributions in the rule for legal point, namely:

(x, y) is legal point IFF x belongs to **fp1** and y belongs to **fp2**
we will get a much reduced decomposition error.

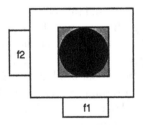

Fig. 2.

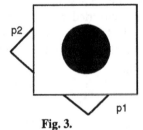

Fig. 3.

2. Essentials of Mass Assignment Theory

In this section we describe the basic ideas of the mass assignment theory and show their relevance for the fuzzy data browser. In order to explain the ideas simply we will use a basic example.

You are told that a weighted dice is thrown and the value is **small** where **small** is a fuzzy set defined as:

$$\text{small} = 1/1 + 2/0.9 + 3/0.4$$

The prior for the dice is:

$$1:0.1, 2:0.2, 3:0.3, 4:0.2, 5:0.1, 6:0.1$$

Can we derive the distribution Pr(dice is i | dice is **small**)?

What is Pr(dice is **about_2** | dice is **small**) where **about_2** is a fuzzy set defined as:

$$\text{about\_2} = 1/0.3 + 2/1 + 3/0.3$$

The most fundamental question we must ask is what do we mean by **small**. What is the semantics of fuzzy sets? To answer this question we will use a voting model involving human voters. The world is not fuzzy. It is continuous and messy and we have to give labels to things we want to recognise as certain objects. We want to categorise and give labels to these categories. There will always be borderline cases. A particular object is neither a tree nor a bush but we do not have a label for it. We must therefore say that it is a borderline case but it may be more like a tree than a bush. We can therefore use graded membership in the nearest and most appropriate categories. We might say the object is a bush with a membership of 0.7 and a tree with a membership of 0.9. But what meaning can we give to this membership value?

Imagine that we have a representative set of people labelled 1 through to 10. Each person is asked to accept or reject the dice score of x as **small**. They can believe x is a borderline case but they have to make a binary decision to accept or reject. We will take the membership of x in the fuzzy set **small** to be the proportion of persons who accept x as **small**.

Thus we know that everyone accepted 1 as small, 90% of persons accepted 2 as small and 30% of persons accepted 3 as small. We only know the proportions who accepted each score and not the complete voting pattern of each person. We will assume that anyone who accepted x as being small will accept also any score lower than x of being small. With this assumption we can write down the voting pattern:

1	2	3	4	5	6	7	8	9	10	persons
1	1	1	1	1	1	1	1	1	1	everyone accepts 1
2	2	2	2	2	2	2	2	2		90% accept 2
3	3	3								30% accept 3

Therefore 1 person accepts {1}, 6 persons accept {1, 2} and 3 persons accept {1, 2, 3} as being the possible sets of scores when told the dice is small. If a member is drawn at random then the probability distribution for the set of scores this person will accept is:

$$\{1\}:0.1, \{1,2\}:0.6, \{1,2,3\}:0.3$$

This is a probability distribution on the power set of dice scores and we will call this a mass assignment and write it as:

$$m_{small} = \{1\} : 0.1, \{1, 2\}: 0.6, \{1, 2, 3\} : 0.3$$

We can determine the mass assignment very easily for a given discrete fuzzy set. The set of values with membership 1 is first selected and given the mass equal to 1 minus the next highest membership value. The next set is chosen by adding to the last set formed the elements corresponding to the next highest membership value and this set is given the mass equal to the difference between the membership value of these added elements and the next highest membership value in the fuzzy set. This is repeated until the last elements are added and the last set takes the value of the membership of the last added elements. Thus for the fuzzy set small we first form:

$\{1\}$ and give it the mass $1 - 0.9 = 0.1$

We then form the set $\{1, 2\}$ and give it the mass $0.9 - 0.3 = 0.6$

We then form the set $\{1, 2, 3\}$ and give it the mass 0.3

It is, of course, a random set and also a basic probability assignment of the Shafer Dempster theory. We give it the name of mass assignment because we use it in a different way to the Dempster Shafer theory.

This mass assignment corresponds to a family of distributions on the set of dice scores. Each mass associated with a set of more than one element can be divided in some way among the elements of the set. This will lead to a distribution over the dice scores and there are an infinite number of ways in which this can be done.

Suppose we wish to give a unique distribution over the dice scores when we are told the dice value is small. How can we choose this distribution from the family of possible distributions arising from the mass assignment? To provide the least prejudiced distribution or the fairest distribution we would divide the masses among the elements of the set associated with them according to the prior for the dice scores. If this prior is unknown then we would use a local entropy concept and divide each mass equally among the elements of its set. The resulting distribution we will call the least prejudiced distribution. This distribution corresponds to the probability of a dice score being chosen if we select a person from the voters at random and then ask that person to select one value from their possible set of accepted values when told the dice value is **small**.

For our case when we know the dice is **small** and has the prior given above we obtain the least prejudiced distribution:

$$1 : 0.1 + 1/3(0.6) + 1/6(0.3) = 0.35$$
$$2 : 2/3(0.6) + 2/6(0.3) = 0.5$$
$$3 : 3/6(0.3) = 0.15$$

Thus:

$$Pr(\text{dice is 1} \mid \text{dice is small}) = 0.35,$$
$$Pr(\text{dice is 2} \mid \text{dice is small}) = 0.5,$$
$$Pr(\text{dice is 3} \mid \text{dice is small}) = 0.15$$

We will also use the notation:

$$lpd_{small} = 1 : 0.35, 2 : 0.5, 3 : 0.15$$

where lpd stands for least prejudiced distribution.

This least prejudiced distribution plays a fundamental role in converting a probability distribution of a given feature to a fuzzy set. Above we found the least prejudiced distribution corresponding to a fuzzy set. For the data browser we reverse this and assume that the feature distribution corresponds to the least prejudiced distribution of a fuzzy set. We work backwards to determine this fuzzy set.

Suppose that the length of papers accepted to date for a given journal has the following distribution:

20 : 0.1, 21 : 0.2, 22 : 0.4, 23 : 0.2, 24 : 0.1

If we treat this as the lpd of the fuzzy set f then f will have the form:

$f = 22 / 1 + 21 / a + 23 / a + 20 / b + 24 / b$

where $b < a < 1$

The mass assignment for f is

$m_f = \{22\} : 1\text{-}a, \{22, 21, 23\} : a\text{-}b, \{22, 21, 23, 20, 24\} : b$

giving the least prejudiced distribution:

$lpd_f = 22 : (1\text{-}a) + 1/3(a\text{-}b) + 1/5b = 0.4$ from distribution above

$\qquad$ 21 and 23 : $1/3(a\text{-}b) + 1/5b = 0.2$ from distribution above

$\qquad$ 20 and 24 : $1/5b = 0.1$ from distribution above

Thus working backwards:

$\qquad b = 5(0.1) = 0.5$

$\qquad a = 3(0.2 \text{ - } 0.1) + b = 0.8$

The fuzzy set for the feature length of accepted paper is:

$\qquad f = 20 / 0.5 + 21 / 0.8 + 22 / 1 + 23 / 0.8 + 24 / 0.5$

We could use this in a rule of the form:

$\qquad$ paper X is acceptable IFF length is $f \wedge \ldots$

where the ... signifies the inclusion of other features in the rule.

The Fril language can determine the least prejudiced distribution for any discrete or continuous fuzzy set. It can also determine the fuzzy set corresponding to any feature distribution treated as the least prejudiced distribution. This is used by the data browser to automatically generate fuzzy sets from the database.

In the case of the prediction problem, the heads of the rules are of the form:

$\qquad$ (value of y is g_i)

For a given case where the values of the features in the bodies of the rules are known, Fril will infer a solution of the form:

$\qquad$ (value of y is g)

where g is a fuzzy set on the Y domain. We require a defuzzified value for y for our prediction. Fril will find the least prejudiced distribution, lpd_g for the value of y, and, if g is a continuous fuzzy set, use this distribution to determine the expected value of y. This expected value is taken as the defuzzified value. We could also obtain a standard deviation for y which would give some measure of confidence in using the defuzzified value. When g is a discrete fuzzy set then the defuzzified value is that value with the largest least prejudiced distribution probability. This method of defuzzification is justified by the voting model semantics and is not as *ad hoc* as that used in fuzzy control.

In the theory above we have shown how to interpret the fuzzy set in such a way as to obtain a least prejudiced distribution. If you are told that the dice value is **small** it makes sense to ask what is the distribution over the possible dice scores for the dice score. This is only a small modification from the following non-fuzzy case. If you are told that the dice score is even then you would say that the scores 2, 4, and 6 were equally likely for a fair dice. In this case you have put a mass of 1 with the set {2, 4, 6} and split this mass equally among the elements of the set of possible scores. The only difference between this and our fuzzy case is that the mass assignment came from a fuzzy set rather than a crisp set. It also makes sense to ask for the probability that the dice value will be in a certain set given that the dice value is in some other set. For example, we can ask what is the probability that the dice value will be {1 or 2} given that it is even:

$$Pr(\{\text{dice value in } \{1, 2\} \mid \text{dice value is even}) = 1/3$$

Similarly we can ask for the probability of the dice value being **about_2** when we know it is **small** where **about_2** is a fuzzy set defined by

$$\textbf{about\_2} = 1 / 0.4 + 2 / 1 + 3 / 0.4$$

The mass assignment for the fuzzy set **about_2** is:

$$m_{\textbf{about\_2}} = \{2\} : 0.6, \{1, 2, 3\} : 0.4$$

We can use this mass assignment with the least prejudiced distribution for small to obtain a point value for Pr(dice value is **about_2** | dice value is **small**). From the least prejudiced distribution for **small** we obtain:

$$Pr(\{2\} \mid \textbf{small}) = 0.5, Pr(\{1, 2, 3\} \mid \textbf{small}) = 0.35 + 0.5 + 0.15 = 1$$

and we define the Pr(dice value is **about_2** | dice value is **small**) as:

Pr(dice value is **about_2** | dice value is **small**) =

$$m_{\textbf{about\_2}}(\{2\})Pr(\{2\} \mid \textbf{small}) + m_{\textbf{about\_2}}(\{1, 2, 3\})Pr(\{1, 2, 3\} \mid \textbf{small})$$
$$0.6 \ 0.5 + 0.4 \ 1 = 0.7$$

We can see the equivalent of this in tabular form as in Fig 4.

	small			
	0.1 {1}	0.6 {1, 2}	0.3 {1, 2, 3}	
0.6 {2}	0	2/3 of (0.6) (0.6) = 0.24	2/6 of (0.6) (0.3) = 0.06	Prior: 1 : 0.1 2 : 0.2
about_2				3 : 0.3
0.4 {1.2.3}	(0.4) (0.1) = 0.04	(0.4)(0.6) = 0.24	(0.4)(0.3) =0.12	4 : 0.2 5 : 0.1 6 : 0.1

Pr ((about_2) | small) = 0.7

Fig. 4.

We are determining the probability of **about_2** when we are given **small**. So for each cell we wish to calculate the probability of the corresponding cell set associated with **about_2** given the corresponding cell set associated with **small**. With each cell we associate a probability equal to the corresponding cell mass of **about_2** and the corresponding cell mass of **small**. Therefore with the topmost cell we associate the probability (0.6)(0.1). We then determine the proportion of these cell probabilities which contribute to Pr(**about_2** | **small**).

The top left cell has entry 0 since the truth of {1} given {2} is false. Thus for this entry we take zero of the cell probability. The second entry in the top row is 0.24 since truth of {2} given 1 is false but the truth of {2} given 2 is true and the 2 occurs with twice the probability of 1 according to the prior. Thus we take 2/3 of the cell probability. The third entry in the top row is calculated in a similar way. The left entry in the bottom row is 0.04 since {1, 2, 3} is true for {1}. Thus we take all the cell probability. The other cells in the bottom row are similar.

The use of the product rule to calculate the cell probabilities assumes that the choice of **about_2** is independent of **small**. We did not take account of small when deciding to use **about_2**.

This process of determining Pr(**about_2** | **small**) is called point value semantic unification. In Fril we also use an interval version of this, called interval semantic unification, where we do not use the prior to select between those values which give true and those values which give false. We simply record in each cell the cell probability, and t corresponding to the truth of the column set given the row set is true or f corresponding to the truth of the column set given the row set is false or u corresponding to the truth of the column set given the row set is uncertain. The total probability for t, f and u are then calculated by adding up the appropriate cell probabilities. This gives an interval for Pr(**about_2** | **small**) as illustrated in Fig 5.

small

		0.1 {1}	0.6 {1, 2}	0.3 {1, 2, 3}
0.6	{2}	f 0.06	u 0.36	u 0.18
about_2				
0.4	{1.2.3}	t 0.04	t 0.24	t 0.12

Pr((about_2) | small) = [0.4, 0.94]

Fig. 5.

In Fril both point and interval semantic unifications can be determined for both discrete and continuous fuzzy sets. The continuous case is treated as a limiting case of the discretised case.

3. Inference Methods for Fril Rules

We will not give the complete inference methods used by the language Fril in this paper but report only those methods used in the data browser as presented here.

Consider the rules:

Value of y is **gi** IFF

feature 1 is **fi1** $\wedge$ feature 2 is **fi2** $\wedge$ ... $\wedge$ feature n is **fin**

for i = 1, ..., m and where fuzzy sets **gi** are such that:

$\mu_{g1}(y) + ... + \mu_{gm}(y) = 1$

Suppose we are given the facts:

feature j is $\mathbf{f'j}$

for $j = 1, ..., n$ where $\mathbf{f'j}$ are fuzzy sets on the appropriate feature spaces.

The support for the body of the rule given the facts is determined using point value semantic unifications.

Let $Pr(\mathbf{fij} \mid \mathbf{f'j})$ be θ_{ij} for $i = 1, .., m$ and $j = 1, ..., n$, where these are determined using the Fril point value semantic unification algorithm.

The support for the body of the ith rule is then given by:

$$\theta_{i1} \theta_{i2} ... \theta_{in} = \theta_i, \text{ say.}$$

This product assumes the features to be independent. This assumption is not necessary in Fril but for this paper we will assume it.

Because the rules are equivalence rules, this support is passed directly to the head of the rule. Thus we infer:

$$\text{Value of y is } \mathbf{gi} : \theta i \quad \text{for } i = 1, ..., m.$$

We now have to combine these results to give a solution of the form

$$\text{Value of y is } \mathbf{g}$$

where $\mathbf{g}$ is a fuzzy set and we defuzzify this result to give us:

$$\text{Value of y is } v$$

where v is the expected value of lpd_g.

How do we determine $\mathbf{g}$ or more importantly how do we determine lpd_g ?

Since $\{\mathbf{gi}\}$ is a fuzzy partition:

$$lpd_g(y) = \sum_i Pr \quad (\text{Value is gi}) lpd_{gi}(y)$$

we have that:

$$v = \sum_i Pr \quad (\text{Value is gi}) \text{ Expected value of } lpd_{gi}(y)$$

Let $\int y.lpd_{gi}(y)dy = \mu_i$

The μ_i, the expected value of the least prejudiced distribution of the fuzzy set in the head of the ith rule, can be determined at compile time, so that:

$$v = \sum_i Pr \, (\text{Value is gi}) \, \mu_i$$

We can re-normalise $\{\theta i\}$ such that $\theta 1 + ... + \theta m = 1$
and equate $Pr(\text{Value is gi})$ with θi, so that:

$$v = \sum_i \theta_i \mu_i$$

This is a simple calculation and provides us with a simple inference rule.

For the classification problem using the rules:

Classification is Ci IFF
    feature 1 is **fi1** $\wedge$ feature 2 is **fi2** $\wedge$ ... $\wedge$ feature n is **fin**.
  for i = 1, ..., m
and the facts:
  feature j is **f'j**
for j = 1, ..., n where **f'j** are fuzzy sets on the appropriate feature spaces
we choose the classification with the highest qi support from:
  Classification is Ci : θ_i
  for i = 1, ..., m
We can now summarise the data browser approach to answering queries by generalising from the supplied database using Fril fuzzy logic rules.

The fuzzy sets in the body of the appropriate rules discussed above are determined from the known cases in the database by finding the frequency distributions for the feature values corresponding to a given classification or head of rule. These frequency distributions are treated as the least prejudiced distributions of the fuzzy sets to be used in the bodies of the rules. The fuzzy sets are determined from the frequency distributions using the backward iteration approach of the mass assignment illustrated above. These rules are then used for new data using the inference rule just derived.

The success of the method will depend on how well the body of a rule discriminates the appropriate head of the rule or classification from the bodies of the other rules. Consider the classification problem depicted in Fig 6.

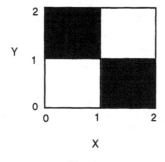

Fig. 6.

The rules found by the above method would be:
    black IFF x is in [0, 2] $\wedge$ y is in [0, 2]
    white IFF x is in [0, 2] $\wedge$ y is in [0, 2]
and there is no discrimination.

In this case we need to cluster the points associated with black and cluster the points associated with white. We will obtain two clusters for black and two clusters for white. We determine a rule for each cluster giving:
    black IFF x is in [0, 1] $\wedge$ y is in [1, 2]
    black IFF x is in [1, 2] $\wedge$ y is in [0, 1]
    white IFF x is in [0, 1] $\wedge$ y is in [0, 1]
    white IFF x is in [1, 2] $\wedge$ y is in [1, 2]

The data browser uses clustering methods prior to finding the rules for generalisation using the above approach.

There is one other point we should discuss. Consider the classification problem when we have a collection of feature vectors, $\{(x1, ..., xn)\}$. Each feature vector has a certain classification and so we can easily partition this collection into the appropriate set of vectors for each classification. For the prediction problem where we use the fuzzy partition $\{gi\}$ for our output space, we cannot determine the subset of feature vectors associated with a given **gi** so easily. Consider a given feature vector $(x1, ..., xn)$. The corresponding output will be y and this will have a membership value in at most two of the fuzzy sets in $\{gi\}$. Suppose these are **gs** and **gt**. Suppose the memberships in these fuzzy sets are µs and µt respectively. Then we can write:

$$y = \mathbf{gs} / \mu_s + \mathbf{gt} / \mu_t$$

where we have that

$$\mu_s + \mu_t = 1$$

since we have a fuzzy partition.

The corresponding mass assignment is:

$$MA_y = \{\mathbf{gs}\} : \mu_s\text{-}\mu_t, \ \{\mathbf{gs}, \mathbf{gt}\} : \mu_t, \ \varnothing : 1 - \mu_s$$

where we assume $\mu_s > \mu_t$.

The mass associated with the null set, $\varnothing$, arises because the fuzzy set y is not normalised. This is a measure of the inconsistency associated with using the labels **gs** and **gt** for the value y.

To find the least prejudiced distribution for y we allocate the mass associated with the null set equally among **gs** and **gt**. In voting model terms this corresponds to choosing a person at random and if this is a person who accepted neither **gs** nor **gt**, forcing this person to choose one of gs and gt. The person would have no other choice than to choose equally likely between all possibilities.

The least prejudiced distribution for y in terms of **gs** and **gt** is therefore:

$$lpd_y = \mathbf{gs} : (\mu_s\text{-}\mu_t) + 1/2(\mu_t) + 1/2(1 - \mu_s), \ \mathbf{gt} : 1/2(\mu_t) + 1/2(1 - \mu_s) = \mathbf{gs} : \mu_s, \mathbf{gt} : \mu_t$$

Thus if we ask a voter drawn at random from our population to allocate y to one of the labels $\{\mathbf{gs}, \mathbf{gt}\}$, the voter will choose **gs** with probability μ_s and **gt** with probability μ_t. We therefore associate the count of μ_s with **gs** and the count of μ_t with **gt** for each value xi in $(x1, ..., xn)$ when determining our frequency distributions for the variables $x1, ..., xn$.

4. Evidential Logic Rule

In the fuzzy data browser we can also use what is called in Fril an evidential logic rule rather than the conjunctive type of rule used above.

In this context the evidential logic rule takes the form:

Classification is Ci IFF **most** {feature 1 is **fi**1 with weight wi1

feature 2 is **fi**2 with weight wi2

$$\cdot \quad \cdot \quad \cdot$$

feature n is **fin** with weight win }

for $i = 1, ..., m$

for the classification problem.

The weights, $\{wij\}$, are understood to be weights of importance associated with the features and are non-negative with the constraint:

$$wi1 + ... + win = 1.$$

The fuzzy sets are feature fuzzy sets found in the same way as previously using the least prejudiced distributions of each feature value associated with classification.

The fuzzy set **most** is defined on the interval $[0, 1]$ and has the form:

$$\mu_{most}(x) = \frac{1}{(b-a)}x - \frac{a}{(b-a)} \quad \text{where } a < b$$

It is shown in Fig 7.

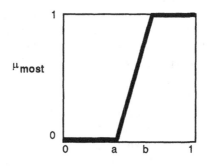

Fig. 7.

The weight for a given feature, k say, in a given rule i measures the power of discrimination that the fuzzy set **fik** associated with this feature has for the classification of this rule. This measure depends on the values of the point value semantic unifications $Pr(fik \mid fjk)$, all j. If the fuzzy set fik is completely separated from the fuzzy sets $fi1, ..., fi(j-1), fi(j+1), ..., \textbf{fim}$ then it discriminates classification i from the other classifications completely. If the fuzzy set fik overlaps completely with some of the other corresponding fuzzy sets in the other rules then there will be no discrimination. Various discrimination formulae can be used for this purpose and this can be chosen by the user in the data browser. The important point to male is that good values of the weights are easily selected by a simple calculation of a few point value semantic unifications.

The choice of a and b for the definition of most is also important. If the fuzzy set **most** is made too broad then we will tend to over-generalise while if it is too narrow we will tend to under-generalise. The best choice of a and b will vary from one rule to the next and some form of iterative optimisation technique is required to find the best values of a and b for each rule.

The features used in the evidential logic rule are not necessarily the known database attributes but can be compound features involving algebraic functions of these attributes. The motivation for using the evidential logic rule is that for many classification problems there is no conjunction of attributes that are satisfied by all members of a given class. All one can expect is that for an object of a given classification most of the relevant features for this classification will be satisfied.

The actual semantics of the evidential logic rule, as far as the generalisation powers it provides, is complicated and not fully understood at this moment. It behaves a little like a constrained neuron.

The evidential logic rule can also be used for prediction although experience indicates that its usefulness for this type of problem is less obvious than for the classification type problems. Once again it is often necessary to cluster first.

5.   An Implementation of the Data Browser

The ideas described above have been implemented as a program — the Data Browser — written in Fril. This program has been applied to a variety of artificial and real-world problems, with excellent results. The system splits into a natural sequence of operations starting from the raw data and ending with a set of Fril rules as shown in Fig 8. The power of generalisation of the rules can be tested by running against unseen data, and, if required, any part of the rules can be altered by the user and the performance of the new rule set assessed. The data browser is an evolving research project, and the applications outlined below give an overview of its capabilities. At the time of writing, an object-oriented version of the data browser is under development, and this will lead to a more flexible architecture where users are able to design their own browsers using a mixture of library-based components and custom-built modules.

The existing system has been implemented entirely in Fril, and runs on all platforms supported by the Fril language, i.e. Macintosh, Windows and Unix. On the Macintosh and Windows systems, a dialog-based front-end (written entirely in Fril) is used to determine user-specifiable parameters and to step through the various stages in the process. On Unix systems, user-specifiable parameters are read from a file of options. The Macintosh front-end has been used below to illustrate the operation of the browser.

5.1   Data Interface

The current implementation assumes that the data is static and resides (conceptually) in a database. For the examples in this paper, the database has been stored as Fril clauses or in external files read by Fril. It is also possible to link in a conventional database, e.g. one stored in Oracle, and pass data between the two systems. This flexibility is achieved by inserting a layer of code between the data browser and the data — this layer forms a data dictionary, specifying:

•   the form of the data (i.e. the tables, attributes, domains);

•   the location of the data (files which must be loaded or read);

- methods to access the data (Fril rules which can be executed by the data browser to extract a tuple or set of tuples from the database).

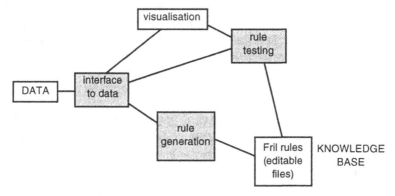

Fig. 8. Schematic architecture of the data browser. The shaded components are the core of the data browser; the visualisation module is implemented externally using Mathematica graphics.

One advantage of storing the data in Fril is that uncertainty in data may be handled naturally. Fril allows uncertainty in attribute values to be represented by a fuzzy set instead of crisp values, and also allows uncertainty in the degree to which a tuple satisfies a relation. Formally if the database contains a relation on $D1 \times D2 \times \ldots \times Dn$:

$R \subseteq D1 \times D2 \times \ldots \times Dn$

$R = \{ti \mid i = 1, \ldots, m\}$ where $ti = (fi1, fi2, \ldots, fin)$ such that $fij \in Dj \lor fij \subseteq_f Dj$

A support pair can also be associated with each tuple $(fi1, fi2, \ldots, fin)$.

5.2   Rule Generation

The data browser forms rules to predict the value of one attribute from other attributes, as discussed earlier in this paper. If y represents the attribute to be predicted then we can write a tuple as $(fi1, fi2, \ldots, fim, y, fim+2, \ldots, fin)$. The rules can be regarded as methods for computing an output value (y) from a subset of the possible input parameters $(fi1, fi2, \ldots, fim, fim+2, \ldots, fin)$. The rules contain fuzzy sets which summarise the possible and likely values for each feature in each rule, where a rule is derived from a set of similar or equal y values in the data. In the current implementation of the data browser, the number of rules is set to a default value by a brief examination of the data — either the number of discrete values taken by the output of the rule, or a sensible guess based on the range and distribution of the target domain. The number of rules is easily overriden by the user, if the default is not appropriate.

The heads of the rules then specify a discrete or fuzzy partition of the domain of y, and we can partition the database according to the membership that the y value for the tuple has in the partition. For each subset of the database, we must examine the distribution of values for the input attributes. In the case of a discrete underlying domain, we form a frequency histogram and derive a fuzzy set as described in section 3. When the underlying domain is continuous, it is necessary to discretise the domain or assume that the data is distributed according to a standard model (e.g. a Gaussian distribution). It may also be necessary to smooth the distribution to avoid noisy fluctuations. This corresponds to a well-known problem in statistics, where it has been noted that slightly different discretisations of the domain can have marked effects on the derived distribution [8]. The mass assignment-based approach is not so dependent on this choice since the fuzzy set defines a family of probability distributions; however, there are still important choices to be made regarding the discretisation of the domain and the degree of smoothing that is applied. For example, consider a domain [0,30] and a set of values:

$$6.1, 6.5, 6.7, 12.8, 12.9, 13.1, 13.2, 13.3, 13.4, 13.5, 13.6, 13.7$$

Discretising the domain into blocks of 10, 5, and 1 produces the histograms shown in Fig 9, and converting to fuzzy sets gives the three possibilities shown. Clearly these have different powers of generalisation, and the effects of discretisation of the domain and smoothing can have considerable effect on the rules.

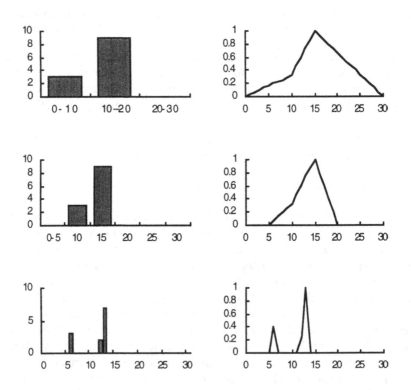

Fig. 9. The effect of different granularity in forming histograms and fuzzy sets from data.

The data browser allows different partitions of the domain, and also offers a method of smoothing the frequency distribution before converting to a fuzzy set. Additionally, a fuzzy histogram method is available — instead of partitioning the domain into crisp subsets such as {[0,10), [10, 20), ...} we use a fuzzy partition. In general, any value has membership in two of these fuzzy subsets, and a proportion is counted in each (calculated according to mass assignment theory). This has the outcome of reducing the effect of sudden jumps near partition boundaries and introducing some automatic smoothing into the process. There is still an important choice in determining the number of fuzzy subsets to use in covering the domain

5.3 Rule Testing

The data browser generates Fril rules as its output. These can be tested against the original data or unseen data by a test harness implemented within the data browser. Figure 10 shows the dialog used to drive this process.

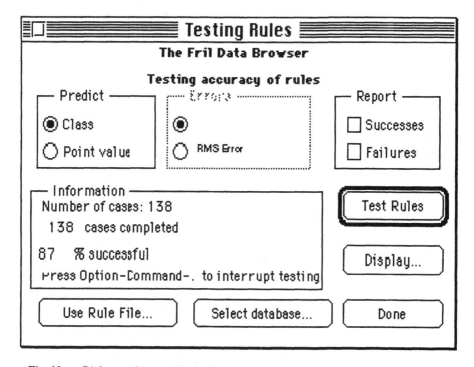

Fig. 10. Dialog used to test the predictive accuracy of rules produced by the data browser. New (unseen) data can be loaded for test purposes.

5.4 Future Development of the Data Browser

The data browser is currently being re-implemented as a suite of objects in the Fril++ language [9, 10]. In addition to components described above, the new system will incorporate clustering methods and the capability to incrementally create rules, i.e. rules which are updated dynamically as data is received rather than being created from a static body of data.

6. Tutorial Example — Ellipse

We consider an artificial problem (see Table 1), to show how the data browser can identify a functional dependency between attributes in the database, and derive rules which make this dependency explicit. Each row (tuple) in the database consists of an index identifying each tuple, an (x, y) pair and a classification of the point (x, y) as legal or illegal. The decision rule for legality is whether or not the point falls within an ellipse, as illustrated in Fig 11. Obviously the entry in the Classification column can be computed from the x-value and y-value; however, it is assumed that this relationship is not known.

Table 1. Artificial problem.

Number	x value	y value	Classification
1	0.3	0.5	legal
2	0.7	1.1	illegal
3	etc.	etc.	etc.

6.1 Use of the Fuzzy Data Browser

Using the x and y features given in the database, Fril is able to derive a set of rules:
((classification of point N is legal) /* IF */
  (xvalue of point N is **xlegal**)
  (yvalue of point N is **ylegal**))
((classification of point N is illegal) /* IF */
  (xvalue of point N is **xillegal**)
  (yvalue of point N is **yillegal**))
where **xlegal, ylegal, xillegal,** and **yillegal** are fuzzy sets derived from the data. Using regularly spaced points, we see in Fig 11 how the classification rules become progressively more accurate with more data. In each case, the boundary is approximately a fuzzy rectangle, rather than an ellipse because of the decomposition error - we should not consider x and y independently when forming the rules, but we should instead consider them jointly. The construction of fuzzy sets on the cross-product space is expensive in computational resources, so we can instead define new features which combine x and y. For example, adding the feature (x-y) to the database used in Fig. 11 (d) increases the classification accuracy from 92% to 94%. Other methods can be used to reduce the decomposition error, as discussed in section 3.

7. Face Recognition

The problem of recognising a face from a 2-dimensional image is a useful testbed for computer vision systems. It has obvious applications in security and access control, and in the provision of user-friendly systems which can recognise a user and adapt to his or her particular mode of working.

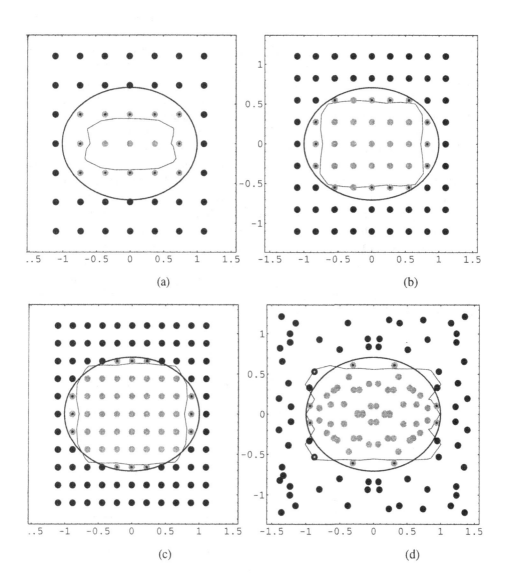

Fig. 11. The Ellipse problem. Three sets of regularly spaced points are shown plus one case of a randomised array of points. Large grey circles represent legal points, and large black circles are illegal points. Where a circle has a smaller point visible in its centre, the Fril rules have made an incorrect prediction. The true and predicted decision boundaries are also shown. Notice that the preponderance of illegal points in (a)—(c) causes the predicted decision boundary to be inside the true boundary.

Here we study a restricted version of the problem, using a dataset taken from the World Wide Web [11, 12], in which the task is to discover whether a face corresponds to a male or a female, given a set of 18 measurements. These measurements are described in Brunelli and Poggio [11] and MIT [12], and refer to features such as thickness of eyebrows, distance from bottom of nose to top of mouth, etc. The features do not concern us here as we seek to produce rules without underlying domain knowledge. The data is therefore treated as a vector of 18 measurements with a label of 0 or 1, and the task is to determine this label from some subset of the other 18.

We adopt a heuristic method to extract a reasonable subset of the 18 features. The data is split arbitrarily into 138 learning cases and 30 test cases. Each attribute is used in turn as the *only* feature in the body of the rule, and those that provide good individual performance are selected for use in a conjunctive fuzzy rule. An alternative heuristic approach to selecting good features is outlined in section 9. We note that this method gives reasonable results, but would not be valid in all cases.

The success rates are shown in Table 2. Features 2, 6, and 14 give a combination of success on the training data and reasonable generalisation (i.e. success on the test data). A rule combining these three features gives even better overall success. It is possible to get success rates of 92—96 % on the training set by careful selection of features; however, these rules do not generalise so well.

Table 2.   Success rates for faces example.

Feature(s) in rule body	Success on training set (%)	Success on test set (%)
Arg2	70	77
Arg3	60	53
Arg4	63	50
Arg5	61	60
Arg6	61	63
Arg7	64	57
Arg8	62	53
Arg9	61	47
Arg10	73	54
Arg11	56	40
Arg12	56	57
Arg13	57	50
Arg14	64	63
Arg15	63	60
Arg16	65	57
Arg17	65	50
Arg18	69	43
Arg19	70	47
Arg2, Arg6, Arg14	83	80

8. Classification of Underwater Sounds

This application [13] concerns the classification of sounds derived from hydrophone recordings, which contain sequences of dolphin sounds set against the ambient noise of the ocean. Dolphins produce whistles, clicks and barks. Recorded audio waveforms have been processed using FFTs resulting in a sequence of instantaneous frequency spectra. Each spectrum is a 32-dimensional multivariate sample giving the instantaneous signal intensity in each of 32 frequency bands linearly spaced over the range 0 to 16 kHz. By way of example, spectral cross-sections from each of four classes of sound are shown in Fig 12. The plots show increasing frequency along the x-axis and increasing acoustical signal power along the y-axis.

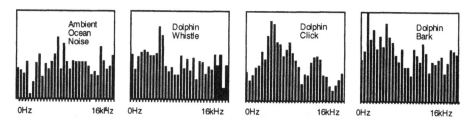

Fig. 12.   Sample frequency spectra for each of the four classes.

The problem is to design a classifier which assigns sample spectra into their correct classes. Separate training and test data sets were used, each containing 3600 spectra drawn in equal number from the four classes above. A high degree of background noise is present in the data, manifested as a comparatively high level of apparently uncorrelated signal across the full frequency range. The random appearance of this noise is evident in the 'ambient' plot in Fig 12. Dolphin whistle sounds appear as a narrow group of correlated high intensity signals superimposed on the ambient noise. The two highest bars in the 'whistle' plot are the whistle signal. Click and bark sounds both appear as a broad spread of low and mid-frequency signals having higher than ambient values. The main distinction between clicks and barks is the duration of the signal — clicks being virtually instantaneous, while bark sounds may be prolonged for up to a few seconds. Due in part to noise and in part to the natural origin of the signals, these sound spectra exhibit a degree of within-class variance often exceeding that between classes. Thus the data set provides a challenging real-world classification problem. An attempt to provide a baseline for comparison of results can be made with reference to results derived using well-known classifier designs. The degree to which the data is resistant to classification is indicated by results of an MoD study quoted by Smith [14]. In this study, many permutations of multi-layer perceptrons were trained and tested on the data. The best result obtained with a multi-layer perceptron is reported as 63.5% of samples being classified correctly.

8.1   Classifier Structure

Structurally, the classifier is organised in two hierarchical levels. At the lower level, a collection of evidential rules describe the instantaneous spectral properties of underwater sounds. The rules at this level may be considered to represent prototypical instances of ocean sound spectra. Generalisation from prototypical cases to other similar instances of sound spectra is empowered through the use of fuzzy feature values within the prototypes. Each prototype is augmented with a symbolic label that describes the class of sound from which its features were derived. For classification of 32-dimensional dolphin sound spectra based on four classes of training data, knowledge of the domain is represented using four evidential rules. The rules are in standard Fril syntax and are of the form <head> IF <body> : <list of support pairs>.

((class of sample is *ambient* if)
        (evlog
                ((feature 1 of sample is $f_{amb,1}$) $w_{amb,1}$
                 ...
                 ...
                (feature 32 of sample is $f_{amb,32}$) $w_{amb,32}$))) : ((1 1)(0 0))
((class of sample is *whistle* if)
        (evlog
                ((feature 1 of sample is $f_{whs,1}$) $w_{whs,1}$
                 ...
                 ...
                (feature 32 of sample is $f_{whs,32}$) $w_{whs,32}$))) : ((1 1)(0 0))

((class of sample is *click* if)
        (evlog
                ((feature 1 of sample is $f_{clk,1}$) $w_{clk,1}$
                 ...
                 ...
                (feature 32 of sample is $f_{clk,32}$) $w_{clk,32}$))) : ((1 1)(0 0))

((class of sample is *bark* if)
        (evlog
                ((feature 1 of sample is $f_{brk,1}$) $w_{brk,1}$
                 ...
                 ...
                (feature 32 of sample is $f_{brk,32}$) $w_{brk,32}$))) : ((1 1)(0 0))

Here the f_{ij} are fuzzy sets defining the jth feature of the ith class of sound spectra, and the w_{ij} are weights of importance corresponding to those features.

Rules of this form are adequate to describe the instantaneous spectral properties of underwater sounds, but are unable to capture temporal features of those sounds. We require therefore to construct a higher level of knowledge which relates to the way in which the different classes of sound behave through time. Such knowledge is acquired by converting the numeric form of the training data into its symbolic representation (using the lower level rules described above) and then by treating short sequences of sample classifications as symbolic feature vectors. Effectively, this process transforms samples from the 32-dimensional Euclidean space into a discrete space based on the set of class labels. In terms of the task of classifying ocean sounds, if we let α denote the set of class-labels {ambient, whistle, click, bark}, and arbitrarily choose to look at sequences of nine samples, then the act of classifying nine samples defines a feature vector in $\{\alpha_1, ..., \alpha_9\}$. In practice a further reduction in dimensionality is enabled by taking the feature vectors in $\{\alpha_1, ..., \alpha_9\}$ and counting the occurrences of class-labels in them to form a final feature vector in $\{N_1, ..., N_4\}$ which we denote as $\mathbf{x} = \{x_1 \, x_2 \, x_3 \, x_4\}$. Here the x_i represent the number of labels 'ambient', 'whistle', 'click' and 'bark' respectively, counted during the classification of a sequence of nine samples. These feature vectors are presented as input sample data to the higher level system of evidential rules. By characterising sequences of samples, projected into a space characterised by their classifications, knowledge of the temporal behaviour of the data may be explored. In terms of the dolphin sound classification problem, temporal knowledge is expressed using the higher level set of evidential rules:

((class of sample-sequence is *ocean-ambient* if)

    (evlog

        ((feature 1 of sequence is $f_{amb,1}$) $w_{amb,1}$

        ...

        ...

        (feature 4 of sequence is $f_{amb,4}$) $w_{amb,4}$))) : ((1 1)(0 0))

((class of sample-sequence is *dolph-whistle* if)

    (evlog

        ((feature 1 of sequence is $f_{whs,1}$) $w_{whs,1}$

        ...

        ...

        (feature 4 of sequence is $f_{whs,4}$) $w_{whs,4}$))) : ((1 1)(0 0))

((class of sample-sequence is *dolph-click* if)

    (evlog

        ((feature 1 of sequence is $f_{clk,1}$) $w_{clk,1}$

        ...

        ...

        (feature 4 of sequence is $f_{clk,4}$) $w_{clk,4}$))) : ((1 1)(0 0))

((class of sample-sequence is *dolph-bark* if)

    (evlog

        ((feature 1 of sequence is $f_{brk,1}$) $w_{brk,1}$

        ...

        ...

        (feature 4 of sequence is $f_{brk,4}$) $w_{brk,4}$))) : ((1 1)(0 0))

As before, the $\mathbf{f}_{ij}$ and w_{ij} are fuzzy feature values and weights respectively, but here the $\mathbf{f}_{ij}$ have membership functions over the domain 'number of sample classifications'. However, the membership functions may be constructed by the same methods used for the lower level features.

Description of the aggregate behaviour of classes of sound using these higher level rules enables a robust characterisation of time-varying features such as click sounds. (In terms solely of their sample classifications, clicks appear to be a sequence of ambient spectra broken for a short period by a bark-like signal.) In addition the higher level rules allow robust classification of noisy time-invariant signals, by incorporating several views of the signal into the derivation of a classification hypothesis, and thus capitalising on redundancy in the signal.

Considering the two levels of knowledge described above, it is evident that, once appropriate feature values and weights of importance are known, it is a simple matter to format these into statements of evidential logic. Evidential logic rules thus defined may be executed as Fril program code and are therefore simultaneously a statement of domain knowledge and an implementation of a pattern classifier. To give some idea of the relative performance of this method, we quote (in Table 3) results obtained using a range of other methods. Further details are in Baldwin, Gooch and Martin [13] and Smith [14].

Table 3. Results of various approaches to classifying underwater sounds.

Method	Result
Supervised Connectionist Learning	
Multi-Layer Perceptron	63.5%
Hybrid Spread-Network/Time Delay NN with hand-crafted receptive fields.	92%
Statistical Pattern Classification	
Closest Class Mean	72.3%
k-Nearest Neighbours	83.0%
Unsupervised Connectionist Learning	
Rumelhart-Zipser	50.5%
Kohonen SO Map	71%
Fuzzy Learning	
Data Browser (evidential logic rules)	89%
Hand Optimised Rules	92%

The results show several interesting characteristics. In particular, the absolute best results both stem from classifier implementations where a little 'human intervention' was applied to optimise the handling of features. However some of the fully automated methods do not lag far behind in performance. Overall, the results indicate the difficulty posed by noisy real-world problems, particularly in respect of learning.

9. A Database of Experimental Measurements

9.1 The Problem

The measurement of aquifer dispersivities is a significant component in modelling the flow of water in rock formations. Predicting the movement and spread of contamination in water supplies is an important application where aquifer dispersivities must be determined accurately. Unfortunately, experimental measurements show a scale dependence which is not predicted by theory; thus values determined experimentally in laboratories are not generally useful in predicting values to be used in large-scale calculations. Some experiments have been performed in the field (i.e. measurements are taken on real aquifers, rather than in the laboratory) and these have been examined closely for use in predicting values to be used in calculations. For example, Gelhar, Welty and Rehfeldt [15] examined a number of field experiments and tabulated over 100 results. These results form our database, which exhibits:

- discrete and continuous data;

- incompleteness (not all experiments take the same set of measurements, so there are gaps in the data);

- uncertainty (many values are quoted as ranges of possible values);

- unreliability (the authors classify each experiment as high, medium, and low reliability).

All of these features are easy to model in Fril. Where ranges appear in the data, these have been modelled by possibility distributions. There are 18 attributes in the database, and 116 tuples. The database attributes are listed in Table 4.

Table 4. Database attributes.

Attribute	Description
Site and Experiment Number	unique identifier for each row in the database (57 sites)
Aquifer Thickness	[0 - 1000] m
Experiment Scale	[0 - 100 000] m
Longitudinal Dispersivity	[0 - 45000]
Transverse Dispersivity	[0 - 1500]
Vertical Dispersivity	[0 - 1]
Material	Sand, Gravel, Alluvial Deposits, ... (26 rock types in total))
Effective Porosity	[0-100] %
Hydraulic Conductivity	$[10^{-8} - 10^{-1}]$
Hydraulic Transmissivity	$[10^{-8} - 20]$
Velocity	[0 - 220]
Flow Configuration	Ambient, Radial Converging, Radial Diverging ...(8 in total))
Monitoring	two-dimensional or three-dimensional
Tracer	Br, Tritium, fluorescein, ... (29 in total)
Input Method	pulse, contamination, step, or environmental
Data Interpretation	2-D Numerical, 1-D Uniform Flow Solution, ... (15 in total)
Reliability	low, reasonable, or high

Much of the data is incomplete, since investigators use different experimental set-ups and methods of analysing data. There is also uncertainty in values, due to the difficulty in measuring or estimating data. Finally, we note that the database is defined on both discrete and continuous domains.

9.2 Use of the Fuzzy Data Browser

To illustrate the fuzzy data browser, we show how rules may be derived which predict one attribute (longitudinal dispersivity) from other attributes. As a rule of thumb, experts in the field recognise that the scale of the experiment and the longitudinal dispersivity are approximately linearly related, although this relationship is not predicted by most theoretical models. Because both quantities vary over several orders of magnitude in the database, it is easier to work in terms of the derived features, Log(Longitudinal Dispersivity) and Log(Experiment Scale), referred to below as LogDispersivity and LogScale. These are defined by Fril rules. The aim is to predict LogDispersivity by means of rules involving the other attributes. The longitudinal, transverse, and vertical dispersivity attributes are omitted from the set of attributes to be considered; also, the material was not considered as no expertise was available to define a similarity relation on the universe of rock types.

Initially, five evidential logic rules were formed, using all available attributes. The LogDispersivity domain is split into five classes LogDispClass1-5, as in Fig 13. Each rule then has the form:

((Predicted value for LogDisp in case (SITEEXPERIMENTNUMBER) is LogDispClass$_i$)

    (evlog

        ((value of LogScale in case (SITEEXPERIMENTNUMBER) is LogScaleClass$_i$) w_{i1}

        (value of Velocity in case (SITEEXPERIMENTNUMBER)) is VelocityClass$_i$) w_{i2})

        ...etc. ...)) : ((1 1) (0 0))

where LogScaleClass$_i$ is a fuzzy set derived from the data, and wij are importances. By examining the importances (as shown in Table 5), we see that LogScale is the most important feature in all cases. As a heuristic in determining the most important features, we also show in Table 5 the average importance of each feature, and calculate its average relative importance as follows.

Let the weight of the ith feature in the jth rule be w_{ij}. The average importance of feature i is:

$$imp_i = \frac{\sum\limits_{j=1}^{m} w_{ij}}{m}$$

where m is the number of rules, and the average relative importance is:

$$\frac{imp_i - \frac{1}{n}}{n}$$

where n is the number of features in the rule (i.e. the number of attributes considered). If features were all equally important, the average relative importance of each feature would be zero. Using this formula we can see which features are more important, and which could perhaps be neglected. In this case, we obtain the results shown in Table 5. Clearly LogScale is the most important feature, followed by the data interpretation method and the effective porosity. In this case, it is not clear whether the high importance of the data interpretation method is valid, since it might be appropriate to define a similarity relation on the domain — for example, cluster together the two-dimensional models, the three-dimensional models, etc.

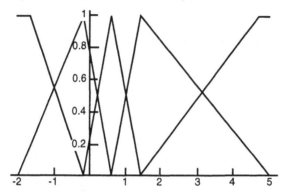

Fig. 13. Fuzzy sets on the Log Dispersivity domain. The sets were chosen automatically by the system, to ensure a roughly equal number of cases in each class. These are referred to in Table 5 as LogDisp Class1 (leftmost fuzzy set) to LogDisp Class5 (rightmost fuzzy set).

Table 5. Importances of each attribute in predicting LogDisp.

	LogDisp Class 1	LogDisp Class 2	LogDisp Class 3	LogDisp Class 4	LogDisp Class 5	Average importance	Average relative importance
LogScale	0.209	0.224	0.198	0.206	0.236	0.215	1.3607
Reliability	0.057	0.014	0.035	0.119	0.109	0.067	-0.266
DataInterpretation	0.119	0.111	0.128	0.126	0.108	0.118	0.3033
InputMethod	0.133	0.136	0.089	0.055	0.061	0.095	0.0396
Thickness	0.061	0.069	0.065	0.065	0.053	0.063	-0.312
HydraulicConductivity	0.049	0.057	0.056	0.060	0.047	0.054	-0.408
HydraulicTransmissivity	0.051	0.059	0.059	0.060	0.047	0.055	-0.395
EffectivePorosity	0.138	0.125	0.091	0.106	0.122	0.117	0.2829
Velocity	0.069	0.078	0.128	0.088	0.063	0.085	-0.061
FlowConfiguration	0.112	0.060	0.053	0.092	0.119	0.087	-0.04
Monitoring	0.002	0.067	0.097	0.023	0.036	0.045	-0.505

Clearly this approach may neglect a feature which is important in one rule but not in any of the others; however, it is adequate in this example. There are two indicators we use to assess the performance of rules. Consider a row in the database. We take the values for the attributes in the bodies of the rules, and find the support for each head, i.e. we obtain:

LogDispClass1 : S1
LogDispClass2 : S2
LogDispClass3 : S3
LogDispClass4 : S4
LogDispClass5 : S5

Comparison of the support pairs S1 — S5 allows us to choose a class from this list; if the actual data value falls within this class, the example has been correctly classified. Alternatively, we can calculate an 'expected value' as discussed in section 3 and compare it to the true value in the database. The average error in the expected value gives an indication of how well the rules perform. The evidential logic rules with all features classify 87% of cases correctly, and give an average error of 9.6% in predicting the point value.

Fuzzy logic rules were generated using the most important three features, LogScale, DataInterpretation, and EffectivePorosity. These rules classify 88% of cases into the correct fuzzy category for LogDispersivity, and give an average error of only 7% when predicting a point value (see Fig 14, where results for LogScale with DataInterpretation and LogScale with Effective Porosity are also shown).

Creating evidential logic rules on the three most important attributes (LogScale, EffectivePorosity, and DataInterpretation) confirms the indication from Table 5, that LogScale is the single most important attribute (see Table 6).

Table 6. Most important attributes.

	LogDisp Class 1	LogDisp Class 2	LogDisp Class 3	LogDisp Class 4	LogDisp Class 5	Average importance	Average relative importance
LogScale	0.448	0.487	0.474	0.470	0.507	0.477	0.4313
DataInterpretation	0.256	0.241	0.307	0.287	0.231	0.265	-0.206
EffectivePorosity	0.296	0.272	0.218	0.243	0.262	0.258	-0.225

Using just the LogScale attribute to build rules gives a prediction rate of 80% and an average error of 9% in the point value predicted by the rule (see Fig 14). This is in accordance with the expert view, that LogScale and LogDispersivity are roughly linearly related. In Fig 14(a), all data points are included; in (b)-(d), one very uncertain point has been omitted from the plots for clarity, although it was used in the calculations.

Figure 14 shows (a) prediction on the basis of LogScale alone — classification success 80%, average error in predicted point value 9%; (b) prediction using LogScale and EffectivePorosity — classification success 79%, average error in predicted point value 8%; (c) prediction using LogScale and DataInterpretation — classification success 85%, average error in predicted point value 8%; (d) prediction using LogScale, EffectivePorosity and DataInterpretation — classification success 88%, average error in predicted point value 7%.

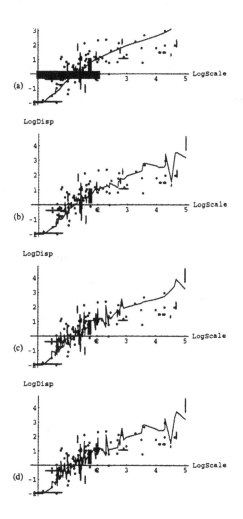

Fig. 14.   Predicted and actual value of LogDispersivity plotted against LogScale.

It is noticeable that the curve predicted in (a) is considerably smoother than in the cases where two or more attributes are considered, since there is no third/fourth dimension to consider in (a). The extra degrees of freedom afforded by considering additional attributes may fit the existing data better, but the rule is less general, i.e. it is less good at predicting unknown cases.

10. Conclusions

The methods described in this paper are based on the unifying theoretical framework of mass assignment theory, which allows us to deal with both fuzzy and probabilistic uncertainty. The fuzzy data browser is a working implementation of these ideas, giving a useful tool in fuzzy modelling. It allows large tables of data to be summarised with a flat or hierarchical set of rules, which can be output as Fril fuzzy or evidential logic rules. The Fril rules can be executed efficiently and also understood easily by a human expert. Each rule corresponds to a summary of several 'similar' cases in the database into a fuzzy prototypical rule. The value in a new case then corresponds to an interpolation between these fuzzy prototypes. The browser can be used to explore intuition about the underlying relationships in the data, or left to run autonomously and discover relations which can be presented to the user. In addition to the examples above, the fuzzy data browser has been used to extract fuzzy models in diverse areas such as:

- monitoring data from an aircraft black-box flight recorder, to detect anomalous readings — these either indicate that a piece of equipment is malfunctioning, or that measurements are being reported incorrectly;

- detecting change in satellite images;

- generating rules for hand-written character recognition.

Further work is examining use of genetic programming to generate compound features. A general implementation of the data browser using the Fril++ fuzzy object-oriented programming language is under way, which should lead to a framework for the user to custom-build a data browser for a specific application.

References

1. Baldwin J F, Martin T P and Pilsworth B W: 'FRIL manual (version 4.0)', Fil Systems Ltd, Bristol Business Centre, Maggs House, Queens Road, Bristol, BS8 1QX, UK (1988).

2. Baldwin J F, Martin T P and Pilsworth B W: 'FRIL — fuzzy and evidential reasoning in AI', Research Studies Press, John Wiley (1995).

3. Baldwin J F: 'A theory of mass assignments for artificial intelligence', Proc IJCAI Workshop on fuzzy Logic, Australia (1991).

4. Baldwin J F: 'The management of fuzzy and probabilistic uncertainties for knowledge based systems', in Shapiro S A (Ed): 'Encylopedia of AI', John Wiley, pp 528—537 (2nd edition) (1992).

5.   Baldwin J F: 'Mass assignments and fuzzy sets for fuzzy databases', in Fedrizzi M, Kacprzyk J and Yager R R (Eds): 'Advances in the Shafter Dempster Theory of Evidence', John Wiley (1992)

6.   Baldwin J F: 'Knowledge from data using Fril and fuzzy methods', in Baldwin J F (Ed): 'Fuzzy Logic in AI', pp 33—76 John Wiley (1996).

7.   Baldwin J F, Martin T P and Pilsworth B W: 'Genetic programming for automatic feature discovery in a fuzzy data browser', to be published.

8.   Silverman B W: 'Density estimation for statistics and data analysis', Chapman & Hall (1986).

9.   Baldwin J F and Martin T P: 'Fuzzy objects and multiple inheritance in Fril++', Proc EUFIT-96, Aachen, pp 680—684, Germany (1996).

10. Baldwin J F, Martin T P and Vargas-Vera M D S: 'Frill++: object-oriented fuzzy logic programming', submitted for publication.

11. Brunelli R and Poggio T: 'Caricatural effects in automated face perception', Biological Cybernetics, 69, pp 235—241 (1993).

12. MIT: http://www.ai.mit.edu/projects/cbcl/old-course9.520/faces (1995).

13. Baldwin J F, Gooch R M and Martin T P: 'Fuzzy processing of hydrophone sounds', Fuzzy Sets and Systems, 77, No 1, pp 35—48 (1996).

14. Smith D: 'The application of artificial neural networks to the classification of underwater cetacean sounds', Exeter (1993).

15. Gelhar L W, Welty C and Rehfeldt K R: 'A critical review of data in field-scale dispersion in aquifiers', Water Resources Research, 28, No 7, pp 1955—1974 (1992).

Towards Soft Computing

E H Mamdani

Department of Electrical and Electronic Engineering, Imperial College,
Exhibition Road, London, SW7 2BT, UK.
E-mail: e.mamdani@ic.ac.uk

It is not clear who coined the term soft computing but one of its greatest promoters has been none other than Lotfi Zadeh — the inventor of fuzzy sets theory. He sees soft computing as an extension of fuzzy logic by merging it with neural networks, (or neurocomputing — NC as he puts it) and evolutionary computing. He should certainly be acknowledged as the earliest founders of soft computing which he promoted as head of the Berkeley Initiative in Soft Computing — the BISC group. Zadeh advocates soft fomputing as the means by which we may go beyond what AI has been able to achieve during its 40 years' existence. In this paper we try and look more deeply into what Zadeh has to say about both the motivation for and the methodology of soft computing.

1. Introduction

Symbolic logic is the cornerstone of AI, but we should look at its developments once again. It is not coincidental that the Greek classical period is credited both with heralding a major departure in the history of mankind and also with the first statements by Aristotle on the rules of Logic. Kitto [1], in his history of the Greeks, gives a fine insight into the mind of the Greeks. Not only the philosophers, but artists and politicians as well, started discussing and referring to abstract, that is to say, universal knowledge dealing both with natural phenomena and human affairs. This is knowledge not just about everyday, individual events, but about regularities behind such events — about invariances if you like — and composed of universal statements. Such abstract knowledge is moral laws, political theories and what we now regard as scientific knowledge. It is often said that "Plato's philosophy rejects scientific rationalism (establishing facts through experiment) in favour of arguments, because mind, not matter, is fundamental, and material objects are merely imperfect copies of abstract and eternal ideas". But perhaps, this is reading too much into Plato. There was no scientific knowledge at that time in the form we recognise it today. Plato may have been simply emphasising the use of human reason in elucidating such knowledge. Plato also

This paper was given as a keynote address at the Expert systems 95 conference and first appeared in the proceedings of that conference. It is reprinted here with their permission.

believed this knowledge to be present in nature so that it could be discovered if one looked deeper beyond everyday life. What we call Plato's epistemology is the belief that there is an absolute perfect knowledge out there that we as scientists can go and try to discover. We can apply scientific rationality to this view of knowledge by both experimentation and a deeper, rigorous enquiry through reductionism. This is the view of the world adopted by most scientists and particularly the mainstream AI community. Below we argue that this is an inappropriate view and in the case of AI, where normal scientific experiments are not possible, it has prevented useful advances to be made.

2. There is Logic and there is Fuzzy Logic

Other civilisations before the Greeks had also acquired worthwhile abstract knowledge. However, they mainly went about using it and applying it, whereas the Greeks discussed it critically. Now, in order to discuss abstract knowledge, which is made up of universal (i.e. in the language of predicate calculus, universally quantified) statements, it is necessary to carry out logical deductions. It is not surprising, therefore, that rules of logic were also first articulated in that same period by Aristotle. According to him one of the main principles of logic was the law of excluded middle. Like Plato he too believed that his logic was a discovery about the law of nature. (It is stated that Descartes questioned how we know the Aristotelian laws of logic to be correct, but concluded that God would not deceive us.) His laws were accepted without any questions for 2000 years.

In the last 100 years or so, the realisation has gradually dawned on philosophers and mathematicians that logic and mathematics are not creations of nature (or God) that man gets to discover, but creations of the human mind and as such they are inventions not too dissimilar to other physical objects man has invented. Boole's book on the "Laws of Thought .." should be a required reading for all AI workers even remotely dealing with logic. This is the book that launched symbolic logic but less than half of it deals with just binary logic; the rest of the book is concerned with the part played by logic in conjunction with probability theory. The second part is really about probability logic but few AI workers know of it. Reading Boole in a critical fashion leaves a question in one's mind: 'Are his laws of thought a **description** of how humans actually think, or a **prescription** of how they ought to think?' If a description, then they are a discovery, originally that of Aristotle and put in a symbolic form by Boole. If a prescription, then they are an invention and then the Cartesian question must be asked again: 'How do we know that they are correct?' Surprisingly this question was seldom discussed at any length by philosophers. Russell also took logic for granted and indeed strived to make it supreme by trying to show that all of mathematics can be shown to rest on logic. Here is what he felt afterwards:

I wanted certainty in the kind of way in which people want religious faith. I thought that certainty is more likely to be found in mathematics than elsewhere. But I discovered that many mathematical demonstrations, which my teachers wanted me to accept, were full of fallacies, and that, if certainty were ever discoverable in mathematics, it would be in a new field of mathematics, with more solid foundations than those that had hitherto been thought secure. But as the work proceeded, I was continually reminded of the fable about the elephant and the tortoise. Having constructed an elephant upon which the mathematical world rested, I found the elephant tottering, and proceeded to construct a tortoise to keep the elephant from falling. But the tortoise was no more secure than the elephant, and after some twenty years of very arduous toil, I came to the conclusion that there was nothing more I could do in the way of making mathematical knowledge indubitable.

Kline [2] quotes the above passage and goes on to discuss how Russell's difficulties led the Intuitionists to found a new logic that questioned the very founding principle of logic — the law of excluded middle. He says: "This principle, which asserts that every meaningful statement is true or false arose historically in the application of reasoning to finite sets and was abstracted therefrom. Then it was accepted as an independent *a priori* principle and was unjustifiably applied to infinite sets. Whereas for finite sets one can decide whether all elements possess a certain property by testing each one, this procedure is not possible for infinite sets." He then quotes Weyl (one of the founders of the Intuitionist school) thus:

This is the fall and original sin of set theory, for which it is justly punished by the antinomies. It is not that such contradictions showed up that is surprising, but that they showed up at such a late stage of the game.

But they do not seem to have showed up in many AI logicians closed world as yet. Few students are made aware of intuitionistic logic. Many workers continue to cite the lack of the law of excluded middle in fuzzy logic as the reason for rejecting it, whereas it may be argued that the boot is on the other foot.

AI's response to the difficulties caused by the law of the excluded middle has been to invent non-monotonic logics, and mechanisms for belief revision. That itself is an indication that in practical AI systems, there needs to be an explicit way of dealing with what is not represented in the conceptualisation of any specific problem. Every practical application must decide what to represent and what to leave out as only a finite number of things can be represented on computers. The granularity of the conceptualisation must be determined in order to build practical applications. Fuzzy logic can be considered as a way of dealing with the residue, having decided upon an appropriate granularity for the problem at hand. The fact that this leads to lack of the law of excluded middle should surprise no one. It is for this reason that Zadeh says that "within soft computing, the principle contribution of fuzzy logic is a methodology for exploiting the tolerance for imprecision to achieve tractability, robustness, low solution cost and better rapport with reality".

2.1   The Uniqueness Argument

An argument often used against Fuzzy logic has been that whatever can be done using fuzzy logic can be done by other more established methods. When fuzzy logic was first used for control — the so-called fuzzy control — then control engineers argued that fuzzy logic is not necessary as the conventional control theory can already deal with all the control problems (or at least the kind of control problems that most papers on fuzzy control used). More recently Bayesians have stated that the Bayesian approach can be used to replicate the results achieved by fuzzy control. At first sight such arguments are persuasive, and indeed the fuzzy control workers countered them by stating that fuzzy control need only be used where conventional techniques were not easy to use, for example, when it was difficult to derive a mathematical model of the system for one reason or another. In retrospect this has turned out to be incorrect.

Looked at closely, these are not scientific arguments at all but territorial ones. At a scientific level one finds that what was tacitly assumed could only be done by conventional approaches was shown to be possible by rather an unconventional approach of rule based control using fuzzy logic to interpret the rules. Fuzzy control is thus an alternative approach which works. Indeed it has many advantages over the conventional method and that is the reason why it has been so widely adopted in industry. This method is now considered part of a new approach to control and is called intelligent control. It must be said that many practitioners of fuzzy control have themselves failed to realise that there are two separate elements in fuzzy control — the rule-base of empirical knowledge and fuzzy logic used to interpret the rules. The successful use of fuzzy control does not just 'validate' fuzzy logic alone but also 'validates' the empirical knowledge contained in the rules. We will return to this issue later.

In the case of Bayesian logic, it should surprise no one that the Bayes approach can replicate the results of fuzzy control. As long as the same empirical knowledge is used and as long as the two logics are not invalid then they should both give similar results. The fact that the Bayes approach works is not a scientific argument for showing that fuzzy logic is invalid.

Could such uniqueness arguments be the result of a misguided Platonic epistemology? This amounts to the belief that there is only one form of perfect knowledge out there to be discovered and that once one instance of it has been discovered, then any alternative form is either itself invalid or is attempting to prove the existing knowledge invalid. In the case of Bayesian logic there is yet another tacit belief that is brought into question by the advocacy of fuzzy logic, and that is the use of the bell shaped curve by fuzzy set theorists. We have all been educated to believe that all bell shaped curves must be expressions of some statistical process and no one should use such a curve without acknowledging it as some probability distribution function. One suspects that it is the use of the bell shaped curve that is really behind the objections of the Bayesians. However, no purely scientific court has ever grated such a copyright and that court does not acknowledge historical right of way, quite the opposite.

2.2   Reductionism in AI

It is generally believed that given a Platonic epistemology, science advances by a reductionist approach. That is, a given problem has to be reduced to its bare essentials and studied at great depth and with extreme rigour — where rigour is interpreted as the use of mathematical symbolism. This approach may well work when studying the physical world where one is concerned with discovering new empirical knowledge. However, the approach is of doubtful use when applied to computer science and particularly to AI. Someone once remarked that all the disciplines that have a science in their title are not sciences. This remark actually states that science is really about descriptive knowledge and many of the disciplines that have science in their title are largely dealing with prescriptive knowledge. Even so, it is possible to study prescriptive knowledge with something approaching scientific rationalism. As we shall see below, prescriptive models should fit real world problems and should not have obvious inconsistencies. Such models should be falsifiable, but may not be unique in representing a given reality. In any case, their mathematical form, and internal symmetry or nice closure properties are never appropriate scientific grounds for adopting or rejecting them.

After 40 years of AI one gets the feeling that while there are many people working in AI, there is very little AI being done. An immense amount of output of a mathematical nature is not helping to advance the field, and is often concerned with stating the obvious and trivial using mathematical symbolism. The chief motivation within AI must always come from good intuition that has first to be implemented and only later mathematised to investigate its limitations. The underlying motivation of Soft computing should be that AI systems are open systems that may not be reducible to closed mathematical models. But old habits die hard, career advances require publications, mathematical investigations provide a path of least resistance to obtaining publications and so, even in the field of fuzzy logic and soft computing the reductionist approach will, one suspects, continue.

An unfortunate consequence of applying such a mistaken scientific approach in AI has been that some of the major questions underlying AI have not been tackled. One such is how the neuronal fabric of the brain manages to achieve mental, cognitive behaviour. That is to say, is there any way we can reconcile the two major branches of AI — neural network research and cognitive processing? Another similar question is the part played by the various sensory inputs and many communicative actions in carrying out cognitive processing. In other words how can we bring together the fields of HCI and AI, which to-day are taken as totally different disciplines.

3. An Appropriate Epistemology for AI

An alternative way of looking at the nature of knowledge and particularly scientific knowledge is that put forward by Sir Karl Popper [3]. Popper's epistemology is particularly relevant to AI and so a short examination of it here is considered useful.

As far as the scientific method is concerned we owe it to Popper who has pointed out that all knowledge is conjecture. Scientific knowledge should be falsifiable and that theories are not proved they can only be falsified. For theories to be accepted as scientific it is necessary that they should be stated in such a way that there are clear tests that can be used to falsify them. Unfortunately, often knowledge that purports to be scientific is stated such that it is immunized against falsification. As far as logical systems are concerned, what this means is that we cannot validate any logic, but only try and invalidate one. As long as a logical system is not known to be invalid, we are at liberty to use it. Competing logical systems are simply trying to provide rules for constructing arguments concerning the empirical world around us using particular nuances of language in a valid way. Imprecise concepts, possibilities (as opposed to probabilities), quantifiers other than existential and universal, such as some, many, a few, most, are all examples of soft concepts that we have collectively agreed to use for constructing meaningful and important arguments. Note this emphasis on falsifiability of knowledge itself amounts to a rejection of the law of the excluded middle at the philosophical and meta-logical level.

Another important but less known of Popper's many contributions is the notion of world 3. According to him, World 1 is 'the world of physical objects, or the world of physical states'. World 2 is 'the world of states of consciousness, or the world of mental states, or the world of dispositions to act'. Now most AI workers would contend that the field of AI investigates, or is inspired by, the phenomena of this world 2. However, Popper maintains that we also have a world 3 which is the world of objective content of thought scientific, poetic thought and works of art. Other contents of world 3 are: theoretical systems, problems, problem situations, critical arguments, the contents of journals or books and so on. He says, "Traditional epistemology has studied knowledge or thought in a subjective sense ... While knowledge in the sense of .. "I know" belongs to world 2, the world of subjects, scientific knowledge belongs to world 3, to the world of objective theories, objective problems and objective arguments".

Popper gives various theses regarding World 3 that are all relevant here:

- traditional epistemology based on world 2 is irrelevant to the study of scientific knowledge;

- the study of a largely autonomous world 3 of objective knowledge is of a decisive importance for epistemology;

- an objective epistemology that studies world 3 can help to throw an immense amount of light upon world 2, but the converse is not true;

- World 3 is a natural product of the human animal comparable to a spider's web (Dawkins [4] will call this the extended phenotype);

- World 3 is largely autonomous;

- it is through this interaction between ourselves and world 3 that objective knowledge grows and that there is close analogy between the growth (or the evolution) of knowledge and biological evolution [5].

This shows world 3 to be quite different from Plato's ideal knowledge. It is man made, composed of conjectures subject to falsification. It is full of imperfections, antinomies and paradoxes. As scientists we need to treat it with humility and there can never be room for arrogance and certainty.

The problem of reconciling symbolic and sub-symbolic computation arises because our view is based on traditional epistemology focused upon world 2 alone. There is an intimate and a fascinating relationship between language and world 3 and a significant amount of human evolution has occurred in the area of language and world 3. An understanding of this evolution ought to be a matter of great concern to those dealing with AI. Language must have evolved rapidly during the classical Greek period to furnish proper terminology to carry out rational and logical arguments. This terminology and the arguments are not private thought processes but in the public domain of world 3. It is not enough that an individual convinces himself of the correctness of any argument. He must articulate it in such a way that it can in principle be falsified by his peers. Such an extension of the language to permit rational arguments is itself an invention arrived at as a consensus by human society. Once it becomes publicly accepted, i.e. a part of World 3, its rules can be discovered. These are the laws of thought; they are the laws of a human invention and are themselves subject to critical rational analysis.

Furthermore, cognitive processes are also conscious events, and conscious activities are not just related to internal world 2 representations. Conscious thought occurs [6] only when those internal representations get translated into public domain World 3 representations. It is not enough that the soft computing program is understood simply as building applications that variously combine the mathematical models of fuzzy logic, genetic algorithms, neural networks and probabilistic reasoning, etc. The soft computing paradigm must take into account the existence of world 3, its nature and how it has evolved and above all how we individually interact with it. For if we are going to build intelligent machines then we need to decide whether such machines will create their own world 3 that will not be shared by the humans or will they be built around the wealth of world 3 that we humans have evolved over our long existence on this planet. It is important that all further advance in AI takes on board a good symbiosis between man and machine, or carbon and silicon as a colleague recently put it.

4. Conclusions

Soft computing should not be seen merely as a licence to merge fuzzy logic with genetic algorithms and neural networks. It is really about open and interacting intelligent systems. It is also about a better communication between man and machine, though again this should not be understood as more of the same old HCI.

Boole's work, both in its well-known binary form as well as its less well-known probabilistic form is one of the well springs of AI. However, it needs to be brought up to date. Both classical binary and probabilistic logic accept the Aristotelian law of the excluded middle as an immutable law of nature. Belief in that immutability is no more than an act of faith and has no scientific basis. Indeed its limitations have forced AI workers to invent non-monotonic systems of belief revision, and theories of belief functions that permit an explicit representation of ignorance. Fuzzy logic is just another way of acknowledging that any representation of a finite granularity will have residue.

Popper's philosophy and epistemology are particular relevant to AI. The emphasis on falsifiability rather than proof and validity shows world 3 knowledge to be always imperfect, tentative and arbitrary which we accept either as an act of pure faith or if we wish to be rational about it, accept it tentatively until we find that it can be falsified. The assertion and certainty of a unique model belongs to the realm of faith rather than scientific enquiry.

From the day we are born we get exposed not just to the physical world of objects around us (world 1) but also to an immensely complex world of objective knowledge (world 3). Our brain develops in the presence of this world 3 and there can be no doubt that its development is affected by world 3. It is imperative that AI workers ask how a computer is to be exposed to world 3 and how man and machine share this world 3. The soft computing paradigm has to be based on a Popperian epistemology.

References

1. Kitto H D F: 'The Greeks', Penguin Books (1962).

2. Kline M: 'Mathematics — The Loss of Certainty', Oxford University Press (1980).

3. Miller D (Ed): 'Popper Selections', Princeton Paperbacks (1985).

4. Dawkins R: 'The Extended Phenotype', Oxford University Press (1983).

5. Dawkins R: ' The Selfish Gene', Oxford University Press (1978).

6. Dennett D C: 'Consciousness Explained', Penguin Science (1993).

Section 4

Machine Intelligence

The Rise of Machine Intelligence

H S Nwana[1], N Azarmi[1] and R Smith[2]

[1] Intelligent Systems Research, Advanced Applications & Technology Department,
BT Laboratories, Martlesham Heath, Ipswich, Suffolk, IP5 7RE, UK.
E-mail: azarmin@info.bt.co.uk/hyacinth@info.bt.co.uk
[2] Department of Electrical and Electronic Engineering, Imperial College,
Exhibition Road, London, SW7 2BT, UK.

This paper provides a brief historical introduction to the machine intelligence endeavour, and to the discipline of artificial intelligence (AI) whose techniques are employed in building intelligent software systems. It also presents some AI success stories both outside and within BT.

1. Introduction

We draw from the prologue of Kurzweil's excellent book, *The Age of Intelligent Machines* [1], in order to chronicle briefly the genesis of the dream of machine intelligence.

We are currently in the thick of the second Industrial Revolution. The first arguably began when a young Englishman, John Kay, invented his new machine for weaving cloth. Though he died penniless, because he spent all his money on litigation attempting to enforce the patent he had obtained for his invention, little did he know that he had set in motion a revolution that will see the automation of all aspects of the production of cloth by the end of the eighteenth century.

Good ideas are infectious, and others in other industries observed the dramatic rise in productivity that automation had brought to English textiles. The next two centuries after Kay's invention saw the spread of mechanisation to other industries and countries including the rest of Europe, the United States and Japan. The economies of nations shifted from agrarian and craft economies to ones dominated by machines. The chain of successive improvements in automation continues, as we know, to this day, even more speedily after the invention of the transistor which ushered in the second industrial revolution. Such automation naturally presents threats, and in the context of the first industrial revolution, it prompted Ned Ludd to found the Luddite movement which set out to protect the livelihoods (as they saw it) of the textile workers. They failed, and, ever since, the 'automation versus jobs' debate has been a controversial and sensitive issue.

However, Kurzweil correctly points out that the first industrial revolution extended, multiplied and leveraged our **physical** capabilities — making us humans able to manipulate tasks which our muscles cannot, and at speeds which were hitherto unachievable.

The second industrial revolution, the one we are currently in, is based on machines that extend, multiply and leverage our **mental** abilities. Naturally, it is accompanied too by similar economic and social controversies as the first. As *homo sapiens*, we operate with symbols and language — and we are now designing machines which manipulate symbols and languages, though generally not natural languages. These machines or computers of the second industrial revolution are based on transistor and semiconductor technology whose growth over the last three decades has, by all accounts, been phenomenal. Computer power doubles every two years and has done so for decades. Today, machines or computers pervade all aspects of our lives, from the mundane (as in billing systems within a company like BT) to the controversial (as in smart weapons which were deployed during the Gulf war).

Companies or corporations which make most use of these machines now dominate others — the Japanese 'miracle' is an obvious case in point. The use of machines is now a *sine qua non* for international and global trade, so much so that they have been blamed in some quarters for the stock market crash of 1987. While the first industrial revolution was fuelled by natural resources, the second is being fuelled by knowledge — which justifies the fourth century slogan: 'Knowledge is power'. Today, a sure way for a company to commit commercial hara-kiri is by failing to protect its intellectual property (i.e. knowledge) and/or ignoring the machines of the second industrial revolution. Only those companies which make current machines smarter, or exploit them to their advantage, are set to dominate the coming twenty first century.

The dream of the ultimate intelligent machine which Charniak and McDermott [2] dare mention — '...the ultimate goal of AI research (which we are very far from achieving) is to build a person, more humbly an animal' — is being pursued. Whether it is achieved, unlikely most believe, is immaterial to a large degree. The spin-offs to be gained while striving for it are potentially revolutionary. The field which is attempting to realise the machine intelligence dream is called artificial intelligence (AI).

2. Artificial Intelligence — an Historical View

Artificial intelligence is still a young discipline, just forty years old. It certainly did not have an easy birth. A pioneer of no lesser status than John Von Neumann (widely regarded as the father of computing) had written, just before his death, a long argument why computers will never exhibit intelligence. Undeterred, a crop of young scientists persisted, and at the now historic Dartmouth College conference of 1956 where several top American researchers came together to discuss the future of machine intelligence, AI was born. Among the researchers were Claude Shannon, Marvin Minsky, John McCarthy (later, the inventor of the LISP programming language), as the main organisers, plus the late Allen Newell and the Nobel laureate, Herbert Simon. The latter four researchers arguably spearheaded AI research for the next two decades until about the mid-1970s.

The general goal of AI is to achieve some degree of 'intelligence' in machines. We eschew providing a specific definition of AI in favour of providing (or reminding the reader) of the motivations for doing it, not least because there are so many definitions of it anyway. The reader can derive a definition or definitions from the field's motivation which include [3]:

- computers are now an accepted part of our lives — researchers want to make them smarter (i.e. extend their current capabilities);

- some AI researchers would like to model 'intelligence', mind, cognition, consciousness and emotions — many have come into the field to test the validity of their theories on these by programming computer models using AI techniques;

- AI provides a good intellectual pursuit for researchers;

- of course, money must be a factor — it is no coincidence that the major industrialised nations are investing heavily in AI research, since there are enormous financial rewards and power to be accrued from making machines smarter.

Clearly academics draw their inspiration mainly from the first three while industrialists mainly carry out such work primarily because of the fourth reason.

However, the field has been dogged continually by controversy as to its true achievements. To be fair, AI people have arguably been the inventors of their own misfortunes. For example, during the mid-1960s to the mid-1970s, which has been referred to as the romantic period of AI [4], AI researchers pronounced that computers will soon understand stories and dialogue in natural language. Earlier, Herbert Simon, had predicted that we would have a chess champion computer by the mid-1960s. These goals are still outstanding four decades later. There were other spectacular failures. Consider the translation system, which infamously translated the sentence 'the spirit is willing but the flesh is weak' into Russian and then back to English. To the amusement of many AI detractors, it returned the sentence 'the wine is good, but the meat is rotten'. Therefore, even in the 1970s, the euphoria was short-lived, and, by 1975, it was clear that scaling up toy demonstrators to more substantive real-world domains, provide exponential rather than linear problems, and hence are non-trivial.

You would have thought AI researchers would have learnt from the failures of the 1960s and 70s, but during the 1980s they were culpably at it again — hyping the promise of AI with the help of the media and public. Our point is simple. Such hype generates unrealistic expectations. The exaggerated claims, over-expectations and 'over-sell' eventually drown out real (and sometimes excellent) achievements, which never match the hype. The aftermath, in retrospect, was quite predictable — interest in the area waned and, as night follows day, funding cuts followed. In the UK, this was evidenced by Sir James Lighthill's devastating 1973 report for the then Science and Engineering Council [5], which concluded that AI's erstwhile promises were dubious. This effectively killed AI research in the UK for a decade.

Furthermore, in such a climate of virtually inelastic claims, it was only normal to expect virulent attacks to come from the critics, who have argued cogently that AI research was an expensive irrelevance. Some critics, notably the Dreyfus bothers [6, 7], and the likes of Searle [8] arguably have, to some degree, flourished in their careers by engaging in wholesale debunking of the claims of AI. Recently, the Oxford scientist, Roger Penrose has joined this list of AI detractors with the publication of his *Shadows of the Mind* [9]. In it, Penrose argues that the brain/mind is a physical reality whose understanding transcends the computational metaphor which is at the heart of AI. He posits that investigations into quantum mechanics, classical and quantum physics, microbiology, etc, may illuminate further our understanding of the workings of mind, brain and consciousness.

In any case, we contend that most AI people do not bother to understand all these philosophical arguments — to them they are sterile. Others have concluded that these critics' arguments are irrelevancies to the machine intelligence venture. However, while some of their arguments smack of sophistry, some others are very cogent indeed. These critics, notwithstanding, the dream of machine intelligence lives on.

3. Machine Intelligence — Some Success Stories

We split this section into two parts — the first is more general and world-wide in outlook, while the second is more BT-oriented.

3.1 Some General AI Success Stories

Lest the latter part of the preceding section reads as a *mea culpa* of the failings of AI, we now highlight, only briefly, some of its success stories. AI now encompasses many areas of investigation including knowledge-based systems, natural-language processing, speech recognition and synthesis, automated reasoning (rule-based reasoning, case-based reasoning, model-based reasoning, qualitative and/or spatial reasoning, etc), automatic programming, vision, search and knowledge representation, planning and scheduling, neural networks, robotics, distributed AI, soft computing, etc.

AI is now part of our lives in ways unimaginable just a decade ago. Particularly since about 1990, AI's use is now quite widespread. Cars are assembled in factories by robots which employ AI technology. Indeed, Munakata [10] reports that estimates of the number of industrial robots world-wide is of the order of half a million. Vision applications are used to ensure quality control in several industries; for example, it is used in the area of electronic inspection, particularly of very large scale integration (VLSI) chips and circuit boards. Other industrial uses of vision applications are in stereo for terrain extraction, target detection and tracking, and x-ray inspection of jet engine turbine blades [11].

Many (particularly Japanese) banks now use speech recognition systems to handle several thousand customer calls daily; though these systems have limited vocabularies, they increasingly combine speaker-independent speech- recognition and speech-synthesis technologies. AI tech-nology is being exploited in weather prediction, mining and in predicting the share movements on the stock market. Not so long ago, the chess program, Deep Blue, won a game against the long-reigning world chess champion, Gary Kasparov. Herbert Simon's prediction of having a computer world chess champion may soon become a reality.

Knowledge-based (expert) systems (KBS) are now established in permanent and secure roles in industry as assistants to humans, decision-making components of more complex systems, critics, automatic planners, designers and schedulers [12]. Indeed, some current estimates of the total dollar value for the expert systems market range from 800 millions (1990) to 1.6 billions (1995). Whatever the real figure is, there is no denying the fact that there has been a real uptake of the technology. One particular KBS, XCON (DEC's configuration expert system), is claimed to perform six times as many functions as the personnel used to perform and saves DEC about 20 million dollars a year (this is a 1984 figure). Indeed, Kurzweil [1] notes that XCON '...reportedly is doing the work of over 300 human experts with substantially higher accuracy', (p 292). More recently, Hayes-Roth and Jacobstein [12] report that XSEL, one of the systems in the XCON suite, reduced a three-hour system configuration/ alternative generation task to 15 minutes and also reduced the number of non-manufacturable systems specified from 30% to 1%; these savings are claimed to be worth 70 million dollars annually.

On a domestic front, AI technologies have found their way, and are still finding their way, into domestic appliances like washing machines and microwave ovens. For example, washing machines now possess 'fuzzy logic' chips which can determine what type of fabric is being washed, and can set the correct wash cycle. Some even detect how 'hard' the water is in order to determine how much detergent to use. There are now 'one touch' microwave ovens which work out what to do with most foods placed in them — they are able to work out, for example, whether it is frozen (and thus start by defrosting); they can also work out for how long the defrosting should go on, etc. These fuzzy logic chips make such decisions from information obtained from sensors within these appliances. Other household appliances which contain such technology include refrigerators, vacuum cleaners, rice cookers and air conditioners. Widrow et al [13] report the exploitation of neural networks in domains including pattern classification, prediction and financial analysis, and control and optimisation.

We could go on, but we believe these examples amply demonstrate some of the incontestable contributions AI is having on our lives, despite the fact that true machine intelligence has not yet been achieved.

3.2   Machine Intelligence in BT — A Brief Review and Some Success Stories

BT did not start investigating the area of artificial intelligence in earnest until about 1984 when a few AI-related groups established themselves. The main reasons were twofold — firstly, very little AI work proceeded in the UK at that time, other than in pocket areas such as the universities of Edinburgh, Essex and Sussex, thanks to the Lighthill report mentioned earlier. Secondly, very few industrial research organisations in the UK were investing in AI-related R&D while the majority of the companies were cautiously awaiting the area to gain sufficient credibility and self-assurance. With some help from the AI and expert systems craze of the mid-1980s and hard work of some internal champions, groups were set up in BT for knowledge-based systems, natural-language processing, speech processing, speech synthesis and recognition, and data mining. Over the years, some of the groups have evolved tremendously, and addressed different areas of AI. For example, the original knowledge-based systems (also known as advanced information processing (AIP)) group, towards the late 1980s and early 1990s, also began investigating domains including machine learning, distributed AI, and planning and scheduling. Currently, this group is called the Intelligent Systems Research (ISR) group, and its researchers are investigating novel tech-nologies including advanced planning and scheduling, software agents, adaptive learning and soft computing.

- Why does/should BT strive for machine intelligence? There are several general reasons. We believe AI techniques would contribute towards the following:

- to facilitate BT in providing better-quality, and a wider range of, services as well as providing 'value-added' services to new and existing customers;

- to facilitate BT in managing its vast national and international telecommunications networks and reducing its operational cost;

- to facilitate BT in responding to the needs of its customers and hence not only keeping but attracting new customers;

- to facilitate BT in expanding into the global telecommunications market;

- to provide 'proof of concept' demonstrators that will open exploitation paths within BT — several of which are presented in this issue;

- to seek routes to downstream already-proven ideas to the rest of the BT business;

- to increase BT patents portfolio, its visibility of public domain results and its international R&D reputation;

- to develop core skills in machine intelligence and intelligent software systems.

So far, there have been many success stories within BT; a few recent and nascent ones are highlighted here.

- Intelligent scheduling and resource management — effective resource management has a major impact on BT's telecommunications network performance and profitability, and significantly contributes to the advantages provided to its customers. The ISR group at BT Laboratories (BTL) has developed intelligent resource management systems capable of providing flexible planning, scheduling and allocation of resources in dynamic environments such as visual broadcast service routeing, workforce scheduling, etc. These systems are developed using AI-based technologies such as constraint modelling, satisfaction and optimisation techniques, stochastic search and distributed problem-solving techniques, and constraint logic programming (see BT's external Web server[1]).

- Speech synthesis — BT's speech group has developed the Laureate text-to-speech system [14], which enables customers to access easily text-based information, anywhere, anytime, using an ordinary fixed or mobile telephone. Its performance betters that of many commercial speech-synthesis systems; at normal listening levels, it betters any other system against which it has been tested. It has been easily integrated into a number of different systems which include telephone access to e-mail, road traffic congestion, weather forecast, WWW pages and medical information lines. It can be found on BT's external Web server[2].

- Text summarisation — we are living in the era of information overload, and it will only get worse. The language group at BTL has developed Netsumm[3] — a text summariser that accepts plain-text documents, and automatically picks out the 'most important' parts of the text, e.g. by highlighting them. Alternatively, it can extract the sentences from the text to produce an abridgement of the article. The results of this prototype, which is still being evaluated, are so far very encouraging.

- Movie recommendation — the ISR group has developed MORSE, an agent which provides personalised movie recommendation. It works by first asking the user to rate as many films he/she has seen as possible. Using this data, MORSE recommends films which others with 'similar tastes' have rated highly. MORSE's performance so far equals and even betters other similar systems (see Fisk [15], and BT's WWW server[4]).

It is perhaps useful to note that special issues of the BT Technology Journal on some of the more established AI sub-areas mentioned earlier, relative to soft computing and software agents, already exist. Some recent issues with AI-related themes or which include a significant number of AI-oriented papers include the following (see BT's external Web server[5]):

- Network Management, BT Technology Journal, Volume 9, Number 3, July 1991;

- Artificial Neural Networks, BT Technology Journal, Volume 10, Number 3, July 1992;

- Modelling Change in Telecommunications, BT Technology Journal, Volume 12, Number 2, April 1994;

---

[1] http://www.labs.bt.com/bookshop/bttj/v13n1/index.htm
[2] http://www.labs.bt.com/innovate/speech/laureate/index.htm
[3] http://www.labs.bt.com/innovate/informat/netsumm/index.htm
[4] http://www.labs.bt.com/innovate/multimed/morse/morse.htm
[5] http:/www.labs.bt.com/bookshop/bttj/index.htm

- Computer-Aided Decision Support, BT Technology Journal, Volume 12, Number 4, October 1994;

- Advanced Information Processing Techniques for Resource Scheduling and Planning, BT Technology Journal, Volume 13, Number 1, January 1995;

- Speech Technology for Telecommunications, BT Technology Journal, Volume 14, Number 1, January 1996.

4. Conclusions

This paper has provided a brief, historical introduction, to machine intelligence and AI for the uninitiated. It is vital that such domains are investigated because the immense complexity of modern communications systems is forcing BT to seek novel and powerful solutions to meet the challenges of tomorrow's systems. Furthermore, as the convergence of telecommunications and computing gathers pace the difficulties facing global operators such as BT will grow — and this growth in complexity is not set to abate in the next few years.

Artificial intelligence, still a relatively young scientific and engineering discipline, has been (and is still being) successfully applied by BT researchers and systems developers in order to provide solutions to some of the problems envisaged.

Much of the AI research and intelligent systems engineering required to deal with the grand challenges ahead is still outstanding.

References

1. Kurzweil R: 'The Age of Intelligent Machines', Cambridge, Massachusetts, MIT Press (1992).

2. Charniak E and McDermott D: 'Introduction to Artificial Intelligence', Cambridge, Massachusetts Addison-Wesley (1982).

3. Nwana H S: 'Introducing Artificial Intelligence — a gentler and less formal approach', Unpublished manuscript, BT Laboratories (1996).

4. Jackson P: 'Introduction to Expert Systems', London, Addison-Wesley (1990).

5. Lighthill J: 'UK Science and Engineering Report', (1973).

6. Dreyfus H L: 'What computers can't do', New York, Harper & Row (1972).

7. Dreyfus H L: 'What computers still can't do: a critic of artificial reason', New York, Harper & Row (1992).

8. Searle J: 'Is the brain's mind a computer program? no: a program merely manipulates symbols whereas a brain attaches meaning to them', Scientific American, No 1, pp 20—25 (1990).

9. Penrose R: 'Shadows of the Mind: A search for the missing science of consciousness', Oxford University Press (1994).

10. Munakata T: 'Commercial and Industrial AI', Communications of the ACM, 37, No 3, pp 23—25 (1994).

11. Grimson W E L and Mundy J L: 'Computer Vision Applications', Communications of the ACM, 37, No 3, pp 45—51 (1994).

12. Hayes-Roth F and Jacobstein J: 'The State of Knowledge-Based Systems', Communications of the ACM, 37, No 3, pp 27—39 (1994).

13. Widrow B, Rumelhart D E and Lehr M A 'Neural Networks: applications in Industry, Business and Science', Communications of the ACM, 37, No 3, pp 93—105 (1994).

14. Page J H and Breen A P: 'The Laureate text-to-speech system — architecture and applications', BT Technology J, 14, No 1, pp 57—67 (January 1996).

15. Fisk D: 'An application of social filtering to movie recommendation', BT Technol J, 14, No 4, pp 124—132 (October 1996).

Intelligent Software Systems

R Smith and E H Mamdani

Department of Electrical and Electronic Engineering, Imperial College,
Exhibition Road, London, SW7 2BT, UK.
E-mail: e.mamdani@ic.ac.uk/Robin.Smith@btinternet.com

During the last four decades the field of artificial intelligence has made impressive progress. It is true that not all the promises generated during the enthusiasm of the early years have yet been delivered. But the fact remains that today's systems do provide impressive levels of machine intelligence. There are many examples of intelligent software systems which can match human capabilities. However, we must not fall into the trap of wanting computer systems to emulate fully human performance, for therein lie many subtle philosophical, scientific and engineering pitfalls. This paper provides a personal account of the progress of AI and offers an optimistic viewpoint.

1. Introduction

We are poised at a threshold — a threshold that clearly delineates two epochs in human development. All history that preceded us will, in the future, characterise man as the tool user. At some point in the near future mankind will, for the first time, enjoy a cognitive partnership, a symbiotic relationship with its own creation — the intelligent computer. Fanciful ideas maybe, but all the indications are that the past 50 years or so of research into artificial intelligence are about to bear fruit; and the product of this long and difficult development period will have a profound impact on our lives and future development as a species.

So why do we take this upbeat account of artificial intelligence (AI) research? Is it because there have been spectacular breakthroughs in AI? No. Could it be that there is a universal demand for the products and intuitions of this branch of system engineering and computer science? Again the answer must still be negative. But, and this is the telling argument, what the objective observer should recognise is that the field is making significant incremental advances on a broad front. These advances include:

- the ability to recognise human speech and the meanings contained therein;

- the ability of computer systems to infer information from visual scenes;

- the power of expert systems and knowledge-based systems to undertake very complex diagnostic and analytic tasks;

- the manner in which computer programmes now intrude into human games such as chess and cards;

- the way simple code helps us plan our daily lives and assists us both with routine tasks and in a multitude of other ways where we are now relying on (intelligent) computer systems.

Admittedly, many people will find this upbeat account unacceptable. However, if we go back only a relatively short period of time, we discover that the commonly held view was that people could never travel faster than the speed of a horse; and it was only a few centuries ago that the geocentric universe held sway.

In this paper we want to set out our arguments why we believe an information processing revolution is at hand. We adopt a frankly tendentious stance, while appreciating that there are many eminent scientists and philosophers who are dismissive of the field. We accept the sincerity of these deep mathematical and philosophical arguments but counter- attack with the engineering viewpoint which has been our life-long perspective.

Most of this paper will address the technical and philosophical boundaries that define AI research. We outline both the important (incremental) advances and the significant hurdles yet to be surmounted. We draw from both mainstream AI work and, where necessary to illustrate a point, from the writings of philosophers who have addressed similar issues. Section 2 reviews the overriding need for intelligent systems in our information rich society. Section 3 gives background ideas drawn from the supporting philosophical tradition. Section 4 provides a brief and deliberately incomplete review of the current state of intelligent systems and section 5 gives the other side of the coin by describing the major hurdles yet to be mastered. The paper concludes with a short discussion and an optimistic view of future progress.

2. The Need for Intelligent Software Systems

So why is it that in the closing years of the 20th century the need for intelligent software systems is becoming urgent? The simple answer is, of course, that the world is in the midst of an information revolution. Increasingly all data and information is being captured, transported and processed digitally. The fruits of this digital revolution, which provide instant access to the vast global data warehouse, has brought with it gross data overload. Our human cognitive capabilities, such as memory and comprehension, have not developed (and we would conjecture will not develop) to keep pace with our own invention. What this means is that we now need assistance from intelligent software systems in order to understand the world we are in the process of creating. These systems are intelligent in the sense that they have the capability to conduct information processing tasks which if performed by humans would require a high degree of skill and not inconsiderable intelligence.

A great deal has been written on the need for intelligent systems [1, 2]. For our purposes we can recall a few of these:

- to assist with routine but important tasks;

- to undertake complex tasks rapidly;

- to act as gofers on our behalf;

- to explore large cognitive search spaces to find elusive solutions;

- to deal with the data-rich environment which we have created.

What underpins the systems-engineering approach to all these intelligent software systems to a greater or lesser extent is the desire to capture some aspect of human intellectual capability. Such a desire may be formally stated (the human/computer interface community) or be a trivial anthropomorphic device (smiling face). The reason for this homocentric approach is the recognition that we humans are most comfortable when interacting with other humans. However, it has to be admitted that in certain circumstances, usually of highly personal nature, some people prefer conversing with machines. Therefore we are not pretending that intelligent software-systems technology offers solutions to all human information processing needs — only a large proportion of them.

As the goal of human-oriented computing is ap-proached, the expectation of combining digital speed and precision with human levels of intuition grows.

3. Philosophical Background

Research in artificial intelligence has been founded on the existence theorem which says that if a task can be done by a natural physical organ, i.e. the brain, then it should be possible to devise a man-made device to carry out that task. An additional hypothesis that is usually made is that the best candidate for the man-made device is the digital computer. Even if not explicitly stated, some such belief provides the underlying motivation to all workers in AI. However, as stated above, the theorem begs many questions and lays itself open to challenges on several fronts. Penrose's challenge [3], in simple terms, is just that while the brain is no doubt a purely physical organ, it is governed by physical laws that are little understood at present; that these laws must be related to the finer points of quantum theory and as such AI research is in no position to realise all its ambitions. Dreyfus's challenge [4] is a little different, and appears to us to question that part of the theorem that posits all human intelligence to a single organ, namely, the brain. If this reading is correct, then our position is not too far removed from his; but we argue as engineers and not as AI theoreticians; and Dreyfus does not have any quarrels with an engineering approach to intelligent software systems. We will have more to say on this matter later. As to the additional hypothesis, Dreyfus seems to say that the von Neuman architecture (serial computing) must be an important limiting factor on the conventional AI research programme. Penrose does not consider that to be an important issue, since artificial neural networks (parallel computing) as used by AI workers can always be simulated on a conventional digital computer.

One of the most important questions that the existence theorem raises is indeed concerned with the organ in question, the brain. Each individual's organ is constructed bio-chemically based on the blueprint provided by the owner's genetic material. That blueprint has been subjected to Darwinian evolution and so it is not surprising that while all animals possess a brain, the human animal displays uniquely more powerful intellectual abilities. However, the fact that human intellectual competence varies so widely from one individual to another cannot be explained away easily as purely genetic, although many would have us believe this to be so. Furthermore, the continuing progress of human knowledge since man first evolved, cannot be explained in terms of a continuing evolution of the human brain.

Humans have been around for about 100 000 years or 4000 generations. This is too short a period for the brain to have evolved very much. The 'out of Africa' theory is now well accepted; that the human race evolved in one place — Africa — and then migrated to other parts of the world. There were other humanoid life-forms such as the Neanderthal man, but these did not survive. We assume the human differed from other humanoids because he had a more elaborate language. A distant predecessor of *homo-sapiens*, the *homo erectus* was so called because he was a biped, with two forelimbs available for purposes other than locomotion. He was followed by *homo habilis*, so called because he had dexterous hands which he used for making tools. It is clear that what characterised the *homo sapiens* is that he evolved another set of equally dexterous muscles — the muscles of the mouth; and that is what enabled speech. Human intelligence is attributed to the much larger brain of the *homo sapiens* compared to other homonids. However, it is not this final adult size that is important but the fact that it comes about through the process called neoteny. This process results in the size of the infant brain being only 25% of its final adult size. That is to say the brain grows fourfold after birth and, most importantly, develops in the presence of its environment.

The above facts should lead us to the conjecture that the human adult brain of each individual consists of a complex set of predispositions to act (a wired response, if you will) that is conditioned by that individual's environment, or more precisely from his sensitivities to that environment at every stage of his early development. The many permutations of the environment that we individually encounter, and our constantly changing emotional state, and thus the sensitivity to that environment, is what ultimately produces such a wide spectrum of intellectual competence among us humans. As someone put it in a semi-humourous way, if we clone a number of individuals from Einstein's genetic material, we may not get a number of physics geniuses but only a whole lot of patent office clerks. This would suggest that all brains are substantially the same and that the variation in human competence is predominantly down to environmental factors. That ought to be good news for the supporters of artificial intelligence research.

One of the principal results of the developmental process in an individual is the acquisition of a wide variety of elementary skills. These are largely in the form of sub-conscious habits and often imprinted as what can be described as 'muscle memory'. Therefore, a significant number of skills, habits or muscle memory acquired during the developmental process refer to the muscles of the mouth, i.e. speech. It is noteworthy that people with amnesia may forget many things about themselves, but not the basic skills like walking and talking their mother tongue, indicating that these are a wired or response-muscle memory. It is not too far fetched to say that the human mouth is as important as the human brain for our superior intelligence. Could it be that we should properly call ourselves *homo loquax*, the garrulous man?

Language is the result of our ability to speak. It is primarily a time-invariant regularity for associating sound to things, events, etc. It is this regularity of sounds, or language that gave us the ability to retain the intermediate results of thought and to recall them for further thought — a kind of short-term memory. Gradually it formed our growing and evolving knowledge. The evolution of knowledge and passing it reliably from one generation to the next was greatly increased when humans developed written language somewhere around 5000 years, or 200 generations ago.

We can safely say that while the human brain itself has not evolved over the 4000 generations the knowledge that human society possesses has steadily (and recently rapidly) increased. Indeed most of human evolution over that period has occurred outside the human body — in human knowledge. This has been best described by Sir Karl Popper. Popper is known as an important philosopher of science, but it is his ideas about World 3 [5] that have a very significant relevance for research workers in AI.

According to Popper, World 1 is 'the world of physical objects, or the world of physical states'. World 2 is 'the world of states of consciousness, or the world of mental states, or the world of dispositions to act'. Now most AI workers would contend that the field investigates, or is inspired by, the phenomena of this World 2. However, Popper maintains that we also have a World 3 which is the world of objective content of scientific thought, poetic thought and works of art. Other contents of World 3 are theoretical systems, problems, problem situations, critical arguments, the contents of journals or books and so on. He says: "Traditional epistemology has studied knowledge or thought in a subjective sense ... While knowledge in the sense of .. 'I know' belongs to World 2, the world of subjective thoughts; scientific knowledge belongs to World 3, the world of objective theories, objective problems and objective arguments."

Popper gives various theses regarding World 3 that are all relevant here:

- traditional epistemology based on World 2 is irrelevant to the study of scientific knowledge;

- the study of a largely autonomous World 3 of objective knowledge is of decisive importance for epistemology;

- an objective epistemology that studies World 3 can help to throw an immense amount of light upon World 2 ... , but the converse is not true;

- World 3 is a natural product of the human comparable to a spider's web (Dawkins [6] calls this the extended phenotype).

World 3 is largely autonomous; it is through this interaction between ourselves and World 3 that objective knowledge grows and there is close analogy between the growth (or the evolution) of knowledge and biological evolution [7].

This shows World 3 to be quite different from Plato's ideal knowledge. It is man-made, composed of conjectures, subject to falsification; it is full of imperfections, antinomies and paradoxes. As scientists and engineers we need to treat it with humility and there can never be room for arrogance and certainty. All human intellectual evolution has thus taken place in this Popperian World 3. Neoteny ensures that each child grows up with a different (and hopefully richer and more accurate) World 3 environment. The knowledge an individual forms is then determined by a variety of factors like the mood he is in while he gets introduced to this barrage of World 3 and the sequence in which this exposure takes place. Then, as knowledge evolves, each generation's view of the world changes.

One of the important constituents of this World 3 are models that:

- describe how the physical world around us works;

- prescribe how we should, as social animals, behave; these prescriptive models are pure conjectures and the result of our fertile imagination.

Let us consider the descriptive models first.

Descriptive models — since man began to talk he must have conjectured how the regularities of the physical world came about. These were little different from what we take today to be scientific theories. In time, once the foundations of mathematics were laid, we began creating mathematical models. It took a long time indeed for us to begin to put down the foundations of the scientific method. This method is no more than a few hundred years old and it is the subject of Popper's main enquiry; the part of his work that most lay people are aware of. For him, for any theory (i.e. a descriptive model that is supposed to be about the real world) to be scientific it must be falsifiable. Furthermore, Popper says that there are many descriptive theories that are immunised against falsification. Our World 3 contains many descriptive models that do not measure up to such scientific rigour.

Prescriptive models — we like to think that our prescriptions for day-to-day actions and future behaviour are based upon a knowledge of how the world is; that is to say they are derived from sound descriptive models. Ask anyone why one should behave in some accepted fashion and the tendency will be to reply that because the world is like thus and so. The sad fact is that there are many prescriptive formulae that are not based on any well- founded descriptive knowledge. Often the description is a *post facto* justification for holding on to a given recipe for behaviour; but that is not to say that prescriptive recipes are purely arbitrary and any recipe will therefore do. They have to work, which in fact means that they have to give us an added survival advantage. Having to be fit for the purpose in an economic way, they are thus subject to selection pressure. Prescriptive models are no different from any other invention, and as such it can often happen that although originally intended for one purpose, an invention is actually discovered to be best suited for an entirely different purpose.

Unfortunately many scientists themselves are not very clear about this. Most of the field of computer science is on close scrutiny dealing with prescriptive models (i.e. inventions) of implementing something. Furthermore, given that so much of our knowledge is concerned with models, such models themselves become for many, matters of interest in their own right. Many scientists cannot tell when their focus of study is the structure of the model itself (particularly when the models are expressed mathematically) and when the main interest is to do with the relationship of the models to reality. Much of orthodoxy, in science as elsewhere, arises from a concern to hang on to particular models irrespective of reality.

Dreyfus is correct in focusing his main criticisms on good old fashioned artificial intelligence (GOFAI). Traditionally, AI has devoted more time to human-like sensory performance, rather than human-like motor performance (robotics being the main exception). However, in a major way, it is precisely our muscular dexterity that marks us out as different from other animals. Dogs for example have better hearing than humans, birds of prey have better eyesight than humans, but no animal has as much muscle control over its hands and mouth muscles as we humans do. The brain is important because it co-ordinates and amplifies the best mouth muscles of any animal with a rather mediocre ear, within the animal kingdom. The computer can generate speech, and it can analyse speech, but the computer is seldom made to hear itself speak; the computer brain has so far not been used to co-ordinate the speech input with speech output.

The result is that, at present, our computers have no bodies, i.e. no muscular movements through which they can respond to sense inputs. In the terms used by one faction of AI practitioners, most computer systems are not grounded. These issues are further discussed towards the end of this paper.

4. Progress to Date

Over the past four decades, systems embodying techniques from the field of artificial intelligence have enjoyed spectacular advances. These advances have, of course, been symbiotic with the equally impressive strides made in information technology. However, it has to be admitted that delivered systems do not yet live up to the expectations generated by the earlier enthusiasm.

In the following paragraphs a brief, specially selected, account is given of the current state of the art. These examples are intended to demonstrate the healthy condition of AI as a set of techniques and systems engineering approaches to delivering intelligent software systems.

4.1 Human/Computer Interface

A new user of today's personal computer (PC) or workstation, would find it difficult to comprehend the vast improvement made in the human/computer interface (HCI). When we began utilising computers the 80 column punched card was king! Those men and women who had to program computers in the early days were equally disadvantaged — machine code, or assembly language, was the only option. Today computers are instructed by natural language (text or speech); blocks of text or graphics can be moved or modified by the click of a mouse; following a few keystrokes the World Wide Web provides rapid access to a vast global database; television quality moving images can be called up to illustrate a point or present complex data, etc. On the programming front the progress has been equally spectacular. Relatively short commands in modern high-level languages evoke complex actions by the computer. The compiler performs many levels of consistency checking that was once the bane of programmers.

This level of 'user friendliness' is now expected and provided on entry-level PCs. However, what is by no means generally appreciated is that many of the accepted aspects of computing are the fruits of research conducted in artificial intelligence laboratories back in the 1950s and 1960s. For example, Lisp, the oldest high-level language, is still the language of choice for much current AI research and delivered systems; and now, of course, we are seeing the ready acceptance of agents technology [8] to further adapt the computer to a more human-like entity.

As we noted in section 3, language is crucial to human intellectual development. Therefore it is not surprising that natural language processing (NLP) has been a major pre-occupation in the development of AI techniques. There has been a continuum of research based on the logical analysis of text which has resulted in delivered systems which provide creditable performance at 'understanding' the meaning of sentences. But human communication is very complex and even the most powerful NLP systems can still be defeated. In part this is because we humans use both a vast store of knowledge (Popper's World 3) and are grounded in the real physical world. These issues are being addressed head-on by the AI research community.

4.2   Voice Recognition/Synthesis

Spoken language is the most natural way for humans to communicate. In fact as Wheddon notes [9] speech and language are 'the very essence of social development and have become the key components lying at the humanising heart of the information revolution'. Today speech synthesis is commonplace — automated home banking, information messages from the telephone network, talking computer games to name but a few.

A great deal of work has been carried out to ensure the quality of computer-based text-to-speech systems is acceptable. In fact, powerful commercial systems are becoming available. Laureate [10], developed at BT Laboratories is representative of today's high-quality systems. Speech recognition systems are making equally impressive progress. Single user systems [11] have the capability of recognising many thousands of words following a training session which typically takes an hour or so. Multi-user applications where the system is required to recognise a more limited vocabulary from very many individuals are beginning to make their presence felt in the IT market-place.

What these technological advances demonstrate is that the human user increasingly is being freed from the constraints of textual communications (keyboard and screen) with computers. And this new freedom is providing an interface which is essential for intelligent applications.

4.3   Representation and Reasoning

While the graphical and speech capabilities of present- day computer systems have an immediate appeal and are the showcase for modern information technology, it is the inner core of software where the task at hand is conducted. The following account of current practice does not provide information on mainstream AI research and products, such as expert systems, since there are many sources [12, 13] that provide excellent coverage of the field.

From the outset AI research has been concerned with the twin problems of representing knowledge and reasoning over that knowledge. Until comparatively recently there have been two distinct approaches:

- symbolic AI;

- artificial neural networks.

The first approach is motivated by the thesis that it is possible to extract relevant facts and relationships from the real world, label such information with symbols, and use mathematical logic to derive new information from that symbol system. The history of expert systems shows that, for well-defined partitions of the real world (domains in the language of AI), well-engineered solutions to a wide variety of problems can be developed. This particular branch of inquiry has been extended by building precise descriptive (mathematical) models of the domain and using logic to extract causal relationships, new facts, consequences, etc, from the model. What characterises these methods of delivering intelligent software systems is that the designer must extract the relevant facts and relationships from the real-world domain. This so-called knowledge-engineering task is non-trivial for all but toy examples.

The artificial neural network community sets about the task of extracting domain information in a completely different manner. Here the AI engineer is motivated by an understanding of how biological nervous systems operate. One of the prime drivers is that biological systems are not programmed in the same way as computers. In higher order biological systems many capabilities are learned — wired neither at conception nor birth. This, as noted in section 3, provides the plasticity for an organism to adapt to its ever changing environment. Increasing success in this systems engineering approach to intelligent software will free the programmer from having to specify all the subtleties (search space, conditions, data values, etc) of the cognitive engine.

4.4   Soft Computing

However, the promise of ANN techniques to deliver more human-like intelligent software has been relatively slow and the application areas patchy. This situation has caused many research groups to investigate alternative routes. Soft computing [14] represents one of the best defined of these alternatives and brings with it a refreshingly 'engineering' approach. Soft computing is concerned with the goal of human-oriented computing and not with any particular branch of AI. It will combine techniques as diverse as fuzzy logic, neuro computing, genetic programming, stochastic computing, etc, in a heady, eclectic mix to achieve its goals; and these goals are to make intelligent software systems that are tolerant of imprecision, where the data, and indeed the program, do not have to be 100% accurate or complete. In short, to make cognitive systems which deal with the real world and not some hard, well-bounded and well-specified subset thereof.

5. Pointers to Future Success

Before computer systems that embody AI techniques are accepted as intelligent — intelligent in the way humans choose to define their cognitive abilities — there are a number of important problems to be solved. These problems can be discovered by analysing how humans grow intellectually. Although we still do not have a detailed understanding of how the human brain operates, we can state with some high degree of certainty that humans develop in the presence of four cognitive influences:

- direct experience of the world (grounding);

- guided learning (parents, teachers);

- exposure to global knowledge (Poppers World 3);

- self-criticism (Poppers World 2?).

The computer equivalent of these human developmental influences are now active research fields in AI.

5.1   Grounded Systems — Direct Experience of the World

Most of the work in artificial intelligence is based on the symbol system hypothesis which posits that a cognitive engine operates on a set of symbols which have a defined relationship with the real world. But as made clear by Brooks [15] such symbols are a pale reflection of reality. For instance, if an expert system were reasoning about the solar system, the symbol ☉ hardly conveys the size, energy and central importance for life on planet Earth of the Sun! Brooks reasons that in order for systems of artificial intelligence to truly be able to 'understand' the real world they must interact, through sensors, with that world and build their knowledge in an incremental fashion. His subsumption architecture provides a framework to develop systems in this bottom-up manner. This approach to building intelligent systems (sometimes called nouvelle AI) has a large measure of scientific and engineering credence. On the one hand, it can be considered to mirror biological evolution — the best existence theorem for intelligent systems; following the Darwinian hypothesis, life on Earth evolved from simple fragments of self-replicating biological material to very complex organisms such as ourselves. On the other hand, subsumption-based systems only have one model of the world — the world itself; and this model is the best there is. While such an approach appeals to engineers such as ourselves, we do not underestimate the problems of building subsumption-based AI systems which will be able to converse with humans in natural speech.

Another approach which tackles the grounding issues is that being pursued by Aleksander. His system, MAGNUS [16], is a finite-state automata approach to neural systems. MAGNUS learns to associate words and images in order to build a comprehensive understanding of its world. Its depth of grounding is not so fundamental as the robots being developed in Brook's Laboratory, but nevertheless is far removed from the symbolic approach of traditional AI. MAGNUS stores its knowledge as a set of states on random access memory — like elements modelled on a general- purpose computer.

5.2   Global Knowledge

At the present stage of AI systems development, no single computer program has access to a data store as vast and wide ranging as that possessed by humans. However, research into interface and co-operative agents [17] is one indication of how this situation would change in a relatively short space of time. The World Wide Web provides access to a vast global warehouse. As automatic information extraction and precision techniques gain maturity we could well find intelligent software systems developing their own World 3. And this computer World 3 may not be identical with our own unless we intervene in suitable ways.

- One obvious route to ensuring that intelligent software systems do exercise only knowledge with which we are content is to hand-craft the knowledge base.

- For the past ten years or so the goal of project CYC has been to encode human common sense knowledge into a computer program. Guha and Lenat [18] describe how this common sense knowledge base can be used to aid information management. Since CYC 'knows' a great deal about our world and relationships between people, it is able to undertake complex data validation tasks without being specifically instructed what to investigate. The authors describe CYC's ability to check databases and spreadsheets for consistency. What this common sense knowledge base confers on the application it supports is a human-like capability to take account of a wide range of anthropomorphic facts and causal relationships.

- Lenat [19] notes that CYC has encoded into its knowledge base about 100 000 general concepts spanning human reality and about 1000 000 common sense axioms. This knowledge base is not one vast homogenous structure. Facts and relationships are clustered into contexts and each context has its associated micro-theory. Importantly, CYC's assertions do not have certainty factors, instead CYC assumes each atom of knowledge is true; CYC does not have completeness of inference. What these facts mean is that CYC is a practical demonstration of a system which encodes human common sense knowledge. It uses theoretical approaches to guide construction but does not permit rigour to obstruct progress.

5.3   Computer Self-Awareness

There is a growing body of opinion [20] that in order for computer programs to be able to display credible intelligence they must have a measure of self-awareness; but currently most computer systems (with the exception of Brook's robots) have hardly any sensory perception at all. They have no plasticity through which they can learn any repertoire of muscular habits. They have not yet been designed to co-ordinate sensory and motor nerves, they cannot hear themselves talk such that they may learn to talk in a particular way. Consider the following situation. In many expert system applications, a computer is programmed to utter statements such as "I did ..." or "I said to you ...". Such self-referential statements refer to what the program may have done by sending some data to its output buffer, but not what the computer actually did. For human- like self-reference what is needed is for the computer to perceive, see or observe its own action, recognise that the action was indeed its own as distinct from that of any other entity in its environment, and attribute the responsibility for that action on itself. (The 'I' referred to in the above utterances is mostly in the third person.) This is then the beginning of a semblance of self-awareness. An action produced in response to some sensory input is blind until it itself is sensed and owned up to, whether it subsequently results in a self-referential utterance or not. Indeed the subsequent utterance may be different from what was sensed, thus producing a lie.

For computer consciousness much more than self-awareness is needed. For example, an action cannot be seen simply as a response to some sensual stimulus, but as itself being intended to act as a stimulus upon the outside world. This calls for an adequate model of the world in order to decide what sort of stimulus is appropriate at any given stage.

There is thankfully a considerable amount of research in this area, for example, speech-acts-based research is intended to investigate just such behaviour. The point to be made here is that sensing each one of the machine's own actions, reflecting upon it, monitoring its effect, comparing that effect with the intended effect, and so on, are all essential requirements for any intelligent behaviour.

6.   Discussion

In section 4 we demonstrated that the current state of art in artificial intelligence and IT is in the process of providing an increasingly human-centred computer environment. We choose the term human-centred because the systems are addressable through speech and respond with speech and high-quality graphical images. Progress in this human/computer interface will be accelerated as computers are welcomed in the home and office alike. We readily admit that high-quality and intuitive interfaces do not of themselves make a computer system intelligent, but they do provide accessibility.

Section 5 provided the reasons why we believe software systems are approaching a level of performance that should be considered intelligent. We set out four influences that help shape human intellectual development and demonstrated how AI research is building machine equivalents. It is, of course, not possible to state that this research is mature — far from it. But progress is incremental and monotonic. There have been few of the setbacks that characterised early AI research. It now appears very unlikely that a new Lighthill [21] will reverse the trend.

7. Conclusions

When viewed from our engineering standpoint the dispassionate observer should be able to recognise the immense strides that are being made in the field. The broad incremental advances in AI now provide an impressive array of techniques to implement intelligent software systems; and the modern, eclectic approach to AI engineering, as evidenced, for example, by the soft computing community, will accelerate the trend to ever-increasing levels of machine intelligence. It falls upon system engineers to harness this new form of intelligence for the benefit of mankind.

Acknowledgments

The authors wish to acknowledge the helpful comments provided by Barry Crabtree, Nader Azarmi, Hyacinth Nwana and Ben Azvine.

References

1. Wheeler T E: 'It's the Information Not the Highway', IEEE Communications (December 1995).

2. Smith R: 'Software Agent Technology', Practical Application of Intelligent Agents and Multi-Agent Technology (PAAM) conference, London (1996).

3. Penrose R: 'Shadows of the Mind', Oxford Univ Press (1994).

4. Dreyfus H L and Dreyfus S E: 'Making a mind versus modelling the brain: AI back at a branchpoint', The AI Debate, MIT Press (1988).

5. Miller D: 'Popper Selections', Princeton Paperbacks (1985).

6. Dawkins R: 'The Extended Phenotype', Oxford Univ Press (1983).

7. Dawkins R: 'The Selfish Gene', Oxford Univ Press (1976).

8. Nwana H S and Wooldridge M: 'Software agent technologies', BT Technol J, 14, No 4, pp 68—78 (October 1996).

9. Wheddon C: 'Foreword' in 'Speech Technology for telecom-munications', BT Technol J, 14, No 1, p 7 (January 1996).

10. Page J H and Breen A P: 'The Laureate text-to-speech system — architecture and applications', BT Technol J, 14, No 1, pp 57—67 (January 1996).

11. Scahill F et al: 'Speech recognition — making it work for real', BT Technol J, 14, No 1, pp 151—164 (January 1996).

12. Buchanan B G and Shortliffe E H: 'Rule-based expert systems', Addison-Wesley (1984).

13. Hayes-Roth F: 'The knowledge-based expert system — a tutorial', Computer 9, pp 11—28 (1985).

14. Zadeh L A: 'Software computing and fuzzy logic', IEEE Software, (November 1994).

15. Brooks R: 'Elephants Don't Play Chess', in: 'Designing Autonomous Agents, Theory and Practice from Biology to Engineering', MIT Press (1987).

16. Aleksander I: 'Impossible Minds, My Neurons, My Consciousness', Imperial College Press (1996).

17. Nwana H S: 'Software agents: An overview', Knowledge Engineering Review, 11, No 3, pp 205—244 (1996).

18. Guha R V and Lenat D B: 'Enabling agents to work together', Communications of the ACM, 37 (1994).

19. Lenat D B: 'CYC: A large-scale investment in knowledge infrastructure', Communications of the ACM, 38 (1995).

20. Michie D: 'Consciousness as an Engineering Issue', (1 and 2), Journal of Consciousness Studies (1994—1995).

21. Lighthill J: 'UK Science and Engineering', Council report (1973).

Machine Intelligibility and the Duality Principle

S Muggleton[1] and D Michie[2]

[1] Computing Laboratory, Oxford Unviersity, Wolfson Building,
Parks Road, Oxford, OX1 3QD, UK.
E-mail:Steve.Muggleton@comlab.ox.ac.uk
[2] 6 Inveralmond Grove, Edinburgh, EH4 6RA, UK.
Fax: +44 131 336 4603

The scale and diversity of networked sources of data and computer programs is rapidly swamping human abilities to digest and even locate relevant information. The high speed of computing has compounded this problem by the generation of even larger amounts of data, derived in ways that are generally opaque to human users. The result is an increasing gulf between human and computer abilities. Society's ever more wide-scale dependence on rapidly growing networked sources of software threatens severe breakdowns if machine intelligibility issues are not given high priority.

We argue that lack of machine intelligibility in human/computer interactions can be traced directly to present approaches to software design. According to the duality principle in this paper, software involved in human/computer interaction should contain two distinct layers — a declarative knowledge-level layer and a lower-level functional or procedural-knowledge layer. This extends the formal methods separation of specification and implementation by requiring that the declarative layer be capable of extensive human interrogation at run time. The declarative layer should support simple deductive and inductive inference. The ease with which declarative knowledge can be translated to natural language could be used to provide a human-comprehensible 'window' into the properties of the underlying functional layer. Adaptation of the declarative knowledge in response to human interaction could be supported by modern machine-learning mechanisms. In addition, declarative knowledge could be used to facilitate human-comprehensible communication between programs. Existing well-developed technologies can be commandeered to implement the declarative layer. The obvious language of choice is pure Prolog, augmented with machine-learning mechanisms based on inductive logic programming. The underlying functional layer would be composed of normal procedurally encoded computer programs. It is argued that the duality principle in software design is a necessity for dealing with the demands of wide-scale computer usage in the information age and should be an urgent goal for computer science research at the start of the 21st century.

1. Introduction

In 1964 Gordon Moore, then president of Fairchild, stated that the component density of integrated circuits would continue doubling every year (presently every two years). Such exponential change in both memory cost and computer speed has held true consistently over the last 40 years of computing. This dramatic increase in computing power has led to the widely heralded 'information revolution', the social implications of which are rivalled only by the industrial revolution of the 18th and 19th centuries. Effects include a shift within the industrialised world from manufacturing-based economies to information-based ones.

The consequences of low-cost memory and computer speed have not all been positive. The scale and diversity of data sources is rapidly swamping human abilities to digest and even locate relevant information. The high speed of computing has compounded this problem by generation of even larger amounts of data, derived in ways that are generally opaque to human users. The result is an ever- widening gulf between human and computer abilities.

Thus, although the parameters of computer hardware abilities are increasing exponentially, those of their human users remain constant and are already dwarfed in all respects. Figure 1 (borrowed from Michie [1]) tabulates some of the information parameters of the human brain.

1	Rate of information transmission along any input or output channel	30 bits per sec
2	Maximum amount of information explicitly storable by the age of 50	10^{10} bits
3	Number of mental discriminations per second during intellectual work	18
4	Number of addresses which can be held in short-term memory	7
5	Time to access an addressable 'chunk' in long-term memory	2 sec
6	Rate of transfer from long-term to short-term memory of successive elements of one 'chunck'	3 elements per sec

Fig. 1.   Some information parameters of the human brain — estimation errors can be taken to be around 30 per cent. (Main sources: Miller (1956) Psychology Review 63, pp 81-97, Stroud (1966) Ann N.Y. Academy, and sources cited by Chase and Simon (1974) Cognitive Psychology, 4, pp 55—81).

It is really human comprehension that is the key bottleneck in a number of the related problems of human/computer incompatibility. What is required is both increased intelligence on the part of machines and increased compatibility in human/ computer interaction.

The need to increase the compatibility between computers and their human users necessitates the practical application, integration and extension of existing technologies.

This paper is structured as follows. The motivations for BT's machine intelligence initiative are introduced in section 2. As a response to the urgent need for increased machine intelligibility we introduce the principle of software duality in section 3 as an approach to machine intelligibility. In section 4 previous large-scale artificial intelligence projects are reviewed in the light of the duality principle and lessons are drawn for BT's ongoing machine intelligence initiative [2]. Sections 5 and 6 review relevant ongoing research in autonomous agents and machine learning. It is argued that present research falls far short of addressing the challenges raised by the problems in human/computer incompatibility we have described above. A radically new approach allowing the development of adaptive collaborative software[1] is called for. This approach should both build on and transform existing software technologies. Section 7 summarises and concludes the paper.

2. BT's Machine Intelligence Initiative

Machine intelligence is the software technology of user friendliness at the level of concepts, rather than the level of keystrokes and error messages. The following quote from Smith et al [2] provides the central motivation behind BT's machine intelligence initiative.

> 'Man-to-machine communications is a major business opportunity. The rapid growth in the use (and processing power) of computers both in the home and in the workplace is leading to the situation where the market for 'man-to-machine traffic' is growing fast.'

The development of high-speed communications and cheap high-powered PCs is rapidly steering the dominant use of information technology into the hands of users who are not computer professionals. Despite the wide-scale use of window and mouse interfaces, the level of machine intelligibility is extremely low. The following is a short list of interaction issues familiar to any computer user:

- **program purpose** — it is generally not possible to query the purpose of a computer program's actions;

- **human intentions** — computer programs generally have no model of their human user's aims and motivations, and thus lack the ability to make helpful suggestions;

- **failure diagnosis** — execution failures are generally hard to track down;

---

[1] This terminology is derived from Nwana's classification [3] of intelligent agents. Nwana also notes that no existing agents are both collaborative and adaptive.

- **correction** — erroneous software behaviour will be repeated indefinitely, since present-day software has no way to incorporate corrective feedback;

- **brittleness** — computer programs are unable to make intelligent conjectures in the face of slightly incomplete or incorrect data;

- **hidden interactions** — the communication between programs are opaque to the human user.

Many of these features have for some time acted as nagging irritants to computer users. However, with the wider-scale use of computers such problems start to impinge not only on business profitability, but also, in some situations, on human safety.

In the next section we urge the need for software involved in human/computer interaction to have an extra declarative layer defining program specifications, reaction speeds of sub-modules, goals and intentions as well as models of other computer programs and of human users.

3. Machine Intelligibility and the Duality Principle

We view machine intelligibility as a state of human/computer interaction. It can be defined as follows.

'A two-way interaction with a machine is intelligible to a human user if the (growing) set of the machine's concept descriptions used in the interaction maintain logical equivalence with a (growing) subset of the human's concepts.'

We see the duality principle of software design as a necessary requisite for machine intelligibility. The software duality principle can be stated as follows.

'Software involved in human/computer inter-action should be designed at two interconnected levels: a) a declarative, or self-aware level, supporting ease of adaptation and human inter-action, and b) a procedural, or skill level, supporting efficient and accurate computation.'

4. Diary Example

As an example of software designed without the duality principle, consider the humble electronic diary, available on most PCs and workstations. New entries are put in such diaries by pointing with a mouse at a representation of an open page, clicking and typing text. However, suppose one has a regular meeting every Thursday at 4 pm for a period of 8 weeks. Rather than forcing the user to put in each entry separately some advanced models of electronic diary will provide a simple mechanism for specifying repetitive entries of this kind. However, you cannot specify that these meetings must avoid public holidays, or ask them to take into account the fact that one might want to miss meetings that fall on one's child's birthday. Nor will they take into account the simplest of temporo-spatial rules, such as the fact that a participant of an event cannot be in two distant places at the same time. Present electronic diaries have no facilities to build up such human-oriented concepts, nor to make intelligent human-checkable conjectures in terms of already defined concepts. This is no doubt due to the difficulties of programming such abilities in a procedural programming language.

However, imagine the situation if the duality principle had been applied in the design of an electronic diary. Events with their associated participants and spatial designations are easy and efficient to represent within a declarative language such as the datalog subset of Prolog. Such events could be asserted into a deductive database as a side-effect of mouse clicking. Integrity constraints such as the requirement for a person to be at only one place at any time are again straightforward to encode in datalog. Interaction in a commonly defined declarative representation with other declaratively encoded diary programs/birthday planners/travel planners would allow integrity checking to extend beyond the local knowledge-base. One would certainly not want to burden a user by requiring that they learn mathematical logic before they can operate their electronic diary! However, rules that state that a series of meetings happens every Thursday except during public holidays and your children's birthdays could be conjectured and refined by an inductive logic programming (ILP) [4] system from a handful of examples and counter-examples entered by mouse-clicking. Such rules could be easily translated into natural language for user certification. Within such a diary procedural encoding would still be vital for numerical calculations involving time and space, graphical display and mouse input.

4.1 Declarative and procedural knowledge

The divisions between declarative and procedural knowledge have their counterparts not only throughout the behavioural and brain sciences but also throughout computer science. Thus, for instance, Hoare [5] distinguishes between specifications and program as follows.

'Given specification S, the task is to find a program P which satisfies it in the sense that every possible observation of every possible behaviour of the program P will be among the behaviours described by (and therefore permitted by) the specification S'.

Note that, unlike programs, specifications are both declarative and human-oriented. This is typically achieved by making use of variants of first-order predicate calculus such as Z [6]. However, the purpose of specifications is largely fulfilled once the program has been correctly implemented. Specifications are not intended to be used for run time interrogation and they do not include knowledge about the program's use and environment beyond its input/output behaviour. Within the field of AI, the knowledge representation debate has polarised between advocates of purely declarative representations (such as McCarthy) and those supporting purely reactive representations (such as Brooks). This split and its potential resolution via the duality principle will be explored in more detail in section 5.

Intelligent interaction has been a central theme within artificial intelligence. For this reason we review some of the large-scale AI projects and relevant sub-disciplines of AI in the next section.

5. Review of Relevant AI Research

5.1 Review of Previous Large-scale Artificial Intelligence Projects

BT's machine intelligence initiative is both timely and important in addressing the needs for intelligent software in the 21st century. We believe that such a project could substantially alter the landscape of computing. However, to do so it will be necessary to take account of the advances and mistakes of previous large-scale artificial intelligence projects. For these purposes we review the Japanese Fifth Generation project and the US CYC project.

- Japanese Fifth Generation project

  The Japanese Fifth Generation Computing Systems (FGCS) project [7] was one of a number of large-scale computing projects of the 1980s aimed at the construction of intelligent machinery. Intensive planning and research led to the identification of Horn clause logic as the best candidate for a single software representation for all parts of the project. Since this representation was aimed at underpinning a whole new generation of machines, the vision acted as a spur to the logic programming community to remodel all the major constituents of computer science within a logic programming framework. The FGCS project aimed at using logic programming for implementing man/machine communication aids, visual and speech input/output, sensory robot interfaces, and natural-language database interfaces. Efficiency was to be achieved by massive parallelism, based on personal inference machines (PIMs) whose assembly language was an augmented version of Prolog. Cognitive compatibility between the new ultra-powerful machines and their users would be ensured by the use of knowledge-based programming techniques. The result would be intelligent machines which made the fruits of large-scale knowledge bases available to their users via interactive natural-language interfaces. What went right and what went wrong?

  The project met many of its technical aims. At the end of the project large-scale parallelism based on a guarded Horn clause (GHC) language was demonstrated on a number of impressive applications, including a theorem prover which proved an open result in number theory. Despite this success, large-scale knowledge bases were not built and the vision of intelligent natural-language-oriented machines was never realised. In addition, the hardware and software were not taken up by Japanese industry due partly to their incompatibility with existing software.

The lasting value of the FGCS project can be largely attributed to its choice of a single declarative knowledge representation, which connected a large number of disparate problems into a coherent whole[1]. As a side-effect intense international research in the 1980s enabled logic programming to encompass the disparate computer science topics of knowledge representation, semantics, databases, program termination, formal methods, program synthesis, debugging, modularity, constraint solving, induction and natural-language processing (see Ten Year Review Special Issue of the Journal of Logic Programming, Volumes 19/20, 1994). On the other hand, the failure of FGCS to construct large-scale knowledge-bases and natural language capabilities has been attributed [8] to the failure of the planners to recognise the central role that should have been played by machine learning. Professor K Furukawa, Research Director of the Japanese Fifth Generation project, has admitted privately that a central error was the initial omission of computer induction when planning the project. Since 1992, Professor Furukawa [9] has re-focused his main research area on the application of 'Inductive Logic Programming systems to various problems including natural-language processing, skill acquisition and economics'.

- CYC project

In response to the Japanese FGCS project, a US consortium started its own privately funded artificial intelligence project called CYC at MCC in Austin Texas. CYC was under the technical directorship of Doug Lenat, who strongly advocated the need to build up a massive, diverse knowledge source. Unlike FGCS Lenat believed that it was not important to choose a particular knowledge representation from the start, but rather to let one evolve.

The first author of this paper visited MCC in 1984 while carrying out a consultancy at Radian Corporation, also in Austin Texas. Radian's approach to building knowledge bases, much more pedestrian than CYC's, involved the use of 'structured' rule induction. During the 1980s Radian's RuleMaster product was used to build a number of expert systems including an autolander real-time advisor for the Space Shuttle and what is still one of the world's largest expert systems, BMT — 30 000 rules were developed in nine man years of development time. The BMT system was installed at Siemens and is still in full-time use. Simple 'first-generation' machine learning techniques have achieved many other similar successes in application [10].

---

[1] This was a lesson lost on the so-called Japanese Sixth Generation (or real-world computing) project, which after 4 years has yet to make a significant impact outside Japan.

By comparison, after ten years effort and hundreds of million of dollars of funding the CYC [11] system failed to find large-scale industrial application. Like FGCS, the self-imposed requirement to enter all knowledge by hand proved overwhelming. Unlike FGCS, the failure to choose a sufficiently expressive common representation language was discovered as an oversight, near the end of the project. The following is a quote from Lenat [11] on this topic.

'Another point is that a standard sort of frame-and-slot language proved to be awkward in various contexts: ... Such experiences caused us to move toward a more expressive language, namely first order predicate calculus with a series of second-order extensions ...'

Thus the CYC project eventually concurred with the original design choice of FGCS, to use first order predicate calculus as the central declarative knowledge representation.

Can BT's Machine Intelligence project succeed where projects like FGCS and CYC have failed to meet expectations? We would argue that the answer is yes, but only if sufficient note is taken of the lessons to be learned from FGCS and CYC. From the above discussion we take the following to be necessary, though not sufficient, design choices for the project.

- Declarative representation — choose first order predicate calculus as the central declarative knowledge representation, as FGCS did and CYC eventually had to do. In practice this implies coding knowledge-bases in Prolog-like programming languages. This representation is both flexible and supports comprehensibility due to its close relationship with natural language.

- Learning — do not rely on hand-coding of knowledge. Machine Learning, when properly applied can generate hundreds of lines of validated code per day. The advent of ILP [12] ties this point to that of representation, since efficient systems now exist [13, 14] which use logic programming as their sole representation for example databases, background knowledge and constructed theories.

- Duality — build links to existing efficient procedural computer software to avoid recoding and enhance take-up in existing user communities. This approach is exemplified to a limited degree by constraint logic programming [15], in which logical theorem proving interacts with efficient procedurally encoded constraint solving.

An alternative to CYC's approach for obtaining large-scale knowledge structures might be imagined by analogy with the World Wide Web. By this analogy we might expect an interconnected network of interacting simple programs, such as the declarative diary program in section 3.1, to build up a massive executable network of personal and social knowledge by continuous interaction with a population of human users. The inferential power of such a 'knowledge network' would be substantially beyond the hopes or aspirations of either FGCS or CYC.

Two of the most pertinent topics in present machine intelligence research relevant to increased intelligibility in human/computer interaction are intelligent agents and machine learning. Issues related to both topics are thrown up by the declarative diary example of section 3.1. These topics will be reviewed in the following two sections.

6. Review of Agents

A rift has opened up in Artificial Intelligence circles between the advocates of, on the one hand, declarative knowledge-based systems and, on the other hand, reactive knowledge-free systems. These two approaches can be exemplified by the views expressed by John McCarthy (Stanford) and Rodney Brooks (MIT). The distinction between these disparate approaches explains some of the diversity in the usage of the term 'agents' in the recent artificial intelligence (AI) literature.

6.1 The Declarative School

On the declarative side McCarthy [16] claims that nothing short of second-order predicate calculus will do for implementing 'robot consciousness'. He underlines the necessity of agents being able to reason about other agents' beliefs, including their own. Despite its declarative elegance this approach runs into problems with tractability and completeness of inference. Genesereth [17] has followed McCarthy's lead and produced specific plans for agent-oriented software based on the logical communication languages KQML and KIF [18]. These languages, which are extensions of first-order Horn clause logic (in a LISP-like syntax) allow declarative definition and communication of agent knowledge. Genesereth advocates the idea of 'software wrappers' which allow existing legacy software to be converted to agent-oriented form by embedding within a KQML/KIF exterior. For this aspiration to be met on a large-scale would require converting software vendors across the board to the new KQML/KIF standards. This approach is related to the duality principle, though it lays no stress on the importance of machine learning or human/computer communication. Also the KQML/KIF attempts to standardise predicate usage in inter-agent communication have been contended even within the limits of the AI community [19]. It is our belief that, in contrast to Genesereth's top-down approach, large-scale usage of agent software — like large-scale usage of the WWW — is more likely to be achieved bottom-up, by way of adaptive personalised agent interfaces.

One limited form of adaptive personalised agent interface that already exists is the Softbot framework developed by Etzioni and Weld [20]. Softbots employ a first-order predicate calculus representation and are primarily planners. Given an imprecisely specified goal, such as 'set up a meeting on agents with Mitchell at CMU', the Softbot plans a precise set of commands to execute this goal. For example this might include determining the e-mail address of Tom Mitchell at CMU. Although Softbots use an expressive representation, they do not communicate with one another. They perform learning, but only by rote memorisation of plans that succeeded or details that proved useful in the past.

6.2   The Reactive School

At MIT Brooks is advocating and leading a programme for building reactive insect-like robots [21]. High-level cognitive compatibility with humans is abandoned in favour of stimulus-response architectures, which lend themselves to straightforward robot implementations imported from mechanical engineering. Some work in Maes' group at MIT appears to be exploiting some of Brooks' ideas where it is applied to software agents [22, 23]. This approach is sometimes referred to as artificial life and is summarised in the following quote from Maes [24].

> 'The goal of building an autonomous agent is as old as the field of AI itself. The artificial life community has initiated a radically different approach to this goal, which focuses on fast, reactive behaviour, rather than on knowledge and reasoning, as well as on adaptation and learning. Its approach is largely inspired by biology, and more specifically the field of ethology, which attempts to understand the mechanisms animals use to demonstrate adaptive and successful behaviour.'

Maes and her colleagues have demonstrated an artificial dog as well as various reactive agent utilities which learn within a non-declarative representation for tasks such as e-mail filters.

At CMU Mitchell and colleagues have developed a reactive agent called Web Watcher [24] that learns about user interests on the World Wide Web. Like other reactive agents, although it adapts it cannot communicate learned knowledge to other agents or to users. WebWatcher has the merit of being freely available over the Web[1].

Another class of agents that best fits within this category is that of Knowbots [25]. Knowbots perform a task similar to that of Softbots (section 5.1) except that rather than employing planning, they carry out hard-wired commands which are encoded procedurally. Communication between Knowbots is opaque to human users and Knowbots do not learn from experience.

Genesereth's approach lends itself to high-level knowledge communication, inter-robot modelling and collaboration. However, due to the nature of the languages used, no learning has been attempted within this framework. On the other hand, Maes' approach does not support high-level communication but has strengths in the ease of incorporation of low-level learning. However, despite the incorporation of learning within a number of the Maes' agent projects, the assumptions made and learned are opaque to human users.

---

[1] http://www.cs.cmu.edu/afs/cs.cmu.edu/project/theo-6/web-agent/www/project-home.htm

6.3   Bridging the Gap Using the Duality Principle

A pragmatic position has been proposed by Michie [26, 27] on conscious agents which bridges McCarthy's and Brooks' programmes. In settings in which agents interact with human users there is a need to integrate both Brooksian subcognitive software with McCarthyite self-articulate 'conscious' abilities. This approach embodies the duality principle of section 3. We see a clear need for adaptive learning at both cognitive and subcognitive levels. Followers of McCarthy's programme have achieved agents which communicate and are autonomous but do not learn. Followers of Brooks have constructed agents which are autonomous and learn but do not communicate with each other or with humans. Neither of these approaches can be seen to follow the duality principle of section 3. The papers by Sammut et al [28], and Michie and Sammut [29] appear to be the only ones in the literature to have demonstrated autonomous agents which communicate with one another and learn. These agents each control an independent control surface of a simulated Cessna aircraft. Inter-agent communication is achieved via a common 'blackboard' which describes the current state of the aircraft. The control strategy of individual agents is defined by situation/action mappings represented as decision trees. These trees are learned independently from observations of human pilot traces. Since the low level of decision-tree representation impedes communicability of the learned knowledge, Michie [27] suggests the future use of first-order predicate calculus and inductive logic programming for the construction of human comprehensible rules.

This paper further endorses the bridge-building approach. We accept the necessity within agents for efficient and reactive low-level functionality, communication and learning. However, adaptive collaborative agents which interact with human users need a corresponding layer of declarative social and self-knowledge which can be autonomously learned and succinctly and exactly communicated to humans and other agents.

7.   Review of Learning

Unlike the topic of software agents, machine learning (ML) is a well-established field of AI with many international conferences and its own reputable journal. Topics covered range from the highly theoretical to the technical intricacies of implementation design and comparative testing. ML largely involves highly reactive representations for the learned knowledge, ranging from statistical regression equations to neural networks, decision trees, boolean functions and finite state automata. The 1990s have seen the rapid development of inductive logic programming (ILP) [4], the only subarea of ML directed at the declarative representations favoured by McCarthy and Genesereth (see section 5.1).

7.1 Surveys of Applied ML

For the purposes of this paper we will narrow the field to that of real-world applications of ML. Despite the fact that ML is one of the largest and fastest growing areas of AI, until recently relatively few of the numerous industrial applications of ML had been detailed in the computer science literature. There are several reasons for this:

- confidentiality — successful ML applications often involve commercially sensitive data (e.g. personal credit limit information) and often give the users a substantial edge which would be lost on communication of the resulting knowledge to competitors,

- trade publication — unlike academia, there is little advantage to company employees who publish in learned journals; ML applications are often published in the relevant trade journals, or described in advertising material.

However, two recent issues of the Communications of the ACM (March 1994 and November 1995) provide in-depth surveys of real-world applications of ML. These surveys cover case-based learning [30], neural networks [31], genetic algorithms [32], rule induction [10] and ILP [12]. As a prime example Langley and Simon describe a chemical process control application of rule induction which saved Westinghouse ten million dollars per year [10].

All the surveyed ML techniques except ILP are highly efficient and reactive, use relatively simple feature-based representations, employ search techniques with implicit biases which are usually not understood by the user and generally produce results which are relatively opaque. These techniques are ideal for 'black-box' reactive agents. By contrast, ILP is relatively slow in generation of hypotheses, but allows a rich relational representation, has an explicit search bias (background knowledge) and is the only one to have produced discoveries which are not only comprehensible to human experts but also represent new knowledge publishable on its own account in top scientific journals [33, 34, 35].

7.2 The Statlog Project

Whereas the quality of ILP-generated declarative knowledge can be established by its publishability in refereed journals, the contending claims of 'black-box' reactive learning mechanisms can best be judged by head-to-head performance comparisons on extensive datasets. Statlog [36], the largest such comparative machine learning study to date, was an ESPRIT project that ran from 1990 to 1993 and involved six academic and six industrial laboratories. Around 20 reactive rule-induction, neural and statistical-classification algorithms were each tested and compared on around 20 large-scale industrial datasets to produce $20 \times 20 = 400$ large-scale experiments. The results were compared and analysed by academic statisticians. Reactive rule induction algorithms were found to have the best average performance, though they could be outstripped on particular datasets by statistical algorithms which made assumptions appropriate to the dataset. Unfortunately, no attempt was made to assess quantitatively the comprehensibility of the learned information.

The general lesson seems to be that 'black-box' learning should be carried out with whatever algorithm, or combination of algorithms (as long as they are reasonably efficient), gives highest predictive accuracy (or minimum cost given a cost/benefit matrix). However, when learned knowledge must be intelligible to the user, a concise, exact and declarative representation, such as that used by ILP, is ideally suited. It should also be noted that Statlog exclusively investigated unstructured learning. Meanwhile, as is the case with good software engineering practice, the interesting machine learning technologies for large-scale knowledge development will be incremental and will further develop highly structured representations by hierarchical problem decomposition.

8. Conclusions

In this paper we have investigated some of the general issues related to computer science research at the end of the 20th century, and tried to indicate some of the central issues for the next century. In particular we have stressed the human overload dangers inherent in computing technology. These stem from the mass availability of high information capacity, transmission rates and computation rates. Without sufficient intelligent support, human users will be increasingly overwhelmed by computer power. This is a central motivation for BT's machine intelligence initiative. However, we note that similar 1980s projects, namely FGCS and CYC, failed to deliver their promise. We trace this failure largely to the absence of declarative machine learning within these projects. The renaissance of artificial intelligence techniques under the guise of the intelligent agent movement, is in danger of repeating the same mistake as FGCS and CYC. Thus most agent technology has no learning capacity, and those agent techniques that do incorporate learning, do not allow for the communication of learned knowledge to human beings.

Our suggestion is that a new approach be taken to designing software which interacts with human beings. We believe such software should incorporate declarative machine learning at its core. According to our 'duality principle' machine intelligibility can only be obtained by clearly separating the declarative and procedural knowledge components of a program. While the procedural part of the program should carry out low-level communication- inaccessible tasks, this should be directed by high-level, declarative knowledge. This declarative knowledge should be encoded in a logic language, thus making it easily translatable to natural language. This would not only actively support high-level interaction with human beings, but also make inter-program communication transparent to inspection. Using today's machine-learning technology, learning at the declarative level would necessarily be carried out using inductive logic programming. We urge the need for software involved in human/computer interaction to have an extra declarative layer defining program specifications, reaction speeds of sub-modules, goals, intentions as well as models of other computer programs and human users.

We believe that if BT were to take this route with the machine intelligence initiative, they would not only be carrying out developments at the forefront of emerging computer-science technologies, but also be helping to transform the communication and computing industries of the 21st century.

Acknowledgements

The authors would like to thank Nader Azarmi, Robin Smith, Hyacinth Nwana, Ben Azvine and Brian Tester for enlightening discussions on agents and other related topics at BT Laboratories at Martlesham Heath. Thanks are also due for discussions on the topics in this paper with John McCarthy, David Page and Lincoln Wallen. Stephen Muggleton and David Page's work on this topic was supported by a period of consultancy at BT during 1995-1996, as well as by the Esprit Long Term Research Action ILP II (project 20237), EPSRC grant GR/J46623 on Experimental Application and Development of ILP, EPSRC grant GR/K57985 on Experiments with Distribution-based Machine Learning and an EPSRC Advanced Research Fellowship held by Stephen Muggleton. Discussions on these topics between the authors was supported at Oxford University Computing Laboratory by EPSRC Visiting Fellowships granted to Professor Michie in 1994 and 1995. During the discussion period Stephen Muggleton and Donald Michie were supported respectively by an ongoing Research Fellowship and a Visiting Scholarship at Wolfson College, Oxford.

References

1. Michie D: 'The superarticulacy phenomenon in the context of software manufacture', Proceedings of the Royal Society of London, A 40, No 5, pp 185—212 (1986).

2. Smith R, Callaghan J and Azvine B: 'Development of a machine intelligence capability in BT', Internal BT report (1995).

3. Nwana H: 'Smart software agents: an overview', Knowledge Engineering Review, 11, No 3 (1996).

4. Muggleton S and de Raedt L: 'Inductive logic programming: Theory and methods', Journal of Logic Programming, 19, No 20, pp 629—679 (1994).

5. Hoare C A R: 'Programs are predicates', in Proceedings of the Final Fifth Generation Conference, pp 211—218, Tokyo, Ohmsha (1992).

6. Spivey J M: 'The Z notation : a reference manual', Prentice-Hall (2nd edition), New York (1992).

7. JIPDEC Fifth Generation Computing Committee, Preliminary report on study and research on fifth-generation computers in 1979-1980, Technical report, Japan Information Processing Development Centre, Tokyo (1981).

8. Michie D: 'The Fifth Generation's unbridged gap', in Herken R (Ed): 'The Universal Turing machine: a half-century survey', pp 467—489, Oxford University Press, Oxford (1988).

9. Furukawa K, Michie D, and Muggleton S: 'Machine Intelligence 13: machine intelligence and inductive learning', Oxford University Press, Oxford (1994).

10. Langley P and Simon H: 'Applications of machine learning and rule induction', Communications of the ACM, 38, No 11, pp 54—64 (1995).

11. Lenat D B: 'CYC: a large-scale investment in knowledge infrastructure', Communications of the ACM, 38, No 11, pp 33—38 (1995).

12. Bratko I and Muggleton S: 'Applications of inductive logic programming', Communications of the ACM, 38, No 11, pp 65—70 (1995).

13. Quinlan J R: 'Learning logical definitions from relations', Machine Learning, 5, pp 239—266 (1990).

14. Muggleton S: 'Inverse entailment and Progol', New Generation Computing, 13, pp 245—286 (1995).

15. Jaffar J and Maher M J: 'Constraint logic programming: a survey', Journal of Logic Programming, 19/20, pp 503—582 (1994).

16. McCarthy J: 'Making robots conscious', in Furukawa K, Michie D and Muggleton S (Eds): 'Machine Intelligence 15: intelligent agents', Oxford University Press, Oxford (to be published in 1996).

17. Genesereth M and Ketchpel S P: 'Software agents', Communications of the ACM, 37, No 7, pp 48—53 (1994).

18. Finin T, Fritzson R, McKay D, and McEntire R: 'KQML — a language and protocol for knowledge and information exchange', Technical Report CS-94-02, Computer Science Department, University of Maryland and Valley Forge Engineering Center, Unisys Corporation, Computer Science Department, University of Maryland, UMBC Baltimore MD 21228 (1994).

19. Ginsberg M: 'Knowledge interchange format: The kif of death', AI Magazine, 12, No 3, pp 57—63 (Fall 1991).

20. Etzioni O and Weld D: 'A softbot-based interface to the Internet', Communications of the ACM, 37, No 7, pp 72—76 (July 1994).

21. Brooks R: 'A robust layered control system for a mobile robot', IEEE Journal of Robotics and Automation, RA-2, pp 14—23 (1986).

22. Maes P: 'Artificial life meets entertainment: lifelike autonomous agents', Communications of the ACM, 38, No 11, pp 108—114 (1995).

23. Blumberg B: 'Lessons from ethology for autonomous agent architectures', in Furukawa K, Michie D, and Muggleton S (Eds): 'Machine Intelligence 15: intelligent agents', Oxford University Press, Oxford (to be published in 1996).

24. Armstrong R, Freitag D, Joachims T, and Mitchell T: 'Webwatcher: a learning apprentice for the World Wide Web', in AAAI Spring symposium on Information Gathering from Heterogeneous, Distributed Environments, Stanford, (1995), also at: http://www.cs.cmu.edu/afs/cs.cmu.edu/project/theo-6/web-agent/www/project-home.htm

25. Droms R: 'The Knowbot information service', FTP Report, Corporation for National Research Initiatives (CNRI) (December 1989).

26. Michie D: 'Consciousness as an engineering issue, Pt 1', Journal of Consciousness Studies, 1, No 2, pp 182—195 (1994).

27. Michie D: 'Consciousness as an engineering issue, Pt 2', Journal of Consciousness Studies, 2, No 1, pp 52—66 (1995).

28. Sammut C, Hurst S, Kedzier D and Michie D: 'Learning to fly', in Sleeman D and Edwards P (Eds): 'Proc of the Ninth International Workshop on Machine Learning', pp 385—393, San Mateo, CA, Morgan Kaufmann (1992).

29. Michie D and Sammut C: 'Behavioural clones and cognitive skill models', in Furukawa K, Michie D and Muggleton S (Eds): 'Machine Intelligence 14: applied machine intelligence', Oxford University Press, Oxford (1995).

30. Allen B P: 'Case-based reasoning: business applications, Communi-cations of the ACM', 37, No 3, pp 40—44 (1994).

31. Widrow B, Rumelhart D E and Lehr M A: 'Neural networks: applications in industry, business and science', Communications of the ACM, 37, No 3, pp 93—105 (1994).

32. Goldberg D E: 'Genetic and evolutionary algorithms come of age', Communications of the ACM, 37, No 3, pp113—119 (1994).

33. Muggleton S, King R and Sternberg M: 'Protein secondary structure prediction using logic-based machine learning', Protein Engineering, 5, No 7, pp 647—657 (1992).

34. King R, Muggleton S, Lewis R, and Sternberg M: 'Drug design by machine learning: The use of inductive logic programming to model the structure-activity relationships of trimethoprim analogues binding to dihydrofolate reductase', Proc of the National Academy of Sciences, 89, No 23 (1992).

35. King R, Muggleton S, Srinivasan A, and Sternberg M: 'Structure-activity relationships derived by machine learning: the use of atoms and their bond connectives to predict mutagenicity by inductive logic programming', Proc of the National Academy of Sciences, 93, pp 438—442 (1996).

36. Michie D, Spiegelhalter D J and Taylor C C: 'Machine learning, neural and statistical classification', Ellis Horwood, London (1994).

Index

Springer
and the
environment

At Springer we firmly believe that an international science publisher has a special obligation to the environment, and our corporate policies consistently reflect this conviction.
We also expect our business partners – paper mills, printers, packaging manufacturers, etc. – to commit themselves to using materials and production processes that do not harm the environment. The paper in this book is made from low- or no-chlorine pulp and is acid free, in conformance with international standards for paper permanency.

Lecture Notes in Artificial Intelligence (LNAI)

Lecture Notes in Computer Science